THE IMPERATIVE OF INTEGRATION

THE IMPERATIVE OF INTEGRATION

ELIZABETH ANDERSON

PRINCETON UNIVERSITY PRESS   PRINCETON AND OXFORD

Copyright © 2010 by Princeton University Press
Published by Princeton University Press, 41 William Street,
Princeton, New Jersey 08540
In the United Kingdom: Princeton University Press, 6 Oxford Street,
Woodstock, Oxfordshire OX20 1TW

press.princeton.edu

Library of Congress Cataloging-in-Publication Data

Anderson, Elizabeth.
The imperative of integration / Elizabeth Anderson.
p.   cm.
Includes bibliographical references and index.
ISBN 978-0-691-13981-4 (cloth : alk. paper)
1. Equality—United States. 2. Race discrimination—United States. 3. Segregation—
United States. 4. Affirmative action programs—United States.
5. Minorities—United States—Social conditions. 6. United States—Race relations.   I. Title.
HN90.S6A64 2010
305.896'073—dc22   2010023222

British Library Cataloging-in-Publication Data is available

This book has been composed in Sabon

Printed on acid-free paper. ∞

Printed in the United States of America

1 3 5 7 9 10 8 6 4 2

TO RACHEL AND BENJAMIN

CONTENTS

PREFACE

In 1988 I needed to move from Ann Arbor to the Detroit area to spare my partner, a sleep-deprived medical resident at Detroit's Henry Ford Hospital, a significant commute to work. As I searched for housing in the metropolitan area, I discovered some surprisingly sharp residential patterns. In the lovely community of Oak Park, just north of Detroit, blocks of carefully tended middle-class homes with impeccable lawns were divided between all-black neighborhoods to the south and all-white, largely Jewish neighborhoods to the north. In Southfield, I examined some apartments and homes for rent north of 10 Mile Road, two miles north of the Detroit border. Prospective landlords assured me, a white woman then in her late twenties, that I had no reason to worry about renting there since "we're holding the line against blacks at 10 Mile Road." One of them then showed me a home with a pile of cockroaches in the kitchen. Landlords in the Detroit metropolitan area appeared confident that whites would rather live with cockroaches as housemates than with blacks as neighbors.

We decided to rent a house in South Rosedale Park, a stable working/middle-class Detroit neighborhood with beautiful 1920s brick homes. The tree-lined streets were divided by grassy strips adorned with flowers planted each spring by the residents as a communal activity. We were welcomed to this effort by our friendly homeowning neighbors. Our neighborhood, which was about 80 percent black, was a model of cordial race relations.

Matters were different in my place of employment, the University of Michigan in Ann Arbor. At the time a rash of racially hostile incidents targeting black, Latino, Native American, and Asian students was raising alarms across campus. One case involved flyers posted on campus that depicted a lynching along with the statement, "Niggers ought to be hanging from trees." Although such overtly racist incidents got the most publicity, they did not constitute either the dominant or, in terms of aggregate effects, the most damaging mode of undesirable racial interactions on campus. More pervasive, insidious, and cumulatively damaging were subtler patterns of racial discomfort, alienation, and ignorant and cloddish interaction, such as classroom dynamics in which white students focused on problems and grievances peculiar to them, ignored what black students were saying, or unwittingly expressed insulting assumptions about them.

I wondered whether there was a connection between the extreme residential racial segregation in Michigan and the patterns of infelicitous interracial interaction I observed at the university, where many students were functioning in a multiracial setting for the first time. It seemed that this was an area where education could do some good. I joined an organization of faculty that sought to address these problems in part through curricular reform. Unlike the many multicultural curricular initiatives that were sweeping college campuses at the time, our initiative focused on the study of race-based inequality rather than the exploration and celebration of cultural diversity. We hoped to provide protected spaces in which students of different racial identities could jointly and cooperatively contend with the history, causes, and consequences of racial inequality in the world in an intellectually responsible and mutually respectful way, without feeling personally threatened by frank discussions of controversial issues. The combination of intellectually serious inquiry about these issues in a context that facilitated interracial interaction on terms of equality would, we hoped, help students equip themselves to participate more competently and respectfully in multiracial settings in the wider world, as well as to better understand problems of inequality.

The premise of our courses reflects, in microcosm, the premise of this book: that integration of racial, ethnic, and other groups that mark significant lines of social inequality is a vital ideal for a democratic society, necessary for its basic institutions to function successfully. This book is the product of investigations inspired by teaching my students in such courses.

So it is fitting to begin by thanking my many students whose arguments, comments, skepticism, and enthusiasm helped make this book possible. Given the number of years I have been thinking about these problems with my students, I cannot name them all. Many are now professors at other institutions. I would like to offer special thanks to Kayla Arslanian, William Berger, Aaron Bronfman, Stephen Campbell, Vanessa Carbonell, Rutger Claassen, Nathaniel Coleman, Steven Daskal, Craig Duncan, Max Florka, Alexa Forrester, Robert Gressis, Christie Hartley, Warren Herold, Jeff Jones, Robin Kar, Eric Li, Eleni Manis, Steven Mazie, Giacomo Mollo, Stephen Nayak-Young, Sven Nyholm, Blaine Neufeld, Bogdan Popa, Amanda Roth, Alexander Silk, Daniel Singer, Will Thomas, Amanda Tillotson, and David Wiens. Numerous current and former colleagues at the University of Michigan have provided helpful comments on this book or on earlier works that informed it, including Gordon Belot, Sarah Buss, Stephen Darwall, Phoebe Ellsworth, Samuel Gross, Patricia Gurin, Don Herzog, Rick Hills, Donald

Kinder, Mika Lavaque-Manty, Robert Mickey, Sallyanne Payton, Peter Railton, Laura Ruetsche, Rebecca Scott, Jamie Tappenden, David Velleman, Thomas Weisskopf, and Mariah Zeisberg. I would also like to thank the faculty and students who offered helpful comments at other institutions where I have presented parts of my book, including Carnegie Mellon University, Cornell University, Harvard University, Kent State University, MIT, New York University, the Spencer Foundation, Stanford University, University of California, Berkeley, University of Copenhagen, University of Illinois Urbana-Champaign, University of Kentucky, University of Oslo, University of San Diego, University of Stockholm, Wayne State University, and Yale University. I offer special thanks to those who have offered detailed and/or especially insightful comments on my work, including Lawrence Alexander, Anita Allen, Lawrence Blum, Joshua Cohen, Derrick Darby, Ronald Dworkin, Richard Fallon, Nancy Fraser, Barbara Fried, Heather Gerken, Thomas Grey, Lani Guinier, Sally Haslanger, Samuel Issacharoff, Meena Krishnamurthy, Kasper Lippert-Rasmussen, Deborah Malamud, Richard Miller, Charles Mills, Martha Minow, Thomas Nagel, Rick Pildes, Robert Post, Jed Rubenfeld, Debra Satz, Thomas Scanlon, Maimon Schwarzschild, James Sterba, and Laurence Thomas. The Jean Beer Blumenfeld Center for Ethics, run by the Department of Philosophy at Georgia State University, ran an exhilarating workshop on my manuscript. I am very grateful to Andrew Altman, Kwame Anthony Appiah, Eamonn Callan, Andrew I. Cohen, Andrew J. Cohen, Ann Cudd, Jorge Garcia, Peter Lindsay, Glenn Loury, and George Rainbolt for the outstanding comments they provided on the penultimate version of this book, and for their intensive scrutiny of it. Rebecca Wolf and Susie Lorand provided indispensable research and editorial assistance. The University of Michigan, Ann Arbor, provided generous funding for my research through a Michigan Humanities Fellowship. I thank Blackwell Press for permission to reprint in chapter 9 portions of my article "The Future of Racial Integration" from *Social Philosophy*, ed. Laurence Thomas, 229–49 (Oxford: Blackwell, 2008). Finally, I would like to thank my husband, David Jacobi, and my children, Rachel and Benjamin, for their love and support.

THE IMPERATIVE OF INTEGRATION

· ONE ·

SEGREGATION AND SOCIAL INEQUALITY

1.1 The Ideal of Integration

This book aims to resurrect the ideal of integration from the grave of the Civil Rights Movement. This may seem a long lost cause. At the height of the Civil Rights Movement, white Americans, while claiming to agree in principle with its goals, in practice vigorously resisted policies that would achieve more than token integration of their neighborhoods and schools.[1] They got their wish. After little more than a decade of energetic federal enforcement of *Brown v. Board of Education*, overwhelming white opposition forced the courts to back down. Since the 1980s courts have largely suspended enforcement of *Brown*, while sharply constraining the freedom of schools to practice voluntary racial integration.[2] Schools have been quietly resegregating—in some regions to levels that exceed those that obtained before the courts began to seriously enforce *Brown*.[3]

One might have expected civil rights activists to press harder for integration. But by the late 1960s, left political movements were shifting priorities from "redistribution" to "recognition"—from socioeconomic equality to equality of respect and esteem for identities and cultures.[4] This shift seemed to make sense in the face of the insult expressed in white opposition to integration: why demean yourself in begging to join a club whose members despise you for your race? Hence, advocates of the Black Power Movement, such as Stokely Carmichael (Kwame Toure) and Charles Hamilton rejected integration, calling instead for black self-reliance and pride in a distinctively black culture with African roots.[5] Although shocked by blacks' calls for "power," many white ethnic groups responded to the allure of identity politics by calling for public recognition of their distinctive cultural heritage. The result, in the standard narrative, was American multiculturalism, reflected in today's motley celebrations of diversity, multicultural sensitivity training, and American history textbooks featuring favorable depictions of the achievements of Americans from different shores. As one conservative commentator puts it, "we are all multiculturalists now."[6]

Multicultural recognition is important; yet it cannot replace efforts to address the continuing reality of racial inequality. Celebrations of diversity cannot make up for the facts that blacks live several years less than whites,[7] that 13 percent of black men are disenfranchised due to a felony conviction,[8] and that more than one-third of black children live in poverty.[9]

The hope of black nationalists and left multiculturalists is that racial equality can be achieved through, or at least notwithstanding, substantial racial segregation. Conservatives have gladly accepted this agenda insofar as it reduces pressure on whites to integrate their social spaces.

This hope is an illusion. Segregation of social groups is a principal cause of group inequality. It isolates disadvantaged groups from access to public and private resources, from sources of human and cultural capital, and from the social networks that govern access to jobs, business connections, and political influence. It depresses their ability to accumulate wealth and gain access to credit. It reinforces stigmatizing stereotypes about the disadvantaged and thus causes discrimination.

Segregation also undermines democracy. The democratic ideal seeks a culture and political institutions that realize society as a system of equal citizens. Democratic political institutions should be equally responsive to the interests and concerns of, and equally accountable to, all citizens. Segregation impedes the realization of this ideal and these principles. It impedes the formation of intergroup political coalitions, facilitates divisive political appeals, and enables officeholders to make decisions that disadvantage segregated communities without being accountable to them. It undermines the competence of officeholders by limiting their knowledge of and responsiveness to the impacts of their decisions on the interests of all.

If segregation is a fundamental cause of social inequality and undemocratic practices, then integration promotes greater equality and democracy. Hence, it is an imperative of justice. It is also a positive good. It should appeal to us as well as command us to action. In our preoccupation with celebrating our particularistic ethno-racial identities, we have forgotten the value of identification with a larger, nationwide community.[10] Integration in a diverse society expands our networks of cooperation and provides a stepping stone to a cosmopolitan identity, which offers the prospect of rewarding relations with people across the globe.

Recognition of the deep connections among integration, equality, and democracy lies at the core of the quiet revival of integrationist thought among American intellectuals.[11] It also grounds affirmative action in education. Alas, we stand at a critical turning point for the prospects of integration. Race-based affirmative action has been prohibited by popular referendum in several states, with more on the way. Integrative policies are in retreat. This book explains why this is a disaster, not just for African Americans, but for America as a whole. Against these trends, we need to restore integration to a central place on our political agenda.

1.2 A Note on Method in Political Philosophy

This is a work in nonideal theory. I do not advance principles and ideals for a perfectly just society, but ones that we need to cope with the injustices in our current world, and to move us to something better. Since this book is a response to current problems, it integrates research in the social sciences in ways not ordinarily found in works of political philosophy.

This method is unorthodox. Nonideal theory is usually regarded as derivative of ideal theory. Don't we first need to know what an ideally just society would be, to identify the ways our current society falls short? Shouldn't the principles for an ideal society be settled first, so that we can work out how to get there from here?

This challenge misunderstands how normative thinking works. Unreflective habits guide most of our activity. We are not jarred into critical thinking about our conduct until we confront a problem that stops us from carrying on unreflectively.[12] We recognize the existence of a problem before we have any idea of what would be best or most just.

Nor do we need to know what is ideal in order to improve. Knowledge of the better does not require knowledge of the best. Figuring out how to address a just claim on our conduct now does not require knowing what system of principles of conduct would settle all possible claims on our conduct in all possible worlds, or in the best of all possible worlds.

In our current world, the problem I propose to investigate is the persistence of large, systematic, and seemingly intractable disadvantages that track lines of group identity, along with troubling patterns of intergroup interaction that call into question our claim to be a fully democratic society of equal citizens. This admittedly inchoate starting point is akin to the complaints of fatigue, insomnia, and headache a patient might bring to her doctor: there seems to be something troubling here, but its precise contours require detailed empirical investigation and await a definitive diagnosis and evaluation.

There are three basic reasons to start political philosophy from nonideal theory—from a diagnosis of injustices in our actual world, rather than from a picture of an ideal world. First, we need to tailor our principles to the motivational and cognitive capacities of human beings. Rousseau famously sought legitimate principles of government, taking people "as they are and laws as they might be."[13] Rousseau's starting point, people *as they are*, is apt. A system of principles that would produce a just world if they regulated the conduct of perfectly rational and just persons will not do so when we ask human beings, with all our limitations and flaws, to follow them. Just institutions must be designed to block, work around, or cancel out our motivational and cognitive deficiencies, to harness our nonmoral motives to moral ends, to make up for each other's limitations by pooling our knowledge and wills. To craft such designs, we must analyze our motivational and cognitive biases, diagnose how they lead people to mistreat others, and how institutions may redirect them to better conduct.

Second, we risk leaping to the conclusion that any gaps we see between our ideal and reality must be the cause of the problems in our actual world, and that the solution must therefore be to adopt policies aimed at directly closing the gaps. Thus if (as some conservatives suppose) the ideal society would be a color-blind one in which everyone adhered to principles of individual responsibility, a work ethic, and traditional family values, the solution would appear to be to end race-conscious policies, preach the right values to individuals, and back them up with punitive measures against those who fail to measure up. Or if (as some on the multiculturalist left suppose) the ideal society would be a system of separate and distinct identity-based communities, each enjoying equal esteem and material resources, the solution would appear to be abundant diversity activities preaching tolerance and celebrating diverse cultures, along with distributions of goods proportional to identity group populations. Such recommendations are like a doctor who prescribes sleeping pills and aspirin to the patient who complains of fatigue, insomnia, and headaches. Without a detailed empirical investigation of the underlying causes of the complaints, we risk missing out on more fundamental and complex diagnoses—for example, that the patient suffers from depression, or a brain tumor—and hence risk missing out on genuine solutions. I believe we have made this mistake for our problems of group inequality. In §4.3 and §§8.2–8.5 I explain why the conservative recommendations are misguided, and in §9.2, why the left multiculturalist recommendations are misguided.

My claim is not simply that those on the left and right adopt insufficient means to ends that remain untouched by empirical inquiry into the causes of our problems. Rather, in the course of investigating these causes, we will find that we need to draw distinctions—for instance, among racial stereotyping, racism, and racial injustice (§3.1), among different racial concepts (§8.2), and among different types of discrimination "on the basis of race" (§3.5, §8.3)—occluded by ideal theories that are founded on inadequate empirical assumptions. And once we draw these distinctions as needed to make sense of our problems, we must reconsider whether the evaluations we adopted toward phenomena falling under the incoherently lumpy concepts (e.g., "racism" and "racial discrimination") make any sense as applied to the newly distinguished phenomena. In other cases, empirical inquiry may show us that certain distinctions—for instance, among civil, political, and social rights—that were thought to designate phenomena meriting distinct evaluations make little sense because empirically, these rights stand or fall together in a republic (§5.1). This recognition in turn forces us to enrich our understanding of the constitutive commitments of republicanism, and thereby to transform that ideal. When we alter our conceptual maps to gain a more empirically adequate understanding of our problems, we also open some and close other evaluative options. New conceptual terrain provides new perspectives from which to engage in evaluation and thereby prompts us to articulate new ideals.

Third, starting from ideal theory may prevent us from recognizing injustices in our nonideal world. Consider how ideal social contract theory works. Social contract theory assumes that the operative principles of society must be justifiable to all its members. A society counts as ideally just so long as the occupants of every representative social position *in that society* would approve of the way it operates, and prefer it to the alternatives. For example, in the ideally just world governed by Rawls's principles of justice, some class inequality will exist.[14] Hence, the principles of justice must be justified to members of each class position.

This orientation raises methodological difficulties when the contractualist ideal is used as a standard of assessment for nonideal societies. For *when we assess whether a society is deviating from ideal justice, we still assess it from the standpoint of representative positions in the ideally just society.* Since no racial positions exist in the ideal society, they do not define a standpoint from which to assess racially unjust societies. Hence, ideal theories that make race invisible fail to supply the conceptual framework needed to recognize and understand contemporary racial injustice. The principled color blindness of ideal theory is epistemologically disabling: it makes us blind to the existence of race-based injustice.[15]

Consider the dilemma of middle-class blacks choosing where to buy a house. Most blacks prefer to live in racially integrated neighborhoods. Most whites prefer to live in neighborhoods that contain no more than token numbers of blacks.[16] Many resist the entry of blacks into their neighborhoods through unwelcoming and hostile behavior. Most of this behavior is legal and would, due to rights of free speech and association, be legal even in an ideal society. Such behavior constitutes a serious dignitary harm to blacks and deters them from seeking housing in overwhelmingly white neighborhoods. The resulting racial segregation of neighborhoods also has adverse material consequences. For example, it isolates blacks from the white-dominated referral networks that govern access to better jobs. Even if egalitarian policies compressed the variation between the most and least advantaged positions, African Americans would still have a just complaint that their segregation deprives them of equal access to better jobs.

Viewing this phenomenon through the color-blind lens of ideal theory, we would assess it not from a racial position, but from an individual or class position. We can recognize an assault on an individual's dignity in the fact that she faces arbitrarily hostile treatment at the hands of others. But this individualistic perspective does not capture all of the expressive harms in the case. To be treated in a hostile way *on account of one's race* injures not only the individual directly targeted, but everyone in her racial group. It brands her and her group with a racial stigma. These expressive injuries are visible from the position of a racially stigmatized group, but invisible from the position of a putatively raceless individual.

The material disadvantages imposed on the African American who, deterred by the prospect of a hostile reception in a white neighborhood, chooses to settle in a poorer black neighborhood are also hard to see from the perspective of a raceless class position. Her class position did not disadvantage her: she was financially able to buy a house in the white neighborhood. She chose not do so because of the costs it entailed for her *as an African American*. From the perspective of a raceless representative position, this is no violation of equality of opportunity, but a voluntary choice not to take advantage of an opportunity. The dignitary harms to her racial identity that she would suffer for taking up the opportunity are not represented.

To capture such race-based injustices, we need a theory that begins from a structural account of the systematic disadvantages imposed on people because of their race in our society. Nonideal theory begins with a diagnosis of the problems and complaints of our society and investigates how to overcome these problems. Nonideal theory does not dispense with ideals but conceives of their function differently from ideal theory. In ideal theory, ideals function as standards of assessment for any society. They are not subject to testing in practice because they set standards, outside of practice, for the success of practice.

In nonideal theory, ideals embody imagined solutions to identified problems in a society. They function as *hypotheses*, to be tested in experience. We test our ideals by putting them into practice and seeing whether they solve the problems for which they were devised, settle people's reasonable complaints, and offer a way of life that people find superior to what they had before.[17] If they pass the test, this does not validate them outside of history. Circumstances change, and new problems and complaints arise, requiring the construction of new ideals. If our ideals fail the test, we need to revise or replace them. This process is not merely instrumental:

it is not a matter of finding better means to a fixed end already fully articulated. Reflection on our experience can give rise to new conceptions of successful conduct. Ideals can be tested in experience because the standards they try to meet are internal to our conception of what we are trying to do—solve a problem, meet a complaint—and we could discover, through reflection on the consequences of following the ideal, that we misconceived the problem, that our proposed solution was confused or incoherent.[18] When a medicine fails to cure the illness, we don't just keep trying other medicines for the same disease. Sometimes we revise the diagnosis.

1.3 A Relational Theory of the Causes of Systematic Group Inequality

This book concerns *group* inequality: modes of social organization whereby bounded social groups are subject to systematic disadvantages in relation to dominant groups. Large, stable, systematic social inequalities across the world are tied to many kinds of group identities, as of race gender, ethnicity, religion, caste, tribe, clan, family line, and national citizenship. Charles Tilly has called these "durable inequalities."[19] I prefer to call them "group" or "categorical" inequalities to stress their ties to paired social categories, such as black/white, male/female, citizen/alien, and Hindu/Muslim, rather than to individual characteristics that vary continuously, such as IQ, height, and skin color. Class inequalities may also ground categorical inequality insofar as privileged classes have been able to lock in their advantages across generations by such practices as monopolistic control of higher education, class-segregated housing, norms against intermarriage, and exclusionary rules of etiquette. This is the case in the United States, where, despite Americans' beliefs that they live in an equal opportunity society, class mobility is low in absolute terms and much lower than in Canada or the Scandinavian countries.[20] However, the latter countries demonstrate that egalitarian social democratic policies can dramatically limit class heritability and prevent class inequality from becoming categorical.

Why do inequalities in material resources, rights, privileges, power, and esteem typically track social group identities? Max Weber argued that categorical inequality arises from social closure. If a group has attained dominant control over an important good, such as land, military technology, education, or purported access to the holy or divine, it often secures this advantage by closing its ranks to outsiders.[21] While it may allow relatively free circulation of this good within the group, it carefully regulates transactions between in-group and out-group members, so as to block outsiders' access to these goods, or allow access only in ways that exclude out-groups from the full value added of their efforts. Charles Tilly, building on Weber's account, calls the first mechanism (blocking access) "opportunity hoarding" and the second (allowing access but depriving out-groups of part of their productive contribution) "exploitation."[22]

Examples abound of the ways opportunity hoarding underwrites durable inequalities. The Japanese samurai caste monopolized power by banning firearms and prohibiting commoners from carrying weapons. "Old boys' networks" limit access to business deals and executive positions to other men in their social circles. U.S. whites have long hoarded opportunities by establishing school systems that provide no, or an inferior, education to blacks, Latinos, and Native Americans. Even nonelites, such as immigrant groups in the United States, hoard opportunities by cornering the market on certain small enterprises—such as Chinese restaurants for Chinese, nail shops for Vietnamese, motels for Indians—and preferentially hiring fellow immigrants to staff them.[23] While such nonelite opportunity hoarding may not secure relative advantages over elites, it often reinforces durable inequalities suffered by other nonelite groups, such as blacks, who have no comparably lucrative opportunities to hoard.

Exploitation is also a common relation between dominant and subordinate social groups. Monopolistic controls over land, labor, or credit by feudal lords, aristocrats, and banking classes have historically constituted fundamental bases of exploitation of other classes. Examples include feudal serfdom and its more modern U.S. counterparts: white landowners imposing debt peonage and oppressive sharecropping arrangements on landless black and Chicano peasants, and the virtual enslavement of many undocumented immigrants today.[24]

Tilly argues that once categorical inequality is secured in one domain, two mechanisms, emulation and adaptation, spread it to new domains, thus making the group inequality pervasive and systematic. By *emulation*, organizations copy categorical inequalities established in other organizations. For example, the division of labor in a factory may assign women to jobs on the assembly line, and men to the higher-paying job of "machine operator" (shutting down the line when a problem arises). Other firms follow suit, assigning women to the inferior job and men to the less tedious, better-paying job. Emulation need not reflect any intent to subordinate women. It can arise from a desire to save setup costs by copying a model proven successful elsewhere. If an enterprise enjoys a competitive advantage from copying existing models, the model can spread in neo-Darwinian fashion in the absence of any sexist intention.[25] For once a particular group-defined intrafirm division of labor becomes widespread, it creates pools of differently experienced workers defined along group lines. Firms save training costs by hiring from the group that contains experienced workers. Thus, competition can lock in group dominance of particular jobs, even if the initial group-defined division of labor was arbitrary.

In *adaptation*, groups that interact according to norms expressing their unequal positions in one domain acquire habits that spread to new domains. For example, when women enter a workplace they may be expected to replicate the domestic services for male workers that they traditionally perform for their husbands at home. They may be expected to pour the coffee for others at a meeting, take their bosses' shirts to the laundry, look pretty, and put up with men's sexual advances.[26] Habits of dominance and subordination thereby spread across domains.

As categorical inequality spreads, people explain and legitimate it by inventing stories about supposed inherent differences between their groups. For example, military castes may acquire dominance in access to food as well as military technology. They thereby grow bigger and stronger than the peasants they oppress and acquire habits of aggression and arrogance. Stunted peasants cower before them not just in battle but, by adaptation, in other domains as well. The military caste thus finds evidence for its legitimating story, that they are by nature strong and brave, the peasants by nature weak and cowardly—and hence, that the peasants are unfit to be warriors and legitimately deprived of access to military technology, and that the warriors are fit to rule the peasants in every domain. Similarly, whites tend to limit access to stable jobs to fellow whites, relegating blacks to temporary, part-time, or marginal jobs in the secondary labor market. Over time, whites acquire résumés documenting long-term stable employment, whereas blacks' résumés evidence a patchy employment record, interpreted as a sign of their poor work ethic, which justifies a reluctance to hire them for permanent jobs in the primary labor market. In both cases, groups are deprived of experiences that would qualify them for access to the goods in question, and that deprivation is turned into a rationale for continued deprivation. Ideologies of inherent group difference misrepresent the effect of group inequality as its cause.[27]

Tilly's theory identifies group segregation as the linchpin of categorical inequality. "Segregation" may refer either to *processes* or *conditions*. Segregative processes consist of any intergroup relations (laws, norms, practices, habits) by which one identity group closes its social network to counterpart groups. Segregation has two basic modes: *spatial segregation*—processes that assign groups to different social spaces and institutions—and *role segregation*—processes that assign groups to different social roles. Such processes are instruments and reflections of the segregation of social networks of affiliation, collegiality, identity, trust, and loyalty. Examples include laws prescribing segregated schools, norms against intergroup marriage, ethnocentric job recruitment practices, emulation of ethnically based job assignments within a firm, and habits of avoidance—such as crossing the street when out-group members are coming one's way—that keep one group out of contact with another. They typically result in the *conditions* of spatial or role segregation, respectively, although such conditions may also arise from other causes.

Segregation typically leads to group inequality when the group practicing social closure controls the allocation of goods critical to securing power or advantage. It may control processes of spatial allocation so as to assign out-groups to spaces lacking the critical goods, and/or control processes of role allocation so as to assign themselves dominant roles and out-groups subordinate roles. Such hierarchical role segregation can survive formal desegregation of facilities, geographical mixing of populations, and even close contact between the groups.

The connection between segregative processes and conditions and group inequality is contingent. A group practicing social closure might not succeed in establishing dominance over others, even if it (initially) controls a critical good. Out-groups may devise means of penetrating the privileged ranks, find alternative modes of access to the critical good, or gain access to other critical goods. If a group does not control a critical good, then neither processes nor the condition of segregation generally cause group inequality. If both groups enjoy parity in control of separate spaces that afford roughly equal opportunities, or if the separate roles they occupy yield comparable advantages, group segregation may not lead to group inequality. For example, Catholics and Protestants in Northern Ireland rigidly segregate themselves by neighborhood, school, church, and friendship but are roughly economically equal.[28] Such segregation is deplorable on cosmopolitan and democratic grounds, but not from an egalitarian perspective.

Several features of Tilly's theory are worth stressing. First, this is a generic theory of categorical inequality. Following Weber, Tilly argues that the same mechanisms generate and sustain group inequality, regardless of the content of group identities—whether these are defined by race, gender, religion, ethnicity, citizenship, tribe, caste, or class.[29]

Second, inequality arises from the relations between groups—that is, intergroup processes or modes of interaction—rather than from characteristics internal and original to the groups as such (for example, distinct group cultures) or from individual characteristics such as intelligence, courage, ambition, shiftiness, or criminal tendencies thought to be inherent in, or intrinsically manifested to a greater degree by, members of a particular group. Inequality may *cause* members of a group to manifest qualities that befit, or seem to befit, them for the superior or inferior positions to which they are assigned. But such differences were not inherent in the groups to begin with. Narratives that trace inequality to primordial group differences are ideological rationalizations of outcomes due to unequal social relations.

Third, the mechanisms that spread inequality need not depend on intentions to do so. Adaptation works by the spread of habits, expectations, and norms of interaction that may operate unconsciously. Emulation may spread through competition. Categorical inequality thus arises as the by-product of unconscious activity or actions aimed at other goals.

Fourth, group stereotypes, ideologies rationalizing group inequality, and accompanying out-group contempt and antipathy are more the effect than the cause of group inequality. Social closure is initially motivated by ethnocentrism (in-group favoritism), not out-group antipathy. However, one leads to the other as advantaged groups cultivate norms of out-group exclusion to police their boundaries, and as ideologies arise that rationalize group inequality. Because prejudice is more the effect than the cause of segregation, we cannot eliminate categorical inequality by working to reduce prejudice, if we leave processes of segregation in place.[30]

1.4 Critique and Extension of the Relational Theory of Group Inequality

Tilly's theory offers a powerful account of the causes of categorical inequality. The centrality of segregation to group inequality, the generality of mechanisms of inequality across different types of groups, the priority of intergroup relations to group differences, the spread of inequality independent of conscious prejudice, and the priority of practices of inequality to identities, prejudice, and ideology are key features of Tilly's theory that I endorse. But Tilly's theory requires modification and extension around the mechanisms underlying group inequality and the basic forms of group inequality.

Mechanisms of Group Inequality

Tilly advances a comprehensive theory of the causes of group inequality in access to material goods, according to which his four mechanisms—opportunity hoarding, exploitation, adaptation, and emulation—all anchored by social closure, explain virtually all group inequality. Tilly's theory focuses on economic (opportunity hoarding, exploitation), cultural (adaptation), and competitive (emulation) mechanisms of inequality, to the exclusion of other causes. A more complete account of causal mechanisms of inequality should include additional mechanisms.

First, violence and conquest have been historically important mechanisms of categorical inequality. Violence was a basic means of spreading racial inequality in the history of imperialism and played key roles in maintaining U.S. slavery and its successor system of white supremacy. Vulnerability to violence remains a central dimension of subordinate social status for many groups, including women and sweatshop factory workers.

Second, inequality also often spreads by "leverage," whereby a group, having attained dominant control over one important good, uses that dominance to extend its control over other goods.[31] Thus, the Chinese literati leveraged their dominance in poetry writing to control over the imperial bureaucracy by installing a rigorous examination system as a hurdle to attaining political office. Other groups have leveraged dominance in religious authority, military prowess, and financial capital into dominance in political power, landownership, and esteem.

Third, political power plays a central role in the construction of inequality. While Tilly rightly emphasizes that categorical inequality can spread and sustain itself through emulation and adaptation, without laws and state policies aimed at institutionalizing it, we should not underestimate the historical importance of state action in extending inequality across domains. Even when it does not directly aim at institutionalizing inequality, it often plays important indirect roles. Where once whites kept blacks down by legally prohibiting anyone from teaching them to read, now an elaborate set of laws—including fragmentation of local governments, zoning regulations, and local financing of schools—works with nonlegal mechanisms sustaining residential racial segregation to exclude blacks from good schools.

Fourth, a comprehensive theory of group inequality must include an account of the psychological mechanisms—stereotyping and prejudice—underlying the intergroup interactions that reproduce inequality. Tilly dismisses group prejudice as merely a byproduct of inequality. He rightly stresses that prejudice does not explain how categorical inequality begins, that segregation plays an independent role in explaining inequality, and that prejudice is caused by inequality. Nevertheless, theories of prejudice and stereotyping must figure in any credible account of the micro mechanisms underwriting adaptation. This is especially important now that antidiscrimination laws and egalitarian norms have forced many boundary maintenance practices underground, to unconscious cognitive processes.

Finally, Tilly's definition of exploitation as the gap between group members' returns on their labor and the value they add to production needs to be modified. In complex economies characterized by a comprehensive division of labor, where everyone's efforts contribute jointly to the production of the economy's total output, and everyone's efforts causally contribute to others' productivity, it makes no normative sense to credit bits of production to the independent efforts of specific producers.[32] One could reconstruct a useful conception of exploitation by shifting from an outcome-based definition in terms of productive contributions to a procedural one based on the interactions of the parties. This would better fit Tilly's relational theory of inequality. A procedural account locates exploitation in such conduct as fraud, discrimination, breach of contract, employer collusion, coercive imposition of contractual terms, and coercive blocking of worker exit. These unjust modes of interaction typify the conditions experienced by today's most highly exploited laborers, such as bonded laborers, sweatshop workers, the victims of trafficking, and undocumented immigrant workers. This procedural alternative captures much but not all of what we would intuitively consider exploitation. As a more comprehensive conception is unnecessary for the purposes of this book, I shall not pursue one.

Forms of Group Inequality

Tilly's theory focuses on material inequalities. We can expand it to cover other types of group inequality by taking Iris Young's typology of unjust forms of intergroup relations as a starting point.[33] According to her, there are "five faces of oppression": exploitation, marginalization, violence, cultural imperialism, and powerlessness. Young's notion of exploitation roughly corresponds to Tilly's. Marginalization captures a subset of extreme cases of opportunity hoarding, whereby a chronically unemployed group is excluded from opportunities to participate in productive life. Young's other three categories have no clear counterparts in Tilly's theory.

Group-based violence is the infliction of physical force against people on account of their social group membership, or on account of their violation of subordinating social norms to which their group is subject. Examples include gangs beating up men because they are gay, and men beating their female domestic partners for talking to other men. The injury of pervasive violence is both physical and expressive. Widespread or normative group-based violence marks victimized groups as lacking moral standing to make claims on those who assault them, and as so inferior or alien that they may be abused with impunity.

Cultural imperialism involves the imposition of a dominant group's culture and interpretations of the world on subordinate groups. It includes the repression of a group's legitimate cultural practices (for example, Turkey's former prohibition of Kurdish language broadcasts), forced conversion of the group to dominant practices (as when Jews were forced to convert to Christianity during the Spanish Inquisition), propagation of stigmatizing representations of the group's culture (as when Islam is portrayed as a terrorist religion), and the erasure of a group's culture from representations of the wider society (as when school textbooks falsely represent everyone as heterosexual). It also includes the propagation of dominant groups' biased perceptions and explanations of group identities and differences as authoritative.

Powerlessness is the condition of being unable to influence one's situation and the world around oneself because others deny one meaningful opportunities to participate in the decision making of the institutions—especially the state—under which one lives with others. It involves the denial not just of formal rights of participation, such as the vote, but of "respectability"—the social status constituted by others' recognition of one's entitlements to have a say in what is going on, to be listened to, and to receive a respectful response.

Young's more expansive typology of modes of intergroup oppression shares with Tilly's theory an emphasis on intergroup relations (systematic interactions) as the fundamental ground of group inequality. Her account helps us see that these social relations are not only causes of unjust distributions of material goods, but unjust in themselves. It also facilitates a more comprehensive view of how segregation is implicated in group inequality.

Consider her concept of marginalization. Young confines it to exclusion from the labor force. This concept can be extended to other domains such as housing (in the case of homelessness), education (in societies where some social groups are denied access to schooling), and public spaces (in societies where certain groups—for example, widows, wives, or people with disabilities—are confined to the home). These are all forms of opportunity hoarding. They amount to systematic exclusion of subordinated groups from access to opportunities to participate meaningfully in social life. They require group segregation, so that goods enjoyed by the dominant group do not circulate beyond its boundaries.

The case of societies in which women (at least of certain castes or classes) are confined to the home illustrates the dual nature of group segregation. Spatial segregation in one domain—public spaces—does not preclude intimate contact between groups in another—the household. Whether segregation takes the form of spatial/institutional separation or role segregation depends on the good being hoarded. In some contexts, as in public facilities, where contact would entail conceding access to the good being hoarded, segregation involves avoidance of intergroup contact. Where contact is permitted, access to critical goods (including power) is denied by ensuring that contact be on terms of domination and subordination. This is a matter of role segregation. Jim Crow segregation illustrates the same two-sided logic. Across-the-board spatial segregation by race was never the norm in a society where middle-class white women considered it their privilege to escape housework by hiring black female domestic servants to do it and entrusted black nannies with their children. Nor does it describe the norm for their husbands and sons, who often raped and sexually harassed their black servants.[34] Racial segregation in public facilities and domains of power went hand-in-hand with interracial intimacy on subordinating terms. Contact was fine as long as it was based on relations of domination and exploitation. Marginalization and exploitation thus represent two different sides of the segregation coin.

Young's category of cultural imperialism conflates two distinct phenomena: cultural imposition and group stigmatization. "Cultural imperialism" usually brings the first to mind: this is the unjust imposition of a dominant group's cultural practices—a language, say, or a religion—on subordinate groups. This framing presupposes a neutral stance between the cultures and argues only against imposition. In this case the remedy may be individualist—let each individual freely choose which practices to accept—or multiculturalist—arrange institutions so as to accommodate or subsidize cultural diversity.

Entirely different is the case of a dominant group's entrenching stigmatizing representations about a subordinate group in public discourse. The subordinate group need not belong to a distinct culture. Men and women do not belong to distinct cultural groups. Rather, stigmatizing representations of women figure in the norms defining gender relations within a *single* culture. In this case neither the individualist nor the multiculturalist remedies are apt. We should not be neutral between stigmatizing and nonstigmatizing representations of innocent groups. The stigma is objectionable in itself.

Group stigmatization legitimates and reinforces the two sides of segregation. It underwrites two different types of attitudes toward segregated, subordinated groups: contempt and aversion (hatred, fear, suspicion, alienation).[35] Stigmatizing stereotypes represent subordinate groups as possessing traits that merit these attitudes. To justify contempt, and hence exclusion from positions of authority and placement in servile, subordinate roles, blacks are stereotyped as stupid and lazy; women, as incompetent, weak, and emotionally unstable. To justify aversion and avoidance, blacks are stereotyped as criminal and violent; women, as sex-crazed harlots threatening to tempt men into sexual sin. The latter stereotype of women in some Middle Eastern, North African, and South Asian societies rationalizes prohibitions on female contact with unrelated men, exclusion from most formal employment, and sometimes extreme marginalization through confinement to the home. The dramatic decline of this stereotype in Western countries reflects the facts that women have advanced their participation in most domains and have thereby undermined the basis for it (which was rooted in part in men's inability to imagine how they could relate to women other than as sex objects).

Violence has often been used as a tool for enforcing segregation. Honor killing of women enforces norms against contact between women and unrelated men. Antiblack lynching traditionally enforced norms against intimate contact between black men and white women. Group-subordinating violence may also include the application of physical force against members' personal property. The antiblack race riots in Tulsa in 1921, which left thousands of blacks homeless and destroyed a thriving black business district, were a case of racial violence that kept blacks in subordinate roles by cutting off their access to forms of property that would support their autonomy and personal independence.

Powerlessness is both a cause and an effect of segregation. The segregation of women from the public sphere and from better-paying "male" jobs makes them more vulnerable to male domination within their families. When state power has been hoarded by dominant groups, they often leverage this power to extend segregation to other domains.

Thus, the different types of unjust group relations form an interlocking set of practices that support group segregation and inequality. All of my proposed modifications of Tilly's theory reinforce his core thesis: that the central cause of categorical inequality is the exclusion of one social group from equal access to critical resources controlled by another. Segregation—social closure—is the linchpin of categorical inequality, since it is needed to keep critical goods preferentially circulating within the dominant social group and out of the hands of the subordinate group, except on disadvantageous terms.

1.5 A Relational Account of the Injustice of Systematic Group Inequality

The relational theory of inequality locates the causes of economic, political, and symbolic group inequalities in the relations (processes of interaction) between the groups, rather than in the internal characteristics of their members or in cultural differences that exist independently of group interaction. It provides a useful perspective for normative purposes because unequal relations among people (that is, modes of social hierarchy), as manifested in their interactions, are proper objects of direct normative assessment in a theory of justice. This relational approach contrasts with views that take de facto inequalities in goods as objects of direct normative assessment independent of the relations through which they are produced or their effects on social relations.

Let us define a *relation* between two people as a mode of conduct—a practice or habit in accordance with a principle, rule, process, or norm—by which one party interacts with (or avoids) the other party, or acts in ways that affect the other party's interests or autonomy. The relation may be face-to-face or mediated by institutions such as the state. It is a *group* relation if the process governs relations between groups. How should we evaluate such relations? I shall advance two approaches to this problem: one broadly contractualist, the other democratic.

Contractualist theories of justice regard persons as self-originating sources of claims:[36] they are entitled to equal standing to demand that others respect their autonomy and interests in accordance with general rules that apply to all and that can be reasonably rejected by none.[37] Since this is a project in nonideal theory, I shall not attempt to construct a contractualist decision procedure that aims to identify an ideal set of rules for interpersonal relations. Instead, I shall use the general contractualist idea to identify objectionable types of interpersonal relations and reasonable alternatives to them. Since this is an investigation into group inequality, I shall focus on intergroup processes that are causally or constitutively connected to categorical inequalities.

In §1.4, I offered a list of types of oppressive group relations, building on Young: marginalization, exploitation, powerlessness, violence, cultural imposition, and stigmatization. Members of all of the types of groups often discussed as subjects of justice—race, ethnicity, nationality, religion, class, caste, gender, sexual orientation—and similar ascriptive identity groups may reasonably reject social arrangements that oppress them in these ways.[38] Contractualists therefore regard such social arrangements as unjust. This conclusion applies across international borders. Thus, distinctions of national citizenship cannot justify opportunity hoarding so extreme as to cause marginalization (mass, chronic unemployment) in other countries. For example, rich country tariffs, agricultural and manufacturing subsidies, and other barriers to trade that prevent poor countries from exporting the principal goods in which they enjoy a comparative advantage, and which thereby cause chronic unemployment in the poor countries, are unjust.

Oppression refers to social inequalities that impose severe disadvantages on its victims. Many cases of socioeconomic inequality are not so extreme. What shall we say about cases in which one social group suffers from higher unemployment rates than another, but not so high as to make it a marginalized group? Without denying that a contractualist approach can help us assess such cases, I suggest that we draw additional evaluative resources from a democratic approach to group inequality.[39] Such an approach initially narrows our focus to social relations within the borders of a democratic state but expands the demands of justice inside those borders.[40] The distinctive normative feature of democratic societies is social equality. All of the members of a democratic society have a just claim to stand in relations of equality with their fellow citizens. As I shall argue below (and in §5.4), this is more demanding than nonoppression in group relations.

Suppose we take the relations between people as primary objects of assessment for the purposes of a theory of justice. We can then derive a standard of justice in distributive outcomes as follows: an inequality in the distribution of some good is unjust if it *embodies* unjust social relations, is *caused* by unjust relations (interactions, processes) among people, or *causes* such unjust relations. This standard enables us to assess as unjust various group inequalities that might not be severe enough to count as forms of oppression, although they violate democratic demands for social equality. (It also reminds us that whether an inequality in the distribution of some good is unjust usually depends on the processes that produce or maintain it.)

Sometimes the distribution of specific goods *embodies* unjust (unequal) social relations. This is true for basic rights and liberties. The all-male franchise exemplifies a distribution that embodies unequal social relations between men and women. Men thereby get to unilaterally set the terms by which men and women interact. (The all-male franchise is also unjust because it is caused by and a cause of further unjust social relations between men and women.) For these sorts of goods, an equal distribution among citizens is usually required for them to stand in relations of equality to one another.

In other cases, the distribution of specific goods *causes* unjust social relations. For example, a system that distributes legal services solely through market provision causes unjust social relations, by making the poor vulnerable to violations of their legal rights by the state and private parties. At least two types of claim follow from the requirement that distributions not cause unjust social relations. First, citizens have a claim to a level of goods sufficient to enable them to participate as equals in society. This claim goes beyond subsistence. It includes, for instance, an entitlement to an income sufficient to purchase good enough clothes that one is able to appear in public without shame, according to prevailing public standards of respectable appearance. It also includes a right to certain configurations of public goods. Those who mobilize by wheelchair are entitled to an infrastructure of public roads, buildings, and transportation that accommodates their needs, lest they be excluded from opportunities to participate in public life. Fair access to responsive public officials also falls under this heading. Second, citizens have a claim to fair opportunities to develop their talents to compete for positions of authority and jobs that pay more than the minimum they can claim under the first principle. A group denied such opportunities, although its members have the potential to serve in such positions, has been relegated to an inferior status, confined to menial, servile occupations. These two types of claim—to minimum levels of goods needed for interaction on terms of equality with others, and to fair opportunities for the development and exercise of talent—are needed to overcome the two dimensions of segregation—exclusion of one group from contact with another, and contact only on subordinating terms.

Finally, the distribution of goods may be *caused* by unjust social relations. Under this heading we include distributions caused by failures to satisfy the preceding requirements—unequal distributions of basic rights and liberties, undemocratic distributions of political influence, failures of access to minimal levels of goods, and unfair distributions of opportunities. We must also include specific discriminatory actions and policies. Unequal distributions brought about through widespread group discrimination exemplify injustices caused by unjust social relations.

In defining unjust intergroup processes, however, we confront a difficulty. A just and democratic society must secure not only the equality of its members, but also their liberties, including their freedom of speech and association. This requirement is in tension with the demands of equal standing because individuals may exercise their freedom of speech by propagating stigmatizing ideas about other groups in society, and their freedom of association by practicing social closure. To evaluate cases, we must distinguish (a) prejudice and stigma from ethnocentrism, (b) the responsibilities of agents in different social domains, and (c) legal from moral claims of justice.

On Tilly's theory, categorical inequality begins with pure ethnocentrism or in-group favoritism. A group that has acquired control over an important good favors its members in granting access to it. Favoring in-group members does not entail any kind of prejudice toward or stigmatizing representations of out-groups.[41] A group may be merely indifferent toward out-groups—or even like them, but favor their own group more. However, prejudice and stigma arise from ethnocentric opportunity hoarding and exploitation through at least two routes. First, advantaged groups may cultivate prejudice and stigma to reinforce group boundaries and motivate in-group members to keep their distance from out-groups. Second, when ethnocentric conduct generates systematic categorical inequalities, dominant groups create stigmatizing stories about marginalized and subordinated groups to explain and rationalize their disadvantage—mainly, by attributing their disadvantage to deficiencies of talent, virtue, or culture intrinsic to the group. Stigma, in turn, often leads to prejudice, since it represents disadvantaged groups as deserving their inferior position and hence as contemptible (if they are exploited or role segregated) or alien (if they are spatially segregated). But this connection, too, is contingent since "cold" cognitive bias (stereotypes) and "hot" (emotional) prejudice are psychologically somewhat independent.[42]

Conduct grounded in group prejudice or stigma toward racial, gender, ethnic, and similar groups is always unjust because it assaults the dignity of groups that do not deserve to be demeaned, and it usually also impairs their access to important goods on unjustified grounds. Those disadvantaged by such conduct have a moral claim that the actors moved by prejudice or stigma stop. Conduct grounded in pure ethnocentrism does not always inflict an expressive harm or violate principles of distributive justice. Whether it does depends on the responsibilities of the agent in the social domain in question. Democratic regimes have a duty to serve all citizens impartially. Ethnocentric conduct by officials is thus unjust since it distributes such services in violation of the public duty of impartiality. It may also be demeaning, if it is systematic enough to amount to a public designation of some groups as more entitled to public service than others. The same considerations apply to operators of public accommodations, including private commercial establishments, who have a duty to serve all members of the public impartially, and to employers and those selling real estate, who are obligated to do their part to ensure fair economic opportunities to all. But individuals acting out of warm feelings for in-group members in the context of personal relations of friendship and intimacy do not demean out-groups or otherwise act unjustly. Out-group members are not morally entitled to demand that these individuals befriend them. This does not mean that such conduct is beyond moral criticism. It contains the seeds of injustice since it may spread its effects beyond the sphere of intimate relations and may lead to categorical inequality, prejudice, and stigma by the routes outlined above.

These moral claims of justice are distinct from legal claims. Even though stigmatizing speech and prejudicial rejection of others in the private sphere are unjust, there are compelling considerations of freedom of expression and association that argue against legally prohibiting such conduct. This does not mean that the state must allow such injustice to spread its effects unimpeded. Public schools play an important role in promoting norms of respectful discourse and undermining prejudice. Nor should the state be passive about private ethnocentric affiliation, even when it is legal and not unjust. Because such affiliation contains the seeds of injustice, the state should take steps to prevent ethnocentric patterns of affiliation from reproducing themselves in institutions of civil society such as public schools. They should take active steps to bring students from different groups together. Ethnocentrism also obstructs the development of a common identity as citizens, which is needed to sustain a vibrant democratic culture and support democratic governance. This gives states further reasons to encourage people to forge more inclusive, less parochial identities in the domains they control.

This book aims to establish integration as an imperative of justice and an ideal of intergroup relations in democratic society. It is not an exercise in ideal theory, which often lacks the ability to identify injustice in our nonideal world. Instead, it begins with a diagnosis of a central social problem: the persistence of systematic group inequalities defined along such lines as race, ethnicity, nationality, religion, class, caste, and gender. Group inequalities arise when a group has acquired a dominant position with respect to a critical good such as land or education and practices social closure to prevent other groups from getting access to these goods, except on subordinating terms. Social closure, or segregation, thus has two sides: suppression of intergroup contact when such contact would cede equal access to the good to outsiders, and promotion of intergroup contact when the advantaged group can relate to outsiders as authorities to subordinates and thereby manipulate the terms of intergroup cooperation to its advantage. A group's dominance over one good then extends to others by emulation, adaptation, leverage, violence, and political control. Group inequality thus arises from the relations or systematic interactions between social groups. The advantaged group may oppress outside groups by reducing them to a marginalized, exploited, powerless, or stigmatized class, vulnerable to group-based violence or denied cultural freedoms. Or it may impose less extreme disadvantages on them: subjecting them to systematic discrimination, denying them equal political influence, and depriving them of the resources they need to stand as equals with others and of opportunities to develop their talents to qualify for positions of authority. Oppressive social relations are unjust because they deprive members of the disadvantaged group of their basic human rights. Less extreme forms of group inequality are unjust because they violate a fundamental norm of democracy, which is social equality. A normative theory that takes social relations as a primary object of normative assessment focuses on such types of injustice. It takes distributions of goods to be unjust if they cause, embody, or are caused by unjust social relations.

The relational theory of group inequality can be used to explain inequalities between any social groups. It offers only an explanatory scheme. In any particular case, the theory must be filled in with a specification of the multiple mechanisms by which group closure generates and reproduces inequality. Such specification is also important for normative purposes. Whether an inequality in distributive outcomes is unjust depends on whether it was caused by, or tends to cause, unjust social relations. Knowledge of causal mechanisms is also needed to fashion remedies, given that our aim is not merely to correct the distributive consequences of unjust social relations, but to eliminate unjust and unequal group relations.

To vindicate and apply the relational theory of group equality, we must therefore fill in the schema by applying it to a particular case. This book takes inequality between blacks and whites as its central case. My choice of this case is partly based on the centrality of black-white inequality to U.S. history and politics. This is also the most intensively researched case in the United States. The quality, range, and abundance of data and theory on black disadvantage, segregation, and their causal mechanisms vastly exceed that for any other racial groups, and for most other categorically unequal groups as well.[43]

In nonideal theory, normative inquiry begins with the identification of a problem. We then seek a causal explanation of the problem to determine what can and ought to be done about it, and who should be charged with correcting it. This requires an evaluation of the mechanisms causing the problem, as well as the responsibility of different agents to alter these mechanisms. If they are unjust, we then consider how these mechanisms can be dismantled. The remaining chapters follow this procedure for our case study. Chapter 2 outlines the direct impact of black-white segregation on black socioeconomic disadvantage. Chapter 3 explores the ways segregation causes racial stigma, and the many ways stigma propagates black disadvantage. Chapter 4 evaluates the causes of racial segregation, tracing them to unjust antiblack intergroup processes. Alternative explanations of black disadvantage that try to dismiss claims that U.S. society is responsible for dismantling its causes, and pin primary responsibility on blacks, are defective on both empirical and normative grounds. Chapter 5 initiates the positive case for racial integration, arguing that it is needed to realize a democratic culture and to fulfill the promise of democratic governance to serve all citizens equally. Chapter 6 examines the causal impact of racial integration, arguing that it improves blacks' access to important goods, reduces prejudice and stigmatization, and improves the competence and accountability of decision-making groups responsible for serving the public. Chapter 7 evaluates four main arguments for affirmative action, arguing that it is best defended as an integrative tool for blocking and dismantling the core causes of race-based disadvantage. Chapter 8 argues that the core "color blindness" arguments against race-based integrationist policies are conceptually confused, empirically mistaken, and lacking a normative rationale. Chapter 9 concludes that, notwithstanding difficulties in the experience of integration, it is an imperative of justice and democracy.

· TWO ·

RACIAL SEGREGATION AND MATERIAL INEQUALITY
IN THE UNITED STATES

2.1 Racial Inequality and Segregation in the United States:
Some Preliminary Observations

In the last chapter I outlined a theory of how segregation is tied to group inequality. Let us now test it for the case of black-white inequality. We begin by considering some important dimensions of black-white inequality in the United States and then consider how black-white segregation causes these inequalities.

Black-White Inequality in the United States

African Americans are worse off than the average American, and worse off than whites, on virtually all major objective measures of well-being. These inequalities are large and enduring and have grown in some cases. Life expectancy for blacks has always been lower than average. For black children born today, it still lags nearly five years behind that of the average American child.[1] The black infant mortality rate is almost twice the U.S. average, growing from 1.5 times the U.S. average since 1950.[2] Blacks are many times more likely than whites to die of AIDS, nearly three times as likely to die from asthma, and well over twice as likely to die from diabetes, kidney disease, or infectious disease. They have higher rates of mortality from heart disease, cerebrovascular disease, cancer, and many other ailments. Many of these inequalities have increased since 1979, and in some cases since 1950.[3]

Black-white economic inequalities are also large and enduring. One quarter of blacks are poor compared to 8 percent of non-Hispanic whites, a 3:1 poverty ratio that has persisted since the 1960s.[4] One-third of black children are poor, compared to 10 percent of white children.[5] Nearly all of these poor black children, while fewer than 1 percent of white children, will experience poverty for ten or more years.[6] The median black household income is two-thirds that of the median white household, a ratio that has widened since 1967.[7] Racial inequalities in wealth are even starker: as of 2005, the median net worth of blacks was less than 10 percent of that of whites.[8] In contrast with middle-class white parents, middle-class black parents have difficulty transmitting their class status to their children. Of children born to parents in the middle income quintile, 45 percent of blacks will fall to the bottom quintile as adults, compared to 16 percent of whites. Two-thirds of whites born to parents in the third and fourth highest income quintiles surpass their parents' real incomes as adults, while only one-third of their black counterparts do so.[9]

Some of these inequalities are due to unequal employment. The black unemployment rate has been twice the white rate for decades.[10] Black male prime-age (25–54) labor force participation rates have also been lower than their white counterparts for decades, with the gap increasing for non–college graduates since 1969. Among male prime-age high school dropouts, the black-white gap in labor force participation is more than 20 percent.[11]

Blacks lag behind whites on every measure of educational attainment. Non-Hispanic whites are almost twice as likely as blacks over twenty-five to have a college degree, and more than twice as likely to have an advanced degree.[12] Black youth are almost twice as likely as white youth to have dropped out of school.[13] Black children enter first grade with lower reading and mathematics skills than their white counterparts and fall further behind in every subsequent grade, even relative to white children who initially scored the same as they did.[14]

The political standing of blacks—their relationship to the state—is also substantially worse than that of whites. The most basic function of the state is to protect its citizens from crime. It does this job less well for blacks than for other Americans. Blacks age twelve and over suffer from violent crime at a rate of 32 per 1,000, compared to 23 per 1,000 whites.[15] Black men are 10.9 times as likely as white men to die of homicide.[16] The state also subjects blacks to far higher rates of criminal punishment than whites. Black men are imprisoned at 6.5 times the rate of white men.[17] The lifetime chance of a black man being imprisoned, if 2001 rates continue, is 32.2 percent, compared to a 5.9 percent chance for white men.[18] For black male high school dropouts born after 1975, it is 69 percent.[19] The incarceration of black men has dramatically increased due to increasingly punitive criminal justice policies enacted since the mid-1970s.[20] Felon disenfranchisement laws have led to mass disenfranchisement of black men. In 1998, 13 percent of black men were disenfranchised, compared to 2 percent of the population overall.[21] In 2008, despite the relaxation of felon disenfranchisement laws in several states, one in eight black men was still disenfranchised.[22]

These inequalities in well-being injure blacks' public standing through the meanings others attach to them. Confronted with evidence of massive racial inequalities, Americans often explain them by invoking contemptuous stereotypes of blacks as lazy, stupid, ignorant, violent, and criminal.[23] In this view, blacks' inferior material condition is due to their personal, cultural, or perhaps biological inferiority, not to injustice. Such widespread stereotypes add profound social stigmatization to blacks' material disadvantages.

Black-White Segregation in the United States

If the stigmatizing explanations of black disadvantage in terms of black cultural or character defects were true, then the case for regarding these disadvantages as unjust would be partially undermined. For whether an inequality is unjust depends in part on the process that brought it about (§1.5). The relational theory of inequality traces these inequalities instead to unjust race relations that systematically exclude blacks from access to important goods. The linchpin of these objectionable relations is racial segregation, understood as processes that prevent interracial contact or structure it on terms of inequality, and resulting conditions of spatial separation by race and disproportionate black occupation of subordinate social roles.

The first step to testing this theory is to document the extent of black segregation in the United States. (In §§4.1–4.2 I will argue that these conditions of black segregation are mainly caused by intergroup processes instigated by whites.) One measure of segregation is the "dissimilarity index," which ranges from 0 to 100. A black-white segregation index of 40 for a metropolitan area at the census tract level indicates that 40 percent of blacks would have to move to a different census tract to establish a black-white ratio within each census tract equal to the overall ratio in the metropolitan area. Some demographers consider a dissimilarity index under 45 to indicate low segregation, 45–60 to indicate medium segregation, and over 60 to indicate high segregation. Another measure of segregation is the "isolation index," which measures the percent of same-race members of a particular unit (neighborhood, school, etc.) that the average member of a given race has. The "exposure index" measures the percent of people of another race that the average member of a given race would meet at random in that unit.

As measured by the index of dissimilarity, residential segregation of blacks with respect to whites is high (65.0); of Latinos, moderate (51.5);

and of Asians, low (42.1). According to Census 2000 data, half of all blacks live in "hypersegregated" census tracts, with an index of dissimilarity of 75 or higher. Only 9 percent of blacks live in census tracts with an index of dissimilarity below 55. At current glacial rates of neighborhood change, it will take forty years for blacks to be as integrated with whites as the next most segregated ethnoracial group, Hispanics, are today. Although non-Hispanic blacks constitute only 12 percent of the U.S. population, their index of isolation is 51.4, indicating that most blacks live in majority-black neighborhoods.[24] Black neighborhoods also tend to be clustered together, concentrated in small areas, and located in inner cities rather than on city/suburban borders.[25]

Public K–12 schools are also highly segregated, largely because they draw from segregated neighborhoods. The typical black student in 2005–06 attended a school that was 52 percent black, 30 percent white, 14 percent Latino, and 4 percent Asian or Native American.[26] In such large states as New York, Michigan, Illinois, and California, less than 25 percent of the average black student's classmates are white.[27] Although *Brown v. Board of Education* led to steep improvements in school integration in the three decades since 1960, since 1990 levels of black-white school integration have stagnated or declined. Now more than half of black students in the Northeast attend schools that are 90–100 percent black.[28]

Segregation is less extreme in the workplace. Data here are spottier and differ depending on the sample and measure of segregation. One survey of jobs in North Carolina found half of all job titles within firms occupied by whites only, and a quarter of blacks working in jobs to which only blacks were assigned.[29] A nationwide study found that the typical black will work in an occupation that, within the firm, is 57 percent black, while the typical white and Latino will work in an occupation within the firm that is rarely more than 4 percent black.[30] Almost a quarter of firms have no black or Latino workers.[31] Segregation varies dramatically according to the race of the firm owner. Of white-owned firms in major metropolitan areas with substantial black populations, 58 percent have no minority employees, whereas 89 percent of black-owned firms have workforces that are at least 75 percent minority. Even if they are located in black neighborhoods, one-third of white-owned firms still have no minority employees.[32] Blacks are also disproportionately assigned to lower-level, poor-paying jobs. Jobs in which blacks are concentrated are paid 17 percent less than jobs occupied mostly by whites, after controlling for the skill requirements of the job.[33] Blacks in managerial positions enjoy less supervisory authority than their white peers.[34]

Informal social integration lags far behind formal integration of schools and firms. More than 90 percent of Americans attend a church in which their ethnoracial group is at least 80 percent of the congregation.[35] Only

12 percent of married or cohabiting couples with at least one black member include a partner of another race, compared to 24 percent of couples with an Asian partner and 26 percent of couples with an Hispanic partner.[36]

Is black-white segregation really due to race, or does it simply reflect socioeconomic differences between blacks and whites? At least with respect to residential, and hence public school, segregation, race trumps class as a factor predicting racial separation. *Levels of residential segregation of blacks from whites do not decline with blacks' attainment of higher socioeconomic status.*[37] This fact justifies expanding the scope of our inquiry into racial inequality beyond the traditionally defined underclass ghetto.[38] We shall see that segregation undermines the opportunities of middle-class as well as poor blacks.

2.2 How Segregation Causes Inequality (1): Spatial Effects in Access to Goods

The most straightforward causal connection between segregation and inequality is spatial. When important goods are asymmetrically distributed across space and groups are sorted into separate spaces containing more or less of these goods, group inequality results. Race-based spatial effects are pronounced for numerous goods, including jobs, consumer goods, professional services, and environmental quality.

Access to Employment: The Spatial Mismatch Hypothesis

The postwar suburbanization boom led millions of whites to leave cities and relocated job growth to suburban areas. Blacks were left behind in economically declining cities with low or negative job growth. These observations led to the spatial mismatch hypothesis, which claims that urban blacks suffer higher unemployment and lower wages than whites due to their difficulties in obtaining distant suburban jobs.[39] Most recent studies confirm the hypothesis; the few that have not typically use methodologies likely to underestimate the effects of spatial mismatch.[40] (Spatial mismatch may also combine with job segregation to reduce black employment: one study finds that the critical predictor of black employment is the proximity of many jobs *occupied by blacks*, suggesting that employers are reluctant to hire blacks into jobs held mostly by whites, or that blacks lack access to the social networks that place people into such jobs.[41])

Several independent lines of evidence support the spatial mismatch hypothesis. Urban employers report far more applications per job opening than suburban employers and take what they perceive as a "captive" urban labor market as a ground for lowering wage rates relative to suburban employers.[42] Wages are lower in black urban neighborhoods than in white suburbs for equivalent low-skilled jobs.[43] Racial inequalities in access to areas of high employment or job growth help explain black-white differences in youth unemployment.[44]

Several mechanisms appear to underlie these results. People who live far from areas of high employment and job growth are less likely to know about job openings there. If they lack cars—a common problem among poor blacks—their access to a job depends on the availability of public transportation within walking distance of both job and home. The lack of effective urban–suburban public transport systems exacerbates the effects of spatial mismatch on unemployment and wage rates. Employers located far from black neighborhoods may be more likely to discriminate against blacks. Urban blacks often fear that they will not be accepted if they venture into white areas.[45]

If living in urban areas impedes urban blacks' access to jobs, why don't they move to the suburbs? Many blacks have moved to the suburbs. But barriers, from housing discrimination to exclusionary zoning, have prevented black population shifts from keeping up with the pace of job shifts.[46] Much black movement has also been to "inner ring" suburbs that suffer from many of the same job losses as the inner cities.[47]

Stephan and Abigail Thernstrom dismiss the spatial mismatch hypothesis on the ground that many Asian and Hispanic immigrants live in the same cities as blacks but do not suffer the same high unemployment rates. They imply that low black employment should rather be credited to a poor work ethic among blacks, who are supposedly unwilling to take the menial jobs that immigrants take.[48] Their argument ignores important differences between immigrants and African Americans. Immigrants can choose not to move to the United States, or to move back home, if they do not find work here. The ones in the United States overwhelmingly belong to the selected group that succeeded in finding work here. Many did so through "chain migration"—a mode of ethnocentric opportunity hoarding, whereby immigrant small-business owners recruit new employees from recently arrived coethnics, rather than from the wider urban population.[49] The most successful immigrant groups to the United States, such as Cubans, Chinese, Koreans, and Indians, arrived with substantial human and financial capital, or access to capital from their home countries, which they used to create businesses and employ their fellow ethnics.[50] Bad schools and barriers to black capital accumulation (§§2.3–2.4) prevent blacks from establishing their own enterprises and taking advantage of ethnocentric hiring to the same degree. Immigrant groups who arrived in the United States with low human and financial capital, such as Cambodians, Hmong, Laotians, and Vietnamese "boat people" (as opposed to relatively elite first-wave Vietnamese who arrived at the fall of South Vietnam and often had strong military or political connections), have economic outcomes in the second generation similar to those of blacks.[51] In addition, as even the Thernstroms concede, employers openly admit that they will not hire blacks if immigrant labor is available.[52]

Access to Retail and Commercial Services

In the late 1980s and early 1990s, when I lived in a majority-black Detroit neighborhood, there was only one restaurant, other than fast-food restaurants, nearby. My neighborhood was solidly working class to middle class; the adjoining neighborhood was even better off. The residents of both neighborhoods had money to spend. Yet we found ourselves spending much of it beyond Detroit's borders because so little retail and entertainment was available in the city. Detroit, then with a population of one million, had no department store. Overall, black neighborhoods have fewer supermarkets, banks, retail outlets, restaurants (other than fast food), movie theaters, and other consumer services than white neighborhoods do. This pattern persists even after controlling for income.[53]

The cost to segregated residents of having to travel outside their cities to spend their money is not limited to the personal inconvenience and cost of travel. The lack of nearby retail and commercial services makes their neighborhoods less attractive to prospective home buyers and thus depresses the value of local housing. Lower housing values, combined with the lack of commercial property, mean that predominantly black cities have a smaller tax base from which to fund city services. Segregated blacks must therefore pay higher local property tax rates than whites for the same level of city services or put up with inferior services—which further lower their home values and tax base. When the lack of local services forces blacks to spend their income in predominantly white cities, their spending stimulates the economies of those cities rather than their own.

It might be argued that the location of businesses is simply efficient. Predominantly white locations offer better opportunities to businesses because they can offer lower tax and crime rates, and hence lower insurance costs and better access to credit. It does not follow that no racial injustices are implicated in the distribution of businesses. That would depend on how city borders came to be drawn along racially segregated lines, and how government policies have helped create and maintain the residential segregation that makes it possible for businesses to be unequally accessible to different racial groups (§4.1).

Moreover, private decisions to develop commercial real estate and locate businesses are not color-blind. Nationwide businesses and real estate investment companies use "cluster analysis" to aid their location decisions. Cluster analysis segments neighborhoods along lines of assumed homogeneity based on their demographic and socioeconomic characteristics.[54] Racial stereotypes concerning presumed consumer demand inform rankings of neighborhoods for business interests. Nationwide Insurance used a cluster analysis that labeled predominantly black neighborhoods of Richmond, Virginia, as "undesirable" as a ground for refusing home insurance to their residents.[55] While the Middle Class Black Families cluster has a homeownership rate higher than the national average, and the highest of all eleven urban clusters, it is ranked only thirty-eighth out of forty clusters for home loan demand—a deterrent for prime lenders.[56] Cluster analysis targets black neighborhoods for subprime and predatory loans at high interest rates.[57]

Cluster analysis has self-fulfilling features. Decisions to locate particular retail and consumer services away from black neighborhoods, on the stereotype of low black demand, limit black demand by limiting black access. Real estate agents and advisors use cluster analysis to steer home buyers to neighborhoods that match their stereotype, thereby perpetuating "homogeneous" clusters. Neighborhood homogeneity serves the interests of demographic companies and their clients in perpetuating the predictive power of their models, but not the civic interests of a democracy in integrated neighborhoods, or the interests of black citizens in having access to consumption opportunities commensurate with their income.

Access to Health-Related Goods and Professional Services

Residence in segregated black neighborhoods is associated with poor health outcomes.[58] Mortality rates are higher, the higher the percentage of blacks in a neighborhood, for black and white residents alike, after controlling for socioeconomic status.[59] Infants born in predominantly black segregated neighborhoods are more likely to have low birth weight, a condition associated with poor health outcomes including infant mortality, childhood illness, and developmental disorders.[60]

Segregation affects health through a lack of retail and consumer services. Residents of segregated neighborhoods have lower access to medical facilities and well-stocked pharmacies.[61] They have lower access to nutritious food, due to the lack of supermarkets.[62] White neighborhoods enjoy one supermarket for every 3,816 residents; black neighborhoods, one for every 23,582 residents.[63] Many blacks therefore eat the food typically offered by small grocery stores: low-quality meats and calorie-dense processed foods, with little fresh produce. Diets reliant on such foods are associated with higher rates of diabetes and mortality.[64]

Segregation also affects health through a relative lack of professional health care services. The physician/population ratio in black communities is substantially lower than the U.S. average.[65] This is not just an effect of class. Predominantly black communities are four times more likely to be underserved than other communities with the same average income.[66] Professionals are less likely to locate in economically depressed and segregated areas, thereby reducing segregated residents' access to professional services.[67]

Segregation also affects health by isolating predominantly black residents from *public goods* that promote health, such as adequate public recreational facilities and streets safe enough for residents to exercise in them.[68] Segregated black neighborhoods also tend to have high concentrations of *public bads* that undermine health. They are targeted for intensive advertising by alcohol and tobacco companies.[69] They concentrate poverty and unemployment, which leads to high crime rates and mortality from homicide.[70] They have higher concentrations of lead, causing their residents to suffer higher rates of lead poisoning.[71] They have more air pollution,[72] which appears to elevate cancer rates.[73] Their poor living conditions increase rates of tuberculosis, while high population density ensures relatively high contagion, and segregation ensures that contagion is racially confined.[74] Hence, as one literature review of this subject concluded, "racial residential segregation is a fundamental cause of racial disparities in health."[75]

2.3 How Segregation Causes Inequality (2): Capital-Mediated Effects

Segregation affects socioeconomic status through its effects on people's ability to accumulate capital. "Capital" designates assets that constitute one's socioeconomic status or enable one to achieve a higher socioeconomic status. Higher socioeconomic status refers not just to higher income, but to positions of authority, power, and prestige, in which one can exercise autonomy, judgment, and varied skills. There are four forms of capital: wealth (financial assets), human capital (marketable skills), social capital, and cultural capital. Social capital refers to networks of associates by which knowledge of and access to opportunities is transmitted, and norms of trust and reciprocity are enforced. Cultural capital refers to facility in the often informal and implicit norms, conventions, and codes of conduct that govern access to advantages. Segregation undermines blacks' ability to accumulate all four forms of capital.

Financial Capital

The auctioneer was having so much difficulty getting people to bid on houses that he had to remind them: "Folks, the ground underneath the house goes with it. You do know that, right?" A string of houses sold for less than $30,000—less than the price of a new car. One four-bedroom house sold for $7,000—less than the price of a used car.[76] The auctioneer was selling homes in Detroit, the most segregated city in the United States. His predicament reflects in extreme form the difficulty segregated blacks have in accumulating assets with appreciating value.

Residential segregation causes blacks and whites to live in neighborhoods with unequal housing values. Even middle-class black neighborhoods suffer disproportionately from numerous disadvantages—distance from areas of job growth; absence of retail outlets; proximity to areas of high crime, poverty, unemployment, and social disorder; high pollution; poor schools; inferior public services; and high taxes—that depress home values and reduce housing appreciation. Since the middle class invests most of its savings in homeownership, confinement to disadvantaged neighborhoods has a substantial impact on blacks' ability to accumulate wealth and entails that blacks enjoy lower returns on housing investment than whites. From 1970 to 1990, white-owned homes appreciated 19.7 percent on average, compared to 5.3 percent for black homes.[77] Living in a neighborhood with 0–2 percent blacks was enough to significantly depress the appreciation of one's home compared to living in a neighborhood with zero blacks.[78] Because credit worthiness depends on wealth, blacks' lower home values mean they are less able to obtain credit on favorable terms than are otherwise similar whites. Full-service banks are less common in black neighborhoods, and finance companies steer blacks into subprime and predatory loans that charge higher rates and fees.[79] In the 1990s blacks paid 0.5 percent higher mortgage rate than whites and suffered a cumulative loss of $24 billion due to denial of mortgages and higher mortgage interest rates. Much of this loss can be attributed to residential segregation, apart from direct discrimination by lending agents.[80] While the losses from systematic predatory lending in black neighborhoods during the 2000s housing bubble have yet to be tallied, preliminary evidence suggests a devastating impact on black communities. Costs include not just the loss of housing and equity due to foreclosure, but lower neighborhood quality and higher taxes endured by those who keep their homes in blocks blighted by abandoned and vandalized houses. One study found that each home foreclosure in a city costs it $34,199. These costs are concentrated in segregated cities.[81]

Lack of access to financial capital is a major cause of lower rates of black entrepreneurship relative to whites. Whites are three times more likely than blacks are to be self-employed, and twice as likely to enter self-employment. This difference is largely due to racial differences in financial assets and rates of paternal self-employment.[82] Fathers often transmit entrepreneurial skills and the business itself to their sons. Half of all privately owned businesses in the United States are acquired by inheritance or purchase; the other half are started by their owners. The legacy of pervasive discrimination left blacks with few businesses to inherit, while segregation reduces their access to the financial capital needed to purchase businesses. Hence, among self-employed blacks, 94 percent started their business from scratch.[83]

Social Capital

Many black residents of Chicago's hypersegregated South Side have never visited downtown. Some have never even left their neighborhoods.[84] Even if they traveled to the next neighborhood, "they would still be unlikely to see a white face; and if they went to the next neighborhood beyond that, no whites would be there either."[85] The social isolation of poor blacks in hypersegregated neighborhoods is an extreme case of a more general tendency of blacks and whites to associate within largely segregated social networks. One study of interracial contact in the Detroit area, including many middle-class subjects, found that only 8 percent of blacks and 5 percent of whites visit the homes of neighbors of the other race.[86]

This segregation of social networks has profound consequences for blacks' access to opportunities, for who one knows matters as much as what one knows in getting ahead. Social capital theory explains how social contacts matter for getting ahead. Social capital refers to networks of people in social relationships that serve as resources for individual and collective action. Social capital serves as a resource in three ways: by providing information channels, supporting cooperation and reciprocity, and sustaining other social norms that coordinate people's behavior.[87] Here I shall focus on social capital as a conduit for information. I consider the other two functions under the rubric of cultural capital.

Social capital may be "bonding" (tie people with common social identities) or "bridging" (tie people with different identities).[88] Social ties may also be "strong" or "weak." Strong ties are characterized by high emotional intensity, investment of time, intimacy, and reciprocity.[89] Weak ties manifest these features to a low degree. Under conditions of segregation, strong ties tend to be bonding (within-race) and bridging ties tend to be weak. However, weak bridging ties have special significance for people's socioeconomic prospects because they give people access to information generated outside their identity group.[90]

Workers often use their personal networks to find out about job opportunities, with weak ties—mere acquaintances—providing a surprising number of successful leads.[91] However, racial segregation depresses blacks' access to white social networks.[92] Such access is important because half of employers frequently recruit new employees by word-of-mouth through a firm's employees or business contacts.[93] If a firm is overwhelmingly white and recruits new employees by employee referral, segregation at work, school, and church and in neighborhoods practically guarantees that few blacks will learn about the firm's job openings. Case studies of working-class men confirm that their differential access to contacts is a critical factor explaining worse outcomes for African American men compared to white men and immigrants.[94] Black women, too, lose out from segregation: they earn less if they depended on a neighborhood contact to get a job, compared to those who obtained a job through an outside contact.[95] Similar considerations apply to educational opportunities. Black students in segregated high schools have lower access to information about predominantly white colleges than do black students in predominantly white high schools, who learn about colleges from white school acquaintances, teachers, and guidance counselors.[96]

Segregation in communities of concentrated marginalization not only limits people's access to weak bridging ties but also undermines their bonding social capital. Levels of trust are extremely low within such communities. Employed blacks are less likely than whites to recommend their unemployed male relatives and friends for a job because they do not trust them to do a good job and worry that this will damage the goodwill they have established with their employers. To save face, unemployed black men adopt a posture of "defensive individualism," avoiding the pain of rejection by not even asking their employed connections to provide a referral. Thus, even when black men have connections, they are not utilized effectively.[97]

Human Capital

Children acquire marketable skills from the social contacts in their community—parents, other relatives, neighbors, and peers. These social relationships are a form of social capital.[98] Economist Glenn Loury was the first to advance a model of the relations among segregation, social capital, and human capital.[99] Suppose we start off with two groups with equal innate potential, but different developed endowments of human capital due to past discrimination in education. If we passed effective antidiscrimination laws, so that individuals with equal developed human capital have equal job opportunities, would this overcome the historic inequality? Loury demonstrated that if there were no group segregation, then children of the disadvantaged group could take advantage of the social capital available in the integrated community and learn valuable skills from everyone. This would reduce the cost to the disadvantaged of acquiring human capital and make convergence between the advantaged and the disadvantaged group very likely. However, if residential, school, and family segregation exists (there is no intermarriage), then children of the disadvantaged will draw from a smaller pool of human capital in the prior generation, and the cost of acquiring more human capital than the average in their community will be high. Segregation ties children to a disadvantaged structure of social capital, thereby perpetuating the effects of historic discrimination in human capital development, even in the presence of effective antidiscrimination law, and even for children with innate potential equal to that of their more advantaged peers.

Recent empirical studies support Loury's theory. George Borjas found that for a wide variety of ethnic groups in the United States, the human capital of the current generation depends not just on their parents' human capital but on the average level of human capital in the ethnic group's previous generation.[100] The human capital possessed by the whole ethnic group, and not just the family unit, influenced children's development. In a later study, Borjas found that the influence of such "ethnic capital" was strongly linked to levels of neighborhood segregation. Even among children who grew up in the same neighborhood, skill levels were associated with frequency of contact with other members of the same ethnic group.[101]

Cultural Capital

Much of what it takes to succeed in school, at work, and in one's community consists of cultural habits acquired by adaptation to the social environment. Such cultural adaptations are known as "cultural capital."

Segregation leads social groups to form different codes of conduct and communication. Some habits that help individuals in intensely segregated, disadvantaged environments undermine their ability to succeed in integrated, more advantaged environments. At Strive, a job training organization, Gyasi Headen teaches young black and Latino men how to drop their "game face" at work. The "game face" is the angry, menacing demeanor these men adopt to ward off attacks in their crime-ridden, segregated neighborhoods. As one trainee described it, it is the face you wear "at 12 o'clock at night, you're in the 'hood and they're going to try to get you."[102] But the habit may freeze it into place, frightening people from outside the ghetto, who mistake the defensive posture for an aggressive one. It may be so entrenched that black men may be unaware that they are glowering at others. This reduces their chance of getting hired.

The "game face" is a form of cultural capital that circulates in seg-regated underclass communities, helping its members survive. Outside these communities, it burdens its possessors with severe disadvantages. Urban ethnographer Elijah Anderson highlights the cruel dilemma this poses for ghetto residents who aspire to mainstream values and seek re-sponsible positions in mainstream society.[103] If they manifest their "de-cent" values in their neighborhoods, they become targets for merciless harassment by those committed to "street" values, who win esteem from their peers by demonstrating their ability and willingness to insult and physically intimidate others with impunity. To protect themselves against their tormentors, and to gain esteem among their peers, they adopt the game face, wear "gangster" clothing, and engage in the posturing style that signals that they are "bad." This survival strategy makes them pari-ahs in the wider community. Police target them for questioning, searches, and arrests.[104] Store owners refuse to serve them, or serve them brusquely, while shadowing them to make sure they are not shoplifting. Employers refuse to employ them.[105] Or they employ them in inferior, segregated jobs. A restaurant owner may hire blacks as dishwashers, but not as wait staff, where they could earn tips.

Cultural differences in communication styles also disadvantage segre-gated blacks. The dialect of segregated inner city blacks, known as Black English Vernacular, has drifted away from Standard American English, which is spoken by nearly all whites. This linguistic drift is a consequence of segregation. The distance between the dialect poor blacks speak at home and that taught in the classroom impedes their educational prog-ress and handicaps them in competing for jobs, especially jobs that re-quire contact with a diverse public.[106]

Differences in cultural capital also disadvantage middle-class blacks who speak Standard American English. Subtle cultural differences in body language, habits of emotional expression and management, styles of personal appearance, and interaction rituals can impair the ability of un-tutored blacks to navigate white-dominated social worlds successfully.[107] One manual, written by Michelle Johnson, a black employment lawyer, advises blacks wishing to pursue careers in white-dominated firms on what topics of conversation to avoid in white social circles, what clothes to wear to put whites at ease, how "black" hairstyles can get one in trou-ble at work, and how to decode indirect styles of speech that appear more prevalent among whites.[108]

The friction and miscommunication caused by differences in cultural styles are a result of ignorance on *both* sides. There is no panculturally valid standard concerning the degree of indirection proper for deliver-ing sensitive information, for example. Yet mutual ignorance reproduces racial inequality when blacks in subordinate positions must pay the price for it. If what most blacks see as ordinary frankness is interpreted by whites as confrontational, the straight-talking black worker in the white-dominated environment will be labeled as having an "attitude," and her career will suffer accordingly.[109]

It is hard to know how far Johnson's experiences of cross-racial miscommunication, drawn from her employment cases, generalize to African Americans and whites overall. Race defines a social identity, not a culture. Cultural variations exist within and not just between racial groups. It is also hard to know how much to credit white perceptions of black workers' "attitude" to impartially applied norms more prevalent among whites, and how much to an unconscious double standard for blacks that demands more deferential speech from them. My point stands independently of any attempt to equate race with culture, however. It is not about within-race homogeneity, but between-race heterogeneity. It views race as significant because it marks the boundary of segregated groups, not because it bears any intrinsic cultural content. When different people belong to distinct social networks, their norms of communication and interaction will diverge in ways that will not be immediately understood by either side. When the segregated groups stand in unequal social relations, the disadvantaged group will tend to bear the costs of misunderstandings arising from their interactions.

Other differences in cultural capital impair blacks' access to elite jobs. Facility with elite leisure activities such as golf, familiarity with cultural reference points that are the basis for small talk with coworkers, mastery of elite norms for circulating among people at a company party, and similar cultural skills have no inherent economic value. They grease the wheels of commerce merely in being shared among those who make business decisions. This has important implications for blacks' careers. A rare inside study of hiring practices by elite firms in law, investment banking, and consulting found that "cultural fit"—similarity to firm members in leisure pursuits, demeanor, sense of humor, and the like—is regarded as one of the two most important qualifications in a job candidate and is cited by 70 percent of decision makers as more important than technical qualifications. While a "fit" match can help job candidates whose identities do not match firm demographics, in practice, lack of facility with "upper-middle-class cultural signals" disproportionately disadvantages black candidates, who are less likely than whites are to share the cultural background of their interviewers.[110]

As people move up a career ladder, the qualifications that matter tend to get "softer" and less objectively observable. Getting one's superiors to feel comfortable in one's presence, winning their trust and confidence, becoming a person to whom they turn for informal advice and off-the-cuff discussions, being perceived as loyal and with leadership potential become increasingly important. Whites' habits of social closure limit the opportunities of blacks to acquire these subjective qualifications and demonstrate to their employers that they have them. This results in racially distinct paths of promotion to managerial and executive occupations. Black workers tend to be confined to narrow paths heavily dependent on demonstration of formal qualifications such as education and years of experience on the job. White workers enjoy access not only to this path, but to informal paths that are less dependent on demonstrations of objective qualifications. They are more likely than blacks with equivalent objective qualifications to win the confidence of an employer that they can handle a job one or two tiers higher than any job in which they have prior experience, and more likely to attract promotion offers from outside employers.[111]

2.4 How Segregation Causes Inequality (3): State-Mediated Effects on Access to Public Goods

Standard measures of poverty focus on individuals' access to income and the commodities it buys. This focus often leads social commentators to argue that the residents of segregated, underclass ghettos do not have such bad lives since most own TVs, consumer electronics, and even expensive athletic shoes. Yet possession of such commodities pales in importance compared to access to public goods. Being able to live in a safe neighborhood, free from threats of gunfire, mugging, and harassment; in a clean neighborhood, free from toxic wastes, air pollution, discarded drug needles, trash-strewn empty lots, run-down and abandoned buildings and cars; in an orderly neighborhood, free from graffiti-marred buildings, open drug dealing, prostitution, and other degrading conduct that expresses contempt for humanity and the interests of others: how many cell phones is that worth? Having access to public parks where one's children can safely play, to well-maintained sidewalks and roads free from potholes likely to disable one's car, to schools that offer an education good enough to qualify one for more than menial, dead-end jobs: how many pairs of fancy athletic shoes is that worth? Enjoying warranted confidence that the police will, if one is innocent of any crime, treat one with the respect one is due, rather than as a criminal suspect, and extend one the protections of the law rather than police harassment, accusation, and prosecutorial abuse: here the question of comparison to consumer goods goes beyond the rhetorical to the absurd. To measure the greatest costs of segregation, then, we must consider its impact on blacks' access to state-provided goods—especially local public services—and exposure to public burdens—notably, taxes, crime, and police abuse.

Access to Public Services

In California, black students have access to substantially fewer AP courses than white students do.[112] Starker inequalities have been found in the most disadvantaged, segregated schools. In the South Bronx, Jonathan Kozol has found classrooms with more students than chairs, and a single windowless classroom filled with four kindergarten classes and a sixth-grade class. One school wasted many hours of the school day showing cartoons and making students line up and wait for lunch and recess.[113] Overall, high-poverty urban schools have higher teacher turnover, teachers with lower qualifications, and lower teacher morale than middle-class suburban schools have.[114] Segregation is directly tied to these outcomes because teacher turnover is higher in schools with high concentrations of blacks.[115] The inexperience of teachers in black schools, in turn, exacerbates the black-white gap in educational achievement.[116]

Individuals mostly depend on their local governments to provide police protection, public order, fire protection, trash removal, streets, parks, public recreational facilities, and schools. Hence, their access to such state-provided goods depends on where they live. American local government is highly fragmented. City borders often divide adjoining, racially segregated neighborhoods. Local governments serving relatively wealthy neighborhoods use zoning—regulations restricting multifamily units, public housing, rental units in predominantly owner-occupied neighborhoods, trailer parks, and other low-income housing, and mandating minimum lot sizes, setbacks, and even expensive amenities—to prevent the entry of less wealthy households inside their borders.[117] Because municipal fragmentation is particularly intense near cities with high black populations, there is reason to believe that whites have used race-based municipal boundary drawing in conjunction with class-exclusionary zoning to exclude blacks from their cities and hence from the public goods they provide through their local governments.[118]

Segregation thus depresses blacks' access to public as well as private goods. Multiple studies find that blacks are less satisfied than whites are with the quality of public services available to them,[119] a response that fits with objective measures of public service quality in segregated black communities.[120] They are also less satisfied, and receive poorer services, when they reside in segregated, fragmented majority-black municipalities than when they are the minority in multiracial, consolidated metropolitan governments.[121]

One reason for these findings is that racial segregation prevents middle-class blacks from practicing class segregation as whites can. When a housing market opens to black entry, poor as well as middle-class blacks enter. Because suburban middle-class blacks are more integrated by class than suburban whites, they share more of the problems of the poor than whites do.[122] This is reflected in the composition of public services their communities provide. Where white suburbs can invest heavily in the type of infrastructure development, such as roads and utilities, that attract businesses and economic growth, black suburbs must spend more on redistributive services such as health care, housing, and welfare services needed to support their poorer residents.[123]

Thus, blacks have poorer opportunities than whites to convert their wealth into access to local public services. Blacks' residential returns on educational attainment are less than half those for whites.[124] Nor can blacks convert their wealth into residence in affluent neighborhoods as whites can. In many metropolitan areas, poor whites (making less than $30,000/year) live in neighborhoods with *higher* median household incomes than affluent blacks (making more than $60,000/year) do.[125] This entails that "the residential returns to being middle class for blacks are far smaller than for middle-class whites."[126] Middle-income whites (making between $30,000 and $60,000/year) are also more willing to share state-provided goods with poor whites than with prosperous blacks. Race trumps class as a barrier to access to these goods.

Segregation enables whites with political power to withhold local public services from blacks even when they live in the same city. Although interracial sharing of public resources is greater in consolidated metropolitan governments than in municipally fragmented regions, residential segregation within these government units impedes the formation of interracial political coalitions and enables groups in control of local government to selectively direct public resources to their own neighborhoods, to the exclusion of other groups' neighborhoods.[127] Selective public disinvestment in segregated black neighborhoods can be devastating. In response to the fiscal crisis of the 1970s, white officials running New York City closed thirty-five fire stations, of which twenty-seven were in poor, segregated neighborhoods that suffered *higher* rates of fire than the rest of the city did. This led to a shocking increase in fires in these neighborhoods, mass abandonment of devastated city blocks, destruction of social networks, and overcrowding of neighboring blocks with those who fled the fires. A public health crisis ensued. The city ignored the chaos it caused because the blacks and Puerto Ricans affected by it were a minority and had no allies in City Hall.[128]

Tax Burdens

Segregated black municipalities, even in the suburbs, have weaker public finances, with weaker tax bases and higher debt loads, than do white communities.[129] Sharply race- and class-segregated white communities can afford high levels of public services at moderate tax rates, or low levels of services at extremely low tax rates. Mixed-class segregated black communities must pay high tax rates for relatively poor services. After controlling for differences in median home values, residents of municipalities with substantial black presence pay tax rates that are 65 percent higher than what residents of white municipalities pay.[130] In highly segregated Allegheny County, Pennsylvania, which is fragmented into 130 local governments, residents of the black majority town of Homestead pay 10.5 mills on their homes and a 1.1 percent income tax, while residents of the white town of McCandless pay 1.3 mills and a 0.5 percent income tax.[131]

Exposure to Crime, Decay, and Police Underenforcement

Of all the public goods that define neighborhood quality, people rate security from crime and absence of blight as the most important.[132] Racial segregation, because it concentrates poverty, tends to create crime-ridden, blighted neighborhoods.[133] To the extent that the state is responsible for creating and maintaining residential segregation (§4.1), it is responsible for the higher rates of crime and decay to which segregated blacks are exposed. Here I focus on the state's indirect responsibility for these conditions, embodied in its failure to enforce the laws. Failures to repair buildings or pick up trash that would generate a citation in a prosperous neighborhood are ignored by city authorities when they take place in poor, segregated neighborhoods. This failure to enforce housing codes contributes to urban decay.[134]

Cities also tend to withhold police resources from segregated black neighborhoods. Los Angeles devotes three times more police officers to its relatively peaceful southeast division than to the nearly equal-sized Compton area, which suffers from the highest homicide rates in the city. Residents of similar neighborhoods in Baltimore complain that the police ignore their calls to close down open-air drug markets. Dallas assigns its least experienced officers to the highest-crime black neighborhoods. It ignores most property crimes there and takes longer to respond to citizen distress calls from these neighborhoods than from others in the city.[135]

This withdrawal of police services from segregated neighborhoods has two effects, both destructive of the rule of law. One is the creation of zones of lawlessness—notably where drug markets and street prostitution are tolerated—in which open lawbreaking and disorder are the norm, rival gangs fight over control of illicit markets, and no one can expect police protection from random violence. The enforcement of laws protecting public order, such as those against public drunkenness, littering, excessive noise, and loitering, is also suspended in these zones.[136] The second effect is the constitution of certain *people* as outlaws—drug dealers, pimps, prostitutes, gang members and their suspected associates, and anyone suspected of being an illegal immigrant or working in the underground economy (which constitutes a substantial proportion of economic activity in the ghetto).[137] Outlaws are held beyond the protection of the law. Police exploit the fact that the outlaws are working in illegal ways to extort sex, drugs, money, and other goods from them and routinely violate their rights to due process.[138]

Social scientists disagree on whether vigorous police enforcement can influence aggregate crime rates. But citizens have an individual claim of justice to police response, or at least to nondiscrimination in police responses. The failure of police to respond to calls for help has other destructive consequences. Blacks express much higher levels of distrust in the police, and in local government more generally, than do whites.[139] In lawless segregated neighborhoods, people realize that they are on their own when it comes to personal protection and resort to solutions, such as joining gangs, that exacerbate violence.[140] They lose trust in the police and refuse to cooperate with them in criminal investigations, for fear of retaliation by criminal suspects.

Overenforcement: Racial Profiling and Harsh Justice

Blacks' mistrust of police, born of long experience with the failure of the police to protect them, ironically reinforces a pathological police *overenforcement* of the law against blacks in other respects. Police respond in kind to distrust and uncooperativeness and become alienated from the residents whom they are supposed to protect. They thereby lose access to the local knowledge of residents and fall back on hostile racial stereotypes that undermine their ability to distinguish criminals from innocents in their midst. Sporadic attempts to reassert police authority in lawless areas therefore often result in harassment, abuse, and even killing of innocents. The police killing of unarmed Amadou Diallo, a black immigrant from Guinea, in a hail of forty-one bullets in the Bronx in 1999 illustrates the deadly impact of race-stereotyped excessive suspicion of black men.[141]

Segregation reinforces racial profiling and a pathological relationship between police and blacks in another way. Because it marks off "black" from "white" neighborhoods, it provides the occasion for generalized suspicion of the presence of blacks in the "wrong" neighborhood. Such racial profiling could not occur in integrated neighborhoods. Racial profiling in turn reinforces racial segregation, by deterring blacks from entering neighborhoods where they fear police harassment.[142]

Blacks are worse off than whites and the average American on virtually every objective measure of well-being, including health, wealth, education, employment, criminal victimization and involvement, and political participation. Blacks are also highly segregated from whites in most domains: neighborhoods, schools, work, churches, and families. The relational theory of group inequality claims that this condition of segregation and the processes that cause it explain observed racial inequalities. Segregation isolates blacks from access to job opportunities, retail and commercial services, and public health goods. It impedes their ability to accumulate financial, human, social, and cultural capital. It deprives them of access to state-provided goods, including decent public schools and adequate law enforcement, while subjecting them to higher tax burdens and discriminatory police practices. To what extent can observed inequality be attributed to segregation? One study found that if segregation were entirely eliminated, so would all of the differences between blacks and whites in income, unemployment, and high school graduation rates, as would two-thirds of the racial difference in rates of single motherhood.[143] Such a finding cannot be taken too literally, as outcomes are sensitive to model specification. Nevertheless, it, along with the other studies surveyed here, gives us strong grounds to believe that the impact of segregation on racial inequality is large. The arguments of this book do not depend on the supposition that segregation is the sole, or even the overwhelming, cause of all of the disadvantages of the black community. I shall discuss other prominent explanations of black disadvantage in §§4.2–4.3. I believe that the evidence presented here shows that segregation is an *important* cause of black disadvantage. As long as that claim is granted, the normative implications of my argument stand.

· THREE ·

SEGREGATION, RACIAL STIGMA, AND DISCRIMINATION

3.1 How Segregation Causes Stereotypes and Attribution Biases

Segregation causes patterns of racial inequality that influence the ways racial groups represent one another. These representations, in turn, reinforce practices of segregation and reproduce categorical inequality. This pattern of explanation, from segregation to categorical inequality to categorical cognitions, follows Tilly's. This chapter explains the psychological mechanisms underwriting it. It also shows how the representations caused by segregation inflict an expressive injury by stigmatizing the disadvantaged.

We have seen in chapter 2 that segregation causes blacks to suffer higher rates of poverty and unemployment and undermines blacks' ability to accumulate financial assets and become entrepreneurs. It causes a divergence between black and white English dialects, and interracial miscommunication due to divergence of other social norms. It concentrates poverty in black neighborhoods and denies them public services such as adequate police and fire protection, trash pickup, and decent schools. It exacerbates social disorders engendered by life in neighborhoods shut off from avenues of opportunity—crime, gang activity, idleness, blight, low school achievement, dropping out, teenage parenthood, absent fathers, and welfare dependency.

Given that practices of social closure make race highly salient as a social category and identity marker, people will try to make sense of the observed effects of segregation by constructing stereotypes about racial groups. The group inequalities generated by segregation provide much of the content of these stereotypes. Thus, people will tend to perceive blacks as (relatively) poor, on welfare, uneducated, idle, prone to form single-parent families at a young age, unlikely to keep up their property, and liable to engage in criminal activity. Such group stereotypes are then used to make inferences about the likely characteristics of individual blacks.

Stereotyping is a universal cognitive process applied to all classes of objects. We have stereotypes about food, cars, trees—virtually any familiar category. The content of stereotypes is not inherently derogatory, nor are stereotypes typically generated by preexisting group prejudice. They are more a matter of "cold" cognitive processing than "hot" emotion. We form and act on them automatically and unconsciously. Stereotypes are simply schemas about classes of objects, used to make inferences about particular objects once they are recognized as a member of a particular class. They are crude, typically unconsciously held heuristics that enable people to economize on information processing and react quickly to situations involving the object. As such, they are not inherently morally objectionable.

Some researchers claim that stereotypes are accurate representations of their objects.[1] In the causal account just suggested, superficial stereotypes about the external behavior and condition of segregated groups typically embody a grain of truth. Blacks really are more likely to be poor, to have dropped out of school, and to be single parents than whites. But stereotypic cognitive processing involves several biases. Stereotypes tend to exaggerate between-group differences and within-group homogeneity. They lead people to exaggerate the conformity of individuals to their group stereotype. They make people more receptive to and better able to recall stereotype-confirming than disconfirming evidence. They lead people to overlook stereotype-independent individuating information about group members.[2]

As so far described, these cognitive biases do not amount to group stigmatization. Stereotypes of a group's external behavior or condition do tend to efface the individuality of group members. And they may support "statistical discrimination"—preference for (or against) individuals on the assumption that they posses the (un)desired traits stereotypically ascribed to their group.[3] While this is unjust, it does not yet amount to a public stamp of dishonor on a group as such. Group stigmatization requires the imputation of dishonorable *meanings* to stereotypes of group difference—public narratives or interpretive frames for explaining perceived group differences in terms that demean the members of the stigmatized group.[4]

These explanations are guided by what social psychologists call "attribution biases." When explaining someone's external behavior or condition, observers may attribute it to dispositional causes (internal to the person) or situational causes (external to the person). Pervasive biases affect this choice. People tend to attribute stereotype-confirming behavior to people's internal dispositions, such as their genes, culture, or voluntary choices, and stereotype-disconfirming behavior to their external circumstances, such as luck or the action of others.[5] Thus, in the aftermath of Hurricane Katrina, news media described stranded blacks as "looting" grocery stores for necessities such as milk and bread, abstracting from the desperate circumstances brought on by the storm, and the fact that the flood would have otherwise destroyed these groceries. The "looting" frame fit their actions into the narratives of inner-city riots, invoking the stigma of inherent black criminality. By contrast, stranded whites hauling groceries from stores were generously inferred to have merely "found" them by innocent luck.[6]

Here lies the core content of group stigma: the attribution of negative stereotypes to dishonorable internal traits, which rationalize antipathy toward the group.[7] The tendency to attribute negative stereotypes dispositionally yields stigmatization of disadvantaged groups. Thus, in several surveys, nearly half of whites agree with the claim that blacks are less intelligent than whites, while hefty majorities agree that they prefer welfare over work.[8]

Six stigma-reinforcing cognitive biases are of particular interest: (1) *In-group favoritism* or *ethnocentrism* is the bias people have in favor of members of groups to which they belong.[9] This leads people to attribute positive behaviors of in-group members dispositionally, and negative behaviors situationally, while reversing these attributions for out-group members.[10] (2) The *shared reality bias* leads individuals to align their perceptions and judgments with those of in-group members, especially if the group is based on personal affiliation.[11] (3) The *illusory correlation bias* disposes people to form stereotypes about a group with which they have little contact on the basis of unusual events, such as sensational crimes, connected to that group.[12] (4) The *stereotype incumbency bias* inclines people to form a stereotype of an effective job-holder as having a particular ascribed identity (as of race, gender, or ethnicity) if the incumbents in that job overwhelmingly share that identity. This bias leads people to perceive individuals with that identity as "fitting in" to that job, and individuals with other identities as ill-suited to it.[13] (5) What I shall call the *power bias* inclines people in positions of power to stereotype their subordinates, and to actively maintain these stereotypes.[14] (6) Finally, the *system justification bias* inclines people to interpret their social world as just, because the thought of living in an unjust world is intolerable. This bias leads individuals to make favorable attributions (dispositional attributions of good behavior and conditions, situational of bad) of high-status people and negative attributions (the reverse) of low-status people.[15]

These biases are generic and not specific to race. However, they interact with racial segregation to enhance black stigmatization. The first three biases link the spatial and social segregation of races to black stigmatization. Spatial segregation entails that whites will belong to few groups that have many black members and will interact mostly with other whites. Hence, they will have few occasions to extend in-group favoritism to blacks, and many more to extend it to fellow whites. The shared interpretations of the social world that they build with their peers will tend to exclude blacks' experiences. To the extent that blacks are more aware than whites are of discrimination and other obstacles to their advancement, insular whites will build a shared reality among themselves that underestimates the extent of these obstacles. This reinforces dispositional explanations of black disadvantage. Whites' infrequent contact with blacks will also make encounters with deviant blacks more salient, following the illusory correlation bias. This will lead whites to form exaggerated ideas about the tendencies of blacks to be deviant.

The second three biases link role segregation—the assignment of blacks to subordinate positions, whites to dominant positions—to racial stigmatization. The stereotype incumbency bias, in conjunction with job segregation, fosters the perceptions that whites are well-suited, and blacks ill-suited, for positions of leadership and responsibility. Hierarchical job segregation thus fosters racial stigmatization and job discrimination. The power bias, in conjunction with such job segregation, tends to reinforce powerful whites' stereotypes of blacks and motivates them to maintain these stereotypes. Finally, the bias toward attributions that legitimate hierarchical job segregation reinforces racial stigmatization—the representation of blacks as incompetent, irresponsible, lazy, and hence unqualified for higher positions.

The preceding account provides psychological microfoundations for the hypothesized connection between racial segregation and racial stigmatization. Processes and conditions of segregation that create and maintain racial disadvantage generate the external racial differences that supply the content of racial stereotypes. The attribution bias in favor of dispositional explanations for stereotype-confirming observations then generates stigmatizing representations of disadvantaged racial groups. Additional cognitive biases interact with segregation to reinforce black stigmatization.

Are people who act out of racially stigmatizing ideas *racist*? Let us distinguish four independent aspects of a representation: content, consciousness, endorsement, and practical engagement. Suppose the content of a representation is stigmatizing. If a stigmatizing representation causes one to act in ways that disadvantage or insult the objects of the representation, then it is practically engaged. Practical engagement does not require being conscious of the representation, much less endorsing it. The operation of cognitive biases is largely automatic and unconscious.[16] In popular moral discourse, the term "racist" is used as a severe character judgment, to label people such as neo-Nazis who consciously endorse particularly hateful beliefs and attitudes toward members of a racial group. To be racist, in this view, requires that one's racial representations possess at least three features: stigmatizing content (perhaps of an extreme sort), consciousness, and endorsement. This combination is certainly sufficient to be racist. Consider, however, the case of someone whose racial representations are stigmatizing and practically engaged, who is conscious of this fact, and who, while not endorsing these representations, is indifferent to the damage they cause and does nothing to stop her injurious conduct or mitigate its consequences. Such conscious, race-based, practical indifference should also qualify as racist.[17]

Some people apply the term "racist" to include any conduct that practically engages stigmatizing ideas in ways that disadvantage or insult their targets, or perhaps any conduct that disadvantages or insults the stigmatized, even if it was not guided by stigmatizing representations. This view denies that, to be racist, one need be aware of or endorse stigmatizing representations of others. I offer three reasons to withhold the label in such cases. First, although people may be justly criticized for unwarranted unconscious and involuntary attitudes,[18] they do not merit the severe moral condemnation implied by the term "racist." Second, to call an idea "racist" is often an attempt to put it beyond the bounds of acceptable discourse. But the ideas in question need to be addressed by argument, reasoning, and evidence—they cannot be disarmed by silencing—and the people who hold them are entitled to be engaged on these terms. Third, "racism" is a highly charged term, both morally and emotionally, which provokes unproductive, defensive reactions and shuts down urgently needed discussion. So let us reserve "racism" for judgments of serious vice, while observing that not all injustice is caused by a vicious character.

A broader concept is racial stigmatization. This can refer either to a condition of a racial group or to an intergroup process relating the stigmatized to other groups. The *condition* of racial stigmatization consists of public, dishonorable, practically engaged representations of a racial group with the following contents: (1) *racial stereotypes*, (2) *racial attributions*, or explanations of why members of the racial group tend to fit their stereotypes, that rationalize and motivate (3) *derogatory evaluations* of and (4) *demeaning or antipathetic attitudes* (such as hatred, contempt, pity, condescension, disgust, aversion, envy, distrust, and willful indifference) toward the target group and its members. *Processes* of racial stigmatization consist of conduct (including habits, norms, and policies) that tends to *produce*, *reinforce*, or *express* that condition. Conduct *expresses* stigma if it insults or disadvantages the stigmatized group in ways that fit the stigmatic ideas (for example, paternalistically controlling those represented as incapable of self-government, shunning those represented as alien, resisting policies that would help those represented as undeserving). This does not require that the actor be conscious of or endorse the stigmatic representations; the actor may be wholly ignorant of them. For example, a hotel guest may unwittingly hand his car keys to a black businessman in the lobby, on the assumption that he is on the hotel staff. This act might be guided by the stigmatic, insulting idea that blacks are a servile class, fit for no higher work than valet parking. But even if it were not (the guest may be a foreigner, unaware of the stigmatization of blacks, and simply mistook the businessman's suit for the uniform of hotel staff), this conduct still expresses racial stigma by reenacting the stigmatic consignment of blacks to servile positions. Finally, conduct can be racially stigmatizing by producing or reinforcing stigma, even if it is not guided by stigmatic ideas. For example, state action out of *purely* ethnocentric attitudes (such as planning bus routes with reference to the interests of only one group) is not guided by stigmatizing ideas. But if it disadvantages an already stigmatized racial out-group, it may magnify salient group inequalities that are interpreted in stigmatizing ways, and thereby be stigmatizing.

The concept of "racially unjust conduct" is even more capacious. It includes both racist and racially stigmatizing conduct (§1.5). It also includes ethnocentric conduct on the part of agents who have a duty of impartiality, even if the conduct is not stigmatizing. For example, a city council in a black-majority town that reserves contracts for black business people, out of pure in-group favoritism (not out of legitimate concerns of corrective justice), unjustly disadvantages white businesses and amounts to a racial injustice on that account, even if its action does not stigmatize whites.[19]

The fact that ideas can be practically engaged without being consciously endorsed helps explain the phenomenon called "aversive racism." This occurs when people sincerely report nonprejudiced attitudes and support for principles of nondiscrimination yet discriminate against stigmatized racial groups in ambiguous situations, where their conduct could be rationalized in nonracial terms.[20] To the extent that cognitive biases lead people to recognize and recall stereotype-confirming evidence more readily, and to attribute white success to virtuous dispositions and black success to accidental circumstance or external help, their own judgments will rationalize treating whites better than blacks on nonracial, meritocratic grounds. Discriminatory treatment mediated by unconsciously biased evaluations acquires the appearance of unprejudiced conduct. While some people may be dissembling about their attitudes in such cases, others may simply be unaware of the ways their stigmatizing ideas are influencing their behavior. Since cognitive biases often operate unconsciously, people are poor judges of whether their conduct is discriminatory or based on stigmatizing ideas.

The fact that cognitive biases typically operate behind people's backs does not entail that there is nothing people can do to block or override their operation. Cognitive biases tend to kick in when people need to make decisions under time pressure, when they are tired, distracted, cognitively overloaded, or under stress,[21] and when a nondiscriminatory rationale for their decision is readily available.[22] They are better able to consciously check their biases when they know they are being observed, are held accountable for their decisions, are reminded of nondiscrimination norms, are given ample time to deliberate, and make evaluations on the basis of objectively measured criteria rather than subjective impressions.[23] In addition, racial integration under certain conditions can also be an effective tool for reducing cognitive bias (§§6.3–6.4).

3.2 The Continuation and Transformation of Racial Stigmatization

The preceding account helps us understand the changing character of racial stigmatization. In the Jim Crow era, racial stigmatization was explicitly racist. It consisted of the following matrix of attitudes, cognitions, and conduct: (1) strongly felt emotions of hatred, coldness, and contempt toward nonwhites; (2) explicit endorsement of racist ideologies representing nonwhites as biologically alien and inferior; and (3) support for explicit practices of racial discrimination, subordination, and segregation. This model still fits some extreme racists today. But the softening of race relations in the wake of the Civil Rights Movement, the discrediting of "scientific" racism, and the triumph of antidiscrimination norms, as ideology if not in practice, has made this model less applicable to Americans today. Since the 1970s, surveys consistently find that few whites endorse theories of black biological inferiority, while overwhelming majorities of whites express support for principles of nondiscrimination.[24]

Some conservative commentators argue that these developments show that antiblack racial antipathy has only a minor presence in the United States today.[25] However, there is much evidence that blacks still suffer from stigma and discrimination. Numerous statistical studies find that blacks do worse than whites in important ways, such as employment and access to credit, even after controlling for nonracial variables, such as human capital and wealth, that could account for these inequalities.[26] These studies support the hypothesis that racial discrimination explains some of the disparities between blacks and whites. Audit studies provide independent evidence supporting the statistical models. In audit studies, carefully matched whites and blacks seek the same opportunities—such as a job, an apartment, or a car—to determine whether they are treated differently. Audit studies have found pervasive discrimination in the housing, mortgage lending, and home insurance markets,[27] in retail car sales and bail bonding[28] and employment.[29] One study found that Milwaukee employers prefer to hire whites with prior felony convictions over equally qualified blacks with no criminal record.[30] Direct testimony reinforces the conclusions of the audit studies. Blacks, even when middle class, report pervasive discrimination in public places.[31] Their reports are confirmed by the surprising willingness of many employers to admit that they practice racial discrimination,[32] and of whites in urban ethnic enclaves to express a determination to keep blacks and Latinos out of their schools and neighborhoods.[33]

Laboratory studies and national surveys underwrite these findings from the field. Experimental research on implicit cognition finds that whites are quicker to associate pleasant ideas with whites than with blacks.[34] Behavioral studies find that whites who avow commitment to color-blind norms discriminate against blacks when they have the cover of "color-blind" explanations of their behavior.[35] Finally, surveys of white opinion consistently find overwhelming verbal support for antidiscrimination norms and equality of opportunity conjoined with opposition to concrete policies that would actually realize these goals.[36] For example, while nearly all whites profess support for equal employment opportunity in principle, half oppose government enforcement of antidiscrimination laws.[37]

Skeptics have offered alternative explanations for these results that exonerate American society from the charge of pervasive racial stigmatization. Statistical models will be flawed if they are missing nonracial variables that correlate with race.[38] Audit studies may fail to match blacks and whites carefully enough.[39] Blacks may be hypersensitive, perceiving racial wrongs when they have not happened.[40] What looks like racial prejudice in survey responses on questions about racial policy may merely reflect Americans' commitment to principles of individualism.[41]

Each of these critiques has been met by advocates of the various methods that find continuing racial stigmatization. Statistical studies,[42] audit studies,[43] and tests of implicit bias[44] that have been adjusted to rule out alternative explanations of racial inequalities continue to find evidence of racial bias. Laboratory evidence shows that blacks are reluctant to blame discrimination for bad outcomes they have experienced.[45] What predicts whites' opposition to policies that help blacks is not their support for group-neutral individualist principles, but rather their endorsement of statements that specifically depict blacks as lazy and dependent, as lacking individualist virtues.[46]

Skirmishes over the interpretation and validity of particular methods and studies continue. Whatever the fate of any particular study, what is most impressive is the *convergence of numerous, independent lines of evidence, using diverse methods, samples, and measurement techniques, on the conclusion that black stigma and discrimination remain pervasive.*

This convergence would be highly improbable if the skeptics were right. Why would *every* available type of test be systematically flawed in the same direction, in favor of spurious findings of black stigmatization, if such stigma were not pervasive? The skeptics, focusing on piecemeal critiques of this or that study or method, have no credible answer to this question.

Black stigmatization thus remains a significant force in the United States. However, many studies point to important transformations in its form and content since the era of white supremacy. Several lines of evidence—notably, laboratory studies of implicit bias in cognition and covert discrimination, and public opinion surveys—support the view that racial stigmatization has gone underground in the face of laws and social norms that discourage racism—that is, explicit expressions of racial antipathy and overt discrimination. In form, racially stigmatizing ideas are now more likely to be embodied in subtle cognitive biases than in strongly felt emotions, more likely to be implicit, unconscious, or deniable than explicit and consciously avowed. In content, people now tend to describe perceived racial differences in terms of statistical tendencies rather than rigid stereotypes. They are also more likely to attribute them to cultural or behavioral tendencies that can be controlled by individuals rather than to immutable biological traits. Thus, familiar stereotypes of blacks as poor students and unmotivated workers, as lacking in entrepreneurship, industry, and determination and prone to poverty, welfare dependency, violence, and criminal activity, are now more likely to be viewed as failures of choice and values rather than reflections of innate, biologically determined inferiority. In this view, blacks do not try hard enough to overcome their problems; they give up too easily and expect others to help them when they should be doing things for themselves. These representations entail a shift in implicit attitudes toward blacks from contempt to resentment, from judgments of inherent biological inferiority to judgments that blacks expect, and are getting, more help than they deserve.[47]

Hence, public opinion researchers today advance theories of "ambivalent,"[48] "symbolic,"[49] or "modern"[50] racism, which differ not just in explicitness but in content from older advocacy of white supremacy. The "new" black stigmatization typically involves (1) subtly felt or unconscious resentment of blacks; (2) representations of blacks as lacking the virtues of self-reliance, enterprise, studiousness, and dedication to hard, honest work, but claiming goods to which they would be entitled only if they had these virtues; and (3) opposition to political programs such as school integration, welfare (perceived to disproportionately aid blacks), affirmative action, active government enforcement of antidiscrimination law, and other state efforts to help blacks. In my terms, racial attitudes have moved from the explicitly racist to the racially stigmatizing.

3.3 Stigmatization as an Expressive Harm

So far, our analysis of racial stigmatization has mainly drawn from cognitive psychology, which represents bias and prejudice in terms of private mental states. But racial stigmatization has a public character that constitutes an expressive harm to blacks *even when all parties to a social interaction reject the stigma*. Consider this illustration. One late night in 2007 I was driving in Detroit when my oil light came on. I pulled into the nearest gas station to investigate the problem when a young black man approached me to offer help. "Don't worry, I'm not here to rob you," he said, holding up his hands, palms flat at face level, gesturing his innocence. "Do you need some help with your car?" I thanked him for his offer and told him I wasn't sure how much oil I needed. He read the dip stick, told me my car needed two quarts, and offered to do the job for free. From the look on his face when I paid him anyway, it was clear that he needed the cash.

This encounter illustrates the *public* standing of racial stereotypes as default images that influence the interactions of black and white strangers in unstructured settings, even when both parties are prepared to disavow them. A little ritual must be performed to confirm that both parties *do* disavow the stigma, so that cooperative interactions may proceed. This is a manifestation of *adaptation* to racial subordination (§1.3), which reproduces the unequal social relations it enacts.

This man suffered a harm of racial stigmatization in this interaction. He was harmed, regardless of how he felt about it, and notwithstanding the fact that I refused to apply the stereotype of the criminally violent black male to him, and that he gained from the transaction. The harm consists in the fact that he walks under a cloud of suspicion in unstructured encounters with strangers. To gain access to cooperative interactions, he must assume the burdens of dispelling this cloud, of protesting and proving his innocence of imagined crimes.

Racial stigmatization, then, does not consist simply in private thoughts isolated in the minds of discrete individuals. It consists in the fact that these thoughts enjoy a certain public standing, coloring the meanings of interactions even among people who would prefer that these meanings not apply. Let us distinguish three dimensions of public standing: (1) common knowledge, (2) public noticeability, and (3) default status. A representation R is a matter of *common knowledge* between A and B just in case A and B entertain representation R, each knows that the other is entertaining R, each knows that each knows this, and so on. (To entertain a representation is merely to have it in mind, not necessarily to endorse it.) R is a matter of *public notice* just in case it is both common knowledge and acceptable to invoke in public discourse. R has *default status* if it is common knowledge that R is taken for granted as a common premise of public discussion and interpersonal interaction, such that people must send countervailing signals to one another to establish a different common premise.

Each of these dimensions of public standing is costly to the stigmatized. Consider the stereotype of black men as violent criminals. That this is a prevailing stereotype is a matter of common knowledge among Americans. Mere common knowledge of the stereotype, apart from endorsement, can interfere with interracial cooperative interaction. Nonstigmatized and unprejudiced whites who have little experience with blacks may feel anxiety about interacting with them, out of fear that the image of the violent black man will taint their behavior even when they do not want it to do so. Such worries cause such individuals to behave awkwardly toward blacks, to experience stress in interracial interaction, and hence to avoid such interaction.[51] The result may be conduct that, in appearance and effect, is discriminatory, even when it is not motivated by racial prejudice. While we should not call this conduct racist, it propagates racial injustice. It also undermines the prospects for smooth and positive interracial interaction that are essential to a flourishing civil society.

The stigma of black criminality is also publicly noticeable. News reports routinely mention the race of a criminal suspect or perpetrator. Contrast this with stereotypes connecting a person's religion with certain crimes. The stereotype of the Jewish shyster is also a matter of common knowledge. But it is unmentionable in mainstream discourse. No one blinks at a news report stating that a twenty-three-year-old black man was arrested for murder. But a broadcast that began "A fifty-five-year-old Jew, David Goldstein, was arrested for stock fraud today" would be condemned as gratuitously stirring up anti-Semitism. A criminal suspect's religion may be publicly noticed only in cases of religiously motivated crime, where a religious organization is involved, or where the criminal used his religious identity for criminal purposes—for example, to gain the trust of his victims. The fact that when a criminal suspect, defendant, or convict is a black man his race is routinely mentioned gives the stereotype of black men as violent a kind of public standing denied to the stereotype of the Jewish shyster. Public noticeability stamps the stigma with an impression of normality, even legitimacy, thereby adding insult to the injury of tainted interracial interaction.

Finally, the stigma of black criminality enjoys default status, as my story of the oil change illustrates. To avoid its application to themselves, black men may need to explicitly ward it off. Jewish lawyers, bankers, and stockbrokers, by contrast, rarely need to contend with the image of the Jewish shyster. Thus, default status poses additional, sometimes insurmountable, obstacles to smooth and cooperative interracial interaction. Blacks cannot count on even a glaring signal being recognized for what it is. For example, middle-class blacks often complain that they are avoided like criminals, even when they go out of their way to dress in respectable clothing.[52]

The public standing of racial stigma is an expressive harm. It is expressive because it is constituted by social meanings. Stigmatization constitutes an assault on one's public reputation. This entails costs over and above the costs of being subject to a single case of unjust perception. To be privately, perhaps unconsciously feared as a suspected criminal does entail certain losses—characteristically, of opportunities for cooperative interaction with those who fear oneself. To be openly feared by a particular other adds insult to this injury. But to be subject as a matter of public reputation to the default presumption of criminal suspicion is not merely to be insulted—a private injury—but to be publicly dishonored and degraded, placed on a lower order of being in a public ranking. The injury of public dishonor is not psychic, but reputational. Even those with thick skins and high self-esteem suffer harm to their public standing due to racial stigmatization.

3.4 Stigmatization as a Self-Confirming Status

Stereotypes cause their own perceived confirmation in at least three ways. First, they selectively favor the recall of stereotype-confirming evidence. Second, they may lead stereotype holders to generate new evidence that confirms the stereotype. For example, police use of racial profiling may lead to a greater proportion of black than white criminals being caught and convicted, which in turn supports an exaggerated representation of racial differences in crime rates. Third, stereotypes can be self-fulfilling prophecies, by inducing their targets to behave in ways that confirm the stereotype.

Some theories of the phenomenon of the self-fulfilling prophecy focus on dyadic interactions between stereotype-holding perceivers and the targets of the stereotype. The general idea is that people will treat blacks and whites differently because of their racial stereotypes; this differential treatment will in turn elicit stereotype-confirming behavior from black and white subjects.[53] For example, there is some evidence that teachers, following prevailing racial stereotypes, express lower expectations about future potential for black students than for whites, in ways that depress black students' academic performance relative to their potentials.[54]

Other theories of stereotype confirmation look beyond dyadic interactions to the causal impact of stigma, understood as a public stamp of dishonor on a group. Consider the stigmatic representation of blacks as poor students who do not value education. One general strategy of the stigmatized for coping with stigma is to disidentify with the domain of achievement in which they are stamped as inferior.[55] Blacks, stigmatized as poor students, may disidentify with school and stake their self-esteem in achieving in other domains. Disidentification impairs school achievement and thereby confirms the stigma. But it spares blacks from internalizing that stigma.[56]

Of course, many blacks are committed to school. However, identification with the domain of stigmatization makes the stigmatized vulnerable to "stereotype threat"—anxiety that one's performance in that domain will confirm the stigma. Blacks who strive for high achievement may find themselves stymied by test anxiety, especially where the racial stigma is salient. Anxiety depresses their achievement and confirms the stereotype.[57] Stereotype threat theory has extensive empirical support applied to many groups, demonstrating that it is a generic, race-neutral response to stigmatization.[58] One recent major study has produced striking confirmation of the theory for vulnerable black freshmen in selective colleges.[59]

Neither disidentification nor stereotype threat involves endorsement by the stigmatized of the stereotype at issue, or interactions with people who endorse the stereotype. The stigma only needs to be "in the air"—a commonly known public image—to generate confirming evidence. That evidence, filtered through the bias that attributes stereotype-confirming behavior to internal dispositions of the stereotyped, reinforces the stigma.

A final route to self-confirming stigmatization focuses on the role of the media. Pervasive segregation by race and class, along with intensive police racial profiling of people whose race makes them look "out of place" in a neighborhood, isolate most law-abiding middle-class whites from contact with most blacks. This makes black-on-white crime a relatively rare event.[60] Hence, if whites had only their personal experiences and those of their social circle to go by, they would have little basis for forming a stereotype of blacks as disposed to crime.[61]

This "evidence gap" is more than filled by the mass media, which relentlessly propagate stigmatizing images of blacks. Local TV news stresses coverage of violent crime. This feeds back into individual perception, memory, and political attitudes, in a vicious circle.[62] News stories tend to portray blacks as perpetrators of violent crime out of proportion to their arrest rates.[63] They highlight black-on-white violent crime far more frequently than its actual rate of occurrence, and they disproportionately portray whites as victims of crime, even though blacks suffer from higher rates of victimization than whites.[64]

The public stigma of the criminal black male then distorts people's memories of crime reports. Reflecting the bias toward stereotype-confirming information, people are more likely to recall the race of a suspect in a news report if the suspect was portrayed as black. When a news report fails to identify the race of the suspect, 60 percent of viewers falsely recall that the suspect's race had been identified, and of those viewers, 70 percent identify the suspect as black.[65] Even when a news story depicts the perpetrator as white, over time white viewers are more likely to mistakenly recall the offender as black.[66] Shown a photo lineup including the offender depicted in a news story about a violent crime, white viewers are also more likely to misidentify the offender (choose an innocent man) when the story depicted a black rather than a white criminal—a reflection of out-group homogenization. This tendency to misidentify violent black perpetrators appears to be due to mere awareness of and not endorsement of the stereotype, since it is unaffected by variations in whites' self-reported prejudice against blacks.[67] Like stereotype threat, it is a function of public stigmatization rather than private conviction.

Some notorious events concerning blacks and crime are linked to the public stigma of black criminality and its attendant stimulation of cognitive biases and prejudice. During the 1988 Bush–Dukakis presidential campaign, a pro-Bush political action committee aired an advertisement criticizing Governor Dukakis's prisoner furlough program, highlighting a mug shot of black convict Willie Horton, who committed violent crimes while on furlough. The producer of the ad described the photograph as depicting "every suburban mother's greatest fear." Horton's notably dark skin likely stimulated the tendency of people to find darker-toned offenders more memorable, and of heavy TV viewers to find crime reports more disturbing, the darker the skin tone of the offender.[68] In the 1999 Diallo case mentioned earlier, New York City police fired forty-one bullets at an innocent, unarmed black man who was reaching for his wallet. His death was likely caused by the same perceptual bias that inclines people playing a video game under time pressure to more readily "shoot" unarmed blacks than unarmed whites, and to misidentify harmless objects as weapons when they are held by blacks[69]—an instance of the more general tendency of people to interpret ambiguous actions by blacks as violent, even though they would not so perceive identical actions by whites.[70] During Hurricane Katrina, major media outlets disseminated many stories of extreme violence among the largely black population that took refuge in the New Orleans Superdome and Convention Center, including sniper fire against rescue helicopters, forty murder victims stuffed in a freezer, and an epidemic of sexual assaults. These reports were fantasies, made credible by prevailing stereotypes of black criminality.[71]

3.5 Stigmatization and Discrimination

This chapter's investigation of stigmatization offers insights into the varied causes of systematic racial discrimination. Several distinctions among mechanisms of discrimination are worth drawing. First, we should distinguish mechanisms grounded in ethnocentrism, or in-group favoritism, from mechanisms grounded in out-group stigma.[72] Second, we should distinguish mechanisms grounded in relatively inarticulate affect from those rationalized in cognition. Third, within the affective type of discrimination, we should distinguish out-group antipathy from out-group anxiety and discomfort. Fourth, within the cognitive type of discrimination, we should distinguish biased representations based on instrumentally rational calculations from biases that irrationally color perception and memory. Since the focus of this chapter is stigma, in the following discussion I set aside ethnocentric discrimination and leave it as an exercise for the reader to consider how the last three distinctions apply to that class.

Within the class of stigmatic discrimination, consider first the traditional understanding of affective discrimination. In this model, individuals consciously and deliberately deprive a racialized person of some good, or impose some bad on her, out of felt animus against her racial group. Call this *prejudicial discrimination*. This is discrimination for its own sake, motivated by strong antipathy—naked racism. "No blacks need apply." Such discrimination still exists, particularly in the housing market, where whites "defend" their neighborhoods against black entry and openly justify their actions in hostile terms.[73] Business owners may also pander to the antipathies of their employees and customers by practicing employment discrimination.[74] This extends the prejudicial model since its ultimate cause is still prejudice; nonprejudiced actors function merely as agents of the prejudiced, catering to their antipathies.

Prejudicial discrimination is not the only kind of affective discrimination. Segregation may make whites feel emotionally distant from blacks, awkward and uncomfortable around them. This can cause whites to treat blacks unfavorably. Whites committed to nondiscrimination may also be vulnerable to stereotype threat: anxious about appearing racist, they may avoid interracial interaction, or act stiffly and formally toward blacks. Such behavior confirms the stereotype they wanted to avoid, since such cool and distant conduct treats blacks less favorably than whites, closing blacks off from relations of affiliation, trust, and loyalty that are critical to economic advancement (§2.3). Call this type of affective discrimination *anxious*. Anxiety is an important factor behind troubled interracial interaction.[75]

Consider now the cognitive type of discrimination. This is distinct from prejudicial discrimination because prejudice (negative affect) and stereotyping (beliefs about racial differences) are only modestly correlated. Each generates a distinct path to discriminatory conduct.[76] Economists developed the idea of *statistical discrimination* to explain how racial discrimination persists in the absence of racist antipathy, which has declined since the Jim Crow era. If race is correlated with economically relevant variables (such as quality of schooling, which may affect productivity), and these variables are costly to measure, then rational actors might use race as a proxy for this information.[77] Discrimination is "rational" (serves the nonprejudiced purposes of the actor), because the racial stereotypes on which it is based reflect real racial differences in economically relevant attributes.

The preceding account of stigma suggests that statistical discrimination is not the only kind of cognitive discrimination. It fails to capture the fact that unconscious stereotypes irrationally bias our thoughts. We do not receive undistorted information about members of different races; our perceptions and memories are colored by racial stigma. To the perceiver familiar with racial stereotypes, that rambunctious black youth shooting hoops in the park *looks* aggressive and hostile, although if he were white, he would be perceived as harmlessly horsing around. Stigmatizing perceptions and memories lead evaluators to draw inferences from them in accordance with stigmatizing attribution biases. This black computer programmer must have been lucky to come across the solution to a problem that had stymied others, but that Asian one showed ingenuity in solving a problem. Call this model *evaluative discrimination.*

These distinctions among causes of discrimination have normative import. While stigmatic categorical discrimination against ascriptive identity groups is always unjust, there are contexts in which ethnocentric discrimination on the basis of such identities is not unjust, although it may be deplorable or unpraiseworthy (§1.5). In addition, while there are contexts in which individuals have a claim of justice against any of the types of discrimination thus far considered, prejudicial discrimination is more vicious than anxious or cognitive discrimination.[78] This illustrates the importance of distinguishing judgments of justice from judgments of virtue and vice (§3.1).

Evaluative discrimination raises normative claims distinct from prejudicial and statistical discrimination. In the case of prejudicial discrimination, the victim's complaint is that her race is not a valid intrinsic basis for denying her access to a good, or for imposing some disadvantage. In statistical discrimination, the victim's complaint is that, in a context where meritocratic selection is normative, he was denied the chance to demonstrate his individual merits. Race may not be fairly used as a proxy for relevant traits, even if it is correlated with them, because its use reproduces categorical inequality by constituting a categorical barrier to opportunity and stigmatizing the excluded group. Where meritocratic selection applies and the underlying merits can be affected by choice, effort, practice, and the like, people are entitled to measures of merit that can be similarly affected, so that those who are able to do the job have a chance to demonstrate that fact.[79] In evaluative discrimination, neither complaint applies. The discriminator has made a sincere individualized assessment of the victim's merits. The victim's complaint is rather that she has been inaccurately evaluated in an unfair way because her evaluator's judgments were distorted by racially stigmatizing ideas. This complaint, in contrast to complaints of prejudicial and statistical discrimination, does not require any imputation of discriminatory purposes or beliefs to the actor. It merely requires the practical engagement of stigmatizing ideas.

Stigma also causes discrimination that does not directly target its objects. Our minds work metaphorically. Stigma is seen as contaminating. Its taint can spread from its immediate targets to anything that has contact with the stigmatized, or that resembles them. This means that stigma attaches not simply to blacks, but to blackness. Adrian Piper calls this phenomenon *second-order discrimination*. This is the origin of skin-tone discrimination, by which people of any race are evaluated and treated more harshly, the darker their skin tone. Thus, people are more disturbed by a crime, the darker the skin tone of the alleged offender.[80] Not only do lighter-skinned blacks earn more than darker-skinned blacks, but lighter-skinned immigrants earn more than darker-skinned ones, even when they have no African ancestry.[81] Not just blacks, but some immigrants too, suffer from the stigma originally attached to blacks.

Second-order discrimination occurs when jobs get downgraded as they are filled by low-status individuals. This is known as a "status-composition effect." As more blacks fill a job, it becomes perceived as a "black" job, which in turn leads employers to reduce the complexity of tasks assigned to the job, strip it of authority, subject its incumbents to closer supervision, and lower its pay. Because such second-order discrimination applies to the "blackness" of the job rather than to the race of its occupants, whites who occupy jobs affected by status composition have lower pay and less desirable jobs than other whites with equivalent human capital.[82]

3.6 Stigmatization and Public Policy

Formally race-neutral policies are often said to be racially discriminatory *in effect* if they have a differential impact on racial groups, allocating benefits and burdens disproportionately among them. As a normative proposal for what should count as objectionable discrimination, this idea is not compelling. It depends on the dubious suppositions that racial groups are fundamental units of consideration for purposes of distributive justice, that they are entitled to a proportional allocation of all benefits and burdens, regardless of other factors that may distinguish their members, and that disproportionate impact can never be an innocent byproduct of otherwise justified policies. As an analytic proposal, this idea is also defective. To count as discriminatory, ideas of racial favor or disfavor have to be implicated in the reasons people had for adopting the policy. The policy, while race-neutral in principle and application, had to be adopted because of ideas connected to the race of its targets.

While a sweeping "differential impact" criterion of discrimination for formally race-neutral policies is too wide for both normative and analytic purposes, a stringent "purposive" criterion is too narrow. This model identifies a race-neutral policy as discriminatory if its criteria for allocating benefits and burdens were deliberately selected because they are close proxies for race, so as to exclude one race from enjoying public benefits or honorable status, or to impose burdens or dishonor on it. The paradigm cases are the complex voting regulations adopted by southern states in the Jim Crow era, such as literacy tests and grandfather clauses. These are fundamentally cases of purposeful, prejudicial discrimination, using formally race-neutral criteria as proxies for race to evade the enforcement of antidiscrimination law. This purposive model is too narrow, for the same reasons that the model of prejudicial discrimination does not capture all of the morally objectionable and causally significant modes by which racial stigmatization causes differential treatment.

To home in on the impacts of racial stigmatization on public policy, we must distinguish ethnocentrism, or in-group favoritism, from out-group animus and stigmatization. In some cases, people support or oppose race-neutral public policies because of their differential racial impact, but out of ethnocentrism. These are often straightforward cases of opportunity hoarding, piggy-backing on segregation. Whites favor tax limitations more strongly in more ethnically diverse jurisdictions so they do not have to share their tax contributions with other groups. Ethnically homogeneous local governments spend a greater proportion of their revenues on public goods used by all, such as education and roads, than ethnically diverse governments, which tend to spend more on patronage directed to particular ethnic groups.[83] To the extent that such opportunity hoarding is based on pure ethnocentrism rather than dishonorable images of out-groups, it does not express racial stigma, although it may cause stigmatization, if it results in or reinforces categorical inequality. Even if it does not cause stigmatization, it can still be unjust in being negligent of out-group interests.

The same biases involved in evaluative and affective discrimination may affect formally race-neutral public policy formation. Models of "modern" and "symbolic" racism combine denial that antiblack discrimination remains significant with beliefs that blacks reject individualistic values of hard work and self-sufficiency, and resentment of what are perceived as their excessive demands and undeserved advantages.[84] High scores for such racial resentment predict opposition to government policies that are perceived to disproportionately help blacks, even when the policies are race-neutral, such as antidiscrimination laws and welfare.[85] They also predict support for highly punitive policies on crime, such as the death penalty and "three strikes" laws.[86] Measures of racial resentment invoke the attribution biases central to racial stigmatization: blaming blacks' disadvantages on internal vices, and blacks' advantages on (undeserved) external help. When whites' racial stereotypes are primed by pictures of or stories about black criminals, or when whites are asked to evaluate black criminals, their support for highly punitive policies increases, whereas the same effect is not observed when they are exposed to stories about white criminals.[87] Whites' support for the death penalty rises when they are told that it disproportionately punishes blacks.[88] An unconscious affective bias appears to be at work here: people feel more fear and discomfort toward crimes committed by blacks and become more concerned about the danger of crime to themselves.[89] So is an evaluative bias: black criminals are judged more harshly than white criminals depicted in otherwise identical stories.[90]

Here lies the heart of racial stigma in public policy: when the target of policy is implicitly or explicitly coded black, the policy response is harsh and punitive; when the target is coded white (or perhaps white middle class), the policy response is sympathetic. White middle-class teenagers with a drug problem get counseling and therapy; black teenagers caught with drugs get thrown in jail for longer and longer terms.[91] Both policies can be in place without violating race-neutrality, as long as they are implemented in distinct, segregated jurisdictions. White upper-middle-class suburbs provide their troubled teens with counseling and rehabilitation; racially mixed cities focus on policing neighborhoods with high concentrations of blacks.

The racial content of such stigmatizing policy responses typically operates beneath the surface. A color-blind story is always available to rationalize the policy. The sharply different reactions people have to policies, depending on the race of the target, are never explicitly juxtaposed, enabling people to continue to regard themselves as color-blind even when their evaluative reactions are influenced by racial stigma.

This is not simply a matter of individual psychology. Racial stigmatization is a public status, not just a concatenation of incidentally coinciding private attitudes (§3.3). The different reactions are triggered by distinct interpretive frames, entrenched in public policy discourse. When what was formerly known as "welfare" (Aid to Families with Dependent Children) was first adopted during the New Deal, the typical recipient was portrayed as a widowed white mother. The interpretive frame for understanding welfare was sympathetic since white women were expected to be free to stay home to take care of the children, and white children's flourishing was seen as dependent on their doing so. By the 1970s the public image of the typical welfare recipient became a single black mother. This did not reflect reality: more white women than black women were on welfare. But black women were disproportionately enrolled, and the media focused disproportionately on them in stories about welfare.[92] Black mothers have never enjoyed the presumption that their children needed them at home since they are expected to work outside the home. The sympathetic interpretive frame for welfare no longer fit the public image of its targets. Instead, its targets were pathologized as lazy, sexually licentious, and poor role models for their children, and this narrative frame fit with the stigma attached to poor black women. No wonder, then, that the more whites thought blacks were disproportionately represented on the welfare rolls, the more they opposed welfare.[93] Thus, whites oppose welfare, not simply because blacks benefit disproportionately from it, but because whites' image of its typical recipient is black, and they transfer their stigmatizing representations of blacks as undeserving, lazy, dependent, and excessively demanding to welfare recipients. This is a case of second-order discrimination: welfare is rejected because welfare is seen as an expression of cultural and character defects that are seen as characteristically "black."

3.7 The Interactions of Segregation and Discrimination

Racial discrimination tends to be seen as the principal situational cause of racial inequality. If racial inequality exists but the proximate cause does not appear to be discrimination, the default presumption is to locate its cause in the internal cultural and character defects of the disadvantaged race. Since racism and discrimination have apparently declined precipitously since the passage of antidiscrimination laws, the stubborn persistence of racial inequality must be due to pathologies internal to blacks and the black community. This presumption—this attribution bias—constitutes part of the racial stigmatization of blacks.

One response to this interpretive frame is to multiply our models of how discrimination works. We found in §3.5 that our standard models of prejudicial and statistical discrimination are not exhaustive. They overlook the roles of implicit and automatic cognition, which cause discriminatory treatment even in the absence of discriminatory beliefs or a conscious intention to discriminate. Hence, the apparent absence of discrimination in some context does not mean it does not exist. This modification of the standard interpretive frame is important, but it does not offer a fundamental alternative.

The alternative frame proposed in this book takes segregation rather than discrimination to be the principal situational cause of racial inequality. Discrimination is a tool of segregation. But segregation propagates many material inequalities on its own, through the numerous mechanisms described in chapter 2. Spatial segregation enables advantaged groups to hoard opportunities without having to actively discriminate, in the legalistic sense of purposely treating two otherwise similarly positioned persons differently on account of their race. Segregation makes it the case that blacks are rarely "similarly positioned" with whites: they live in a different jurisdiction or, due to their spatial segregation, lacked opportunities for human, social, and cultural capital formation needed to compete on a par with whites. Gregory Weiher, investigating the causes of school segregation in St. Louis, found that the

> structuring of political space was far more important in determining the relationships of blacks and whites in the educational system than were particular discriminatory actions. The drawing and redrawing of political boundaries is a more subtle strategy than confrontation, but its effects are more pervasive and enduring. Indeed, if political boundaries are appropriately drawn, confrontation is not required to maintain racial separation. The "second class citizen," though he or she may be relatively disadvantaged, may nevertheless gain some satisfaction by insisting upon the rights shared by all citizens. The *non*-citizen, one who is outside the political space, can make no claim upon the resources or guarantees of the polity, no matter how wretched may be his or her situation. Political boundaries that give geographic manifestation to racial antipathies permit citizenship to be manipulated to serve racial purposes.[94]

Segregation also propagates inequality by playing on people's cognitive biases so as to generate racially stigmatizing representations of blacks, both in individuals' minds (§3.1) and in public discourse (§3.3). Stigmatizing ideas about blacks, in turn, cause discrimination against them. Thus, segregation and discrimination are mutually reinforcing.

Situating discrimination in the context of segregation also expands our conception of its causal impact. In the standard model, discrimination is viewed as a discrete event, a one-time loss accruing to an individual victim, the effects of which extend no further than her dependents. This is a fair model of the causal impact of discrimination on victims who are neither segregated from the mainstream nor publicly stigmatized. It fits the experience of whites in the United States.

However, when the victim belongs to a segregated community, the effects of discrimination spread to other members of the community beyond his family and persist over time. Job discrimination against one member diminishes the social capital of everyone else in that community, depriving them of a potential role model, a source of information about job openings at the firm, and a connection who could provide a credible job reference. This loss is negligible for people who have plenty of other acquaintances with connections to mainstream opportunities. But if segregation means one's social network is limited to mostly disadvantaged people like the victim, their disadvantages become one's own. Once these disadvantages become shared, the community as a whole becomes a site of concentrated and self-reinforcing disadvantage, perpetuating the effects of discrimination over time. Given the invisibility of much discrimination and the attribution biases put into play by segregation, others will tend to interpret the community's disadvantage in stigmatizing terms. The taint of laziness and inadequacy that clouds the reputation of the victim of unseen discrimination spreads to the whole community, dishonoring it in the eyes of others, and in public discourse, where their claims on public policy are framed as the grasping demands of an excessively entitled, undeserving group. For blacks, discrimination is therefore not a discrete, one-time loss. Segregation operates as a discrimination multiplier, spreading its material and symbolic harms to the rest of the community.

Segregation is a fundamental cause of stigmatization. It causes the inequalities that form the basis of racial stereotypes and triggers numerous biases that induce people to explain black disadvantage in stigmatizing terms. The character of black racial stigma changed in the mid-twentieth century, from conscious beliefs that blacks are biologically inferior to cautiously expressed or unconscious stereotypes of blacks as disposed to make morally undeserving choices, and from strongly felt contempt and hatred to often unconscious resentment. These changes have led some observers to hold that blacks no longer encounter substantial prejudice or discrimination. However, the persistence of antiblack attitudes and discrimination is documented by numerous independent lines of evidence, including survey research, laboratory studies, audit studies of discrimination in the field, interviews with discriminating agents and victims of discrimination, and statistical studies. Racially stigmatizing representations do not merely inhabit people's private thoughts; they have public standing as commonly known, publicly noticeable default presumptions for interracial interactions. This public status inflicts an expressive injury on blacks by assaulting their public reputation and degrading them to an inferior status. It impairs the quality of interracial interaction and obstructs interracial cooperation even among people who would prefer to cooperate. It is self-reinforcing through individual behavior as well as biased media reports. Racially stigmatizing ideas underlie several distinct types of discrimination: prejudicial, anxious, statistical, evaluative, and second-order. Mere awareness of racially stigmatizing ideas about blacks can cause people to treat blacks less favorably than whites, even if they do not intend to discriminate, don't endorse the stigmatizing representations, and prefer not to discriminate. The same stigmatic biases that cause discrimination in dyadic interactions also influence whites' public policy attitudes. They lead whites to favor punitive policies when the targets of the policy are perceived to be disproportionately black, and sympathetic policies when the targets of the policy are perceived to be disproportionately white. Segregation, stigmatization, and discrimination interact in complex ways. Segregation has numerous negative impacts independent of discrimination. It enables other racial groups to hoard opportunities without having to engage in direct racial discrimination. Segregation causes racial stigmatization, an expressive harm in itself, and multiplies and spreads the effects of discrimination. Recognition of the importance of segregation and stigmatization as causes of disadvantage through routes other than discrimination enriches our causal model of racial disadvantage and undermines the stigmatizing presumption that, where no discrimination is apparent, the cause of black disadvantage should be attributed to black character and cultural defects.

· FOUR ·

RACIAL SEGREGATION TODAY: A NORMATIVE ASSESSMENT

4.1 The Injustice of the Causes of Segregation

In §1.5 I presented a relational account of the injustice of systematic group inequality. In this account, the bare fact that the distribution of material and symbolic goods across social groups is unequal does not constitute an adequate basis for judging whether that distribution manifests a group injustice. No fundamental principle of justice requires the proportional allocation of goods to social groups as such. Individuals, not social groups, are the fundamental claimants to distributive justice. Nevertheless, individual members of a group may complain that they are victims of a group-based injustice if they suffer disadvantages causally connected to unjust intergroup relations. That is, they may complain if their group membership is implicated in unjust intergroup processes that allocate benefits and burdens to individuals. In general, a group inequality is unjust if it (a) is caused by unjust intergroup relations; (b) causes unjust intergroup relations; or (c) embodies such relations. This and the next two sections of this chapter focus on (a). The remaining sections focus on (b) and (c).

The relational theory of inequality identifies segregation as the linchpin of group inequality. In chapters 2 and 3 I discussed the myriad ways in which segregation of blacks underlies their systematic disadvantages. However, the bare fact that a group inequality was caused by segregation does not provide a sufficient basis for evaluating it or suggesting remedies. There are a variety of mechanisms of social closure, some of which are more objectionable than others, and some of which are perhaps not even unjust, although they may be morally problematic in other ways (§1.5). Thus, to evaluate any particular case of group segregation, we must assess the full range of processes that brought it about.

Controversies arise with respect to three issues.[1] First, to the extent that whites cause segregation and group inequality by means that do not merit the charge of racism (§3.1), such as unconscious stereotypes and ethnocentrism, do they ground claims of injustice? Can people be justly held morally responsible for unconscious and automatic mental states, the operation of which disadvantages blacks? Second, to what extent is segregation caused by morally innocent voluntary choices of blacks? Third, to what extent is racial inequality due to self-destructive conduct for which blacks alone are morally responsible? These controversies mix empirical and evaluative considerations in complex ways. I shall discuss the first and second in §4.2, and the third in §4.3. The remainder of this section makes the case that the causes of black-white racial segregation are due to unjust intergroup relations.

Current patterns of residential racial segregation can be historically traced to the collusion of federal, state, and local governments with white real estate agents, apartment owners, and homeowners to keep blacks out of white neighborhoods. Overt, discriminatory exclusion of blacks from white neighborhoods was the norm in cities that had significant numbers of blacks, from the Jim Crow era through the passage of the Fair Housing Act of 1968.[2] Contemporary studies continue to find high levels of private housing discrimination in areas with significant black presence.[3] Discrimination laws are rarely enforced in this sector of the economy, partly due to the difficulty of detecting discrimination, partly due to state neglect. Although audit studies indicate that thousands of cases of housing discrimination against blacks occur every year, for decades the federal government has prosecuted only a handful of cases annually.[4]

The state's role in constructing segregation has been large. In the postwar era, the Federal Housing Administration (FHA) promoted racial redlining, denying mortgage guarantees in black and integrated neighborhoods. This policy heightened whites' fears of financial ruin were they to allow blacks into their neighborhoods and inspired white flight. The FHA financed white flight by preferentially directing home loans to whites in all-white suburbs and reinforced housing segregation by building highways along the borders of racially distinct neighborhoods. It acceded to white demands that public housing projects be located outside their neighborhoods. It created a system of highly fragmented local public housing authorities, which could offer housing subsidies only within the segregated neighborhoods in which they were located, thereby trapping poor blacks in disadvantaged neighborhoods.[5]

Local governments also facilitated racial segregation. During the suburbanization boom of the 1950s, the most important predictor of the formation of new local governments was proximity to cities with large black populations that had the power to annex new territories. The new governments that formed contained very few blacks. New city formation functioned to block incorporation into mixed-race cities, where whites would have to share public services and tax revenues with blacks. It also enabled class-exclusionary zoning regulations, used to keep relatively poorer blacks from moving in.[6] This is powerful evidence that the formation of new governments in this era was motivated by whites' desire to exclude blacks from their localities. Cities also colluded with private developers to locate public schools in racially exclusive neighborhoods, and close schools with catchment areas including both black and white neighborhoods, thus guaranteeing the racial segregation of schools.[7]

Because children's abilities depend so heavily on the abilities of their parents and ethnic group (§2.3), historical state discrimination in the provision of public schooling is also a significant cause of current racial differences in human capital. Moreover, whites continue to use city boundaries and zoning laws to hoard opportunities in access to public goods.[8] This causes race-based inequalities in human capital and other important goods.

Hence, current patterns of black-white racial segregation, causing the systematic race-based disadvantages documented in chapters 2 and 3, are the legacy of state-sponsored antiblack racial discrimination. These patterns are perpetuated today by massive illegal private housing discrimination, while the state looks the other way. The causes of segregation and resulting inequality can thus be traced to unjust intergroup processes. This generates a powerful claim on the part of those disadvantaged by these processes for their results to be undone.

4.2 Arguments for the Moral Innocence of the Causes of Black Segregation and Disadvantage

Claims of injustice are essentially expressible as complaints addressed to agents who are held morally responsible for correcting or ameliorating the injustice cited in the complaint, and for compensating for damages caused by the injustice. In this case, the complaint against segregation is expressed on behalf of blacks and addressed to the state, private parties such as real estate agents, employers, and others subject to antidiscrimination law, and citizens at large.

Intellectual resistance to the claim that agents external to the black community are morally responsible for black segregation and disadvantage arises from the changed character of the causes of racial exclusion in the post Jim Crow era. Where once racial segregation was legally enforced, today some claim that segregation is due to the voluntary exercise of individuals' rights to freedom of association. Where once racial discrimination was legally permitted and sometimes required, today it often appears to be the product of unconscious and automatic processes that may not be racist, and for which individuals may have diminished responsibility.

That the Causes of Racial Segregation Today Are Morally Innocent

Individuals have a right to freedom of association. They may choose neighborhoods on the basis of considerations of personal advantage, as well as ethnocentrism—feelings of affiliation and loyalty to groups with which they identify. Some argue that these considerations justify much observed residential racial segregation. Three hypotheses figure in this view: that segregation is due to black ethnocentrism, that it is due to class-based ethnocentrism, and that it is due to benign white ethnocentrism.

Stephan and Abigail Thernstrom argue that current patterns of black-white residential segregation are due to voluntary black self-segregation. Survey data show that whites are much more willing to accept black neighbors than in the past. Segregation is due rather to black ethnocentrism. Indeed, few blacks are willing to be racial pioneers in an otherwise all-white neighborhood. Most prefer neighborhoods that are evenly divided between whites and blacks, or neighborhoods where blacks are a majority.[9] If black ethnocentrism rather than white prejudice is driving current patterns of segregation, then it follows that blacks have no just complaint against others for their own segregation.

The Thernstroms' benign view of current racial segregation is not supported by more searching reviews of the evidence. To be sure, many whites avoid neighborhoods with large or increasing numbers of blacks for class-based reasons. However, most whites prefer not to live in neighborhoods with many blacks even after controlling for all of the other factors, such as class composition, that whites cite as influencing their neighborhood preferences.[10]

The motives behind black self-segregation should also be probed. Some black self-segregation is due to ethnocentrism. Many blacks express pride in controlling their own communities and feel more at home in black-majority neighborhoods.[11] However, the obverse of this is that they *do not* feel at home, but rather unwelcome, in majority-white neighborhoods. Fear of white hostility is a more important factor than ethnocentrism in explaining black residential choices.[12] Thus, while some black self-segregation is voluntary, white antipathy toward blacks makes integration an unattractive option for them. This kind of voluntary choice does not justify the restricted range of options blacks face (§1.2).

An alternative hypothesis attributes racial segregation to class-based ethnocentrism. Americans prefer to associate with people who share their socioeconomic status. An elaborate set of state institutions—municipal boundaries, zoning regulations, building codes—caters to this preference by enabling class-based segregation. Howard Husock describes with approval the "unwritten rules" governing class segregation in terms of a "ladder" of economically stratified neighborhoods. In the American ethos, access to higher rungs must be earned by individual hard work and saving. The "responsible" classes may justifiably exclude the "underclass" from their neighborhoods, so that they may create safe communities of their own and secure decent prospects for housing appreciation. In this view, Americans who earned their way into a decent neighborhood by dint of personal striving rightly resent lower-income individuals who manage to move in through government subsidies.[13] To the extent that racial segregation is a byproduct of class segregation, Husock would argue that it is morally justified.

Given that black-white racial segregation is far more intense than class segregation, and that levels of black segregation do not decline with attainment of middle-class status (§2.1), this rationale does not go very far. It can stretch further by joining it with the analysis of Ingrid Ellen, explaining why whites are reluctant to buy homes in neighborhoods with large or increasing numbers of blacks. Ellen argues that few whites avoid these neighborhoods out of racism. Rather, whites engage in racial profiling: they take a significant or increasing presence of blacks in the neighborhood as a sign that it is undesirable for race-neutral, class-based reasons. They see such neighborhoods as likely to harbor low-class residents, suffer from high crime rates, and share other problems of "underclass" urban areas.[14]

"There goes the neighborhood." This thought is not color-blind, nor are the actions associated with it morally innocent. It reflects second-order discrimination, born of racial stigmatization: not just blacks, but things associated with them, are tarred with the stigmas originally attached to blacks (§3.5). The practice of racially profiling neighborhoods is self-confirming: it helps create the neighborhoods of poverty and disadvantage that people are eager to avoid. And it does so in ways that have a harsh impact on blacks, even when they are not "underclass" (§§2.2–2.4). Since this practice expresses racial stigma and causes black disadvantage, it counts as a form of unjust racial stigmatization (§3.1).

One could argue that whites who avoid black neighborhoods for these reasons are not blameworthy. They are not acting out of racist animus. They are simply trapped in a prisoner's dilemma. Although the self-fulfilling prophecy could be avoided if whites collectively refused to racially profile neighborhoods, any individual white who ignores the racial profile risks a large personal loss in access to advantage for a negligible positive impact on the neighborhood's access. Individual whites can hardly be blamed for preferring to buy homes in neighborhoods that can promise decent public services, low tax and crime rates, few blighted lots, and steadily appreciating housing values—especially when their individual choices can do little to improve the neighborhoods that suffer from these problems.

This argument may excuse individual whites who avoid black neighborhoods for class-based reasons, if their perceptions are accurate. But this only shows that substantive responsibility for the problems of class-segregated neighborhoods should not be lodged with individuals. It cannot justify the state's facilitation of class segregation. The analysis of the preceding two chapters provides strong reasons for rejecting the rationale for class segregation underlying America's "unwritten rules." The ladder analogy, and the background meritocratic story according to which the exercise of an individualist work ethic is sufficient to get ahead, presuppose a world in which opportunities are open to all. Yet class segregation is just a form of opportunity hoarding. Segregation of the less from the more advantaged is a generic cause of poverty, unemployment, and poor access to public and private goods (§1.3). The disadvantages of poverty are multiplied when all of one's neighbors are similarly disadvantaged. Thus, class segregation generates more poverty than would otherwise exist. It also causes stigmatizing representations of the poor as "underclass." It buys relatively small advantages to the already advantaged by imposing severe costs on the least. The rungs of the ladder, far from offering opportunities for advancement, function as bars against the advancement of those who occupy the lowest positions. The ladder myth adds insult to injury by reinforcing the "fundamental attribution error": ascribing the economic success of the better-off to their individual virtue alone and the economic failures of the "underclass" to their vices alone, ignoring the negative effects of class segregation on the poor. Even if we grant a rough correlation between hard work and success, this hardly does justice to the many hardworking poor whose opportunities are diminished by class segregation. It also disregards the claims of "underclass" children to minimally decent opportunities, although they bear no responsibility for their parents' behavior.

An alternative account of black-white segregation appeals to white ethnocentrism. Thomas Schelling has demonstrated that high levels of residential segregation can arise without discrimination, simply from individual tastes for in-group affiliation.[15] If both blacks and whites prefer to live in neighborhoods where their race is the majority, only complete segregation will satisfy that preference—even if all would prefer some integration. If most whites prefer to be the overwhelming majority in a neighborhood, and virtually none will tolerate being a small minority, then the entry of just a few blacks can create a "tipping point" leading to mass white flight and segregation levels higher than any individual would prefer.

Arguably, patterns of racial segregation arising from such a process of voluntary moves are not caused by unjust intergroup processes. No discrimination is involved; everyone enjoys freedom to move to the neighborhood of their choice. The motive is ethnocentrism, not out-group stig-matization. While ethnocentrism is hardly a morally admirable motive, it is not intrinsically unjust. Blacks and whites alike express preferences for some degree of in-group affiliation, as do members of other racial and ethnic groups. Individuals are entitled to freedom of association. Hence, the argument goes, no one is entitled to complain about neighborhoods that came to be segregated by ethnocentric sorting processes.

Even if we were to concede this theoretical point, it does not explain how America's neighborhoods have actually come to be segregated.[16] Given the high tolerance of blacks for being a minority in their neigh-borhoods, observed levels of segregation cannot be explained without some discriminatory processes keeping blacks out of white neighbor-hoods.[17] These processes are widely documented in contemporary Amer-ica. Furthermore, white neighborhood preferences cannot be explained in terms of pure ethnocentrism. If in-group affiliation were what motivated white settlement patterns, then whites would also prefer all-white neigh-borhoods to neighborhoods containing significant numbers of Asians and Hispanics. However, after controlling for other factors such as class, whites appear to be virtually indifferent to the numbers of Asians and Hispanics in their neighborhood.[18] This is not so for the numbers of blacks in their neighborhood. This strongly suggests that black stigmati-zation explains white avoidance of neighborhoods with more than token numbers of blacks. In addition, it is hard to see how the mere presence of members of diverse racial groups can pose an obstacle to in-group affilia-tion.[19] America's storied ethnic immigrant enclaves of the first half of the last century, which were far more ethnically integrated than the hyper-segregated black neighborhoods of today,[20] did not prevent the Italians, Jews, and Poles living side-by-side from associating more with their in-group than with other immigrant groups. High levels of majority group segregation require out-group antipathy, not just in-group favoritism.

That the Unconscious Causes of Racial Discrimination Are Morally Innocent

Gregory Mitchell and Philip Tetlock complain that contemporary social psychological theories fail to establish that people's unconscious stereo-types reflect racial animus. They fail to rule out the possibility that mere awareness of racial stereotypes can cause people to more quickly asso-ciate bad qualities with blacks and good qualities with whites, or even that good intentions, such as the desire *not* to be bigoted, can heighten awareness of stereotypes in ways that backfire. Since these alternative explanations of conduct caused by implicit stereotypes suggest that such conduct is morally innocent, social psychologists unjustly infer from their experimental studies that the vast majority of people "are implicit bigots on par with children reared in prejudiced households and taught to hold mean-spirited beliefs about minorities and to act out these prejudices."[21]

This complaint confuses judgments of character with judgments of justice (§2.1). Mitchell and Tetlock rightly observe that many of the causes of systematic race-based disadvantage may not be traceable to racism, understood as a moral vice. Contrary to their charge, social psychological theories of stigmatization acknowledge that many motives, including good intentions, can cause racial discrimination (§3.4, §3.5). However, from the fact that many motives for discriminatory treatment are not evil, it does not follow that blacks have no grounds for complaint about this treatment. They are being treated in a disadvantageous manner, out of racially stigmatizing ideas about their characters and capacities.[22] This treatment is objectionable, even if the people entertaining these ideas are not racists because they do not endorse these ideas and are unaware of their effects. Their conduct amounts to injustice born of negligence. We are all morally responsible for ensuring that our racial stereotypes do not lead to unfair evaluations and treatments of others.

Against this claim, Amy Wax argues that unconscious stereotyping is beyond anyone's control. Since stereotyping is automatic and unconscious, there is nothing we can do to prevent it. Hence, it is unfair and futile to hold people responsible for it.[23]

To assess the unfairness charge, let us distinguish two concepts of responsibility: attributive and substantive. A person is attributively responsible for some mental state or conduct if she is open to moral criticism or praise for it. A person is substantively responsible for some conduct if others may rightly hold her responsible for it, either in making her do or avoid it, or in making her bear the costs of doing or avoiding it. Control is not a necessary condition for either kind of responsibility. We are attributively responsible for any mental state that is, in principle, responsive to reasons, even if we cannot control it at will.[24] For example, although beliefs are not generally subject to our wills, we are still open to criticism for basing our beliefs on insufficient evidence and poor reasoning. Holding unendorsed automatic racial stereotypes is not racist. The moral criticism to which these mental states leave us open must be milder than what we would direct toward avowed racists. But it is not negligible. These stereotypes operate in harmful and rationally unjustified ways. This is sufficient to make them properly subject to moral criticism.

Control is also not necessary for substantive responsibility for the costs of one's unjustified mental habits. The idea that it is relies on the background thought that people are entitled to a chance to avoid the costs in question. However, whenever some conduct has costs for human beings, someone will always have to bear these costs and thus be held substantively responsible for them. This is true whether the conduct is controllable or not. The *victims* of harmful habits lack control over their consequences and never had a chance to avoid these costs.[25] Thus, the principle of control cannot do the work ascribed to it. It gives us no moral reason to prefer that the victims rather than the perpetrators of harmful conduct should bear its costs.

Turn now to Wax's futility charge. Valid claims of justice must be addressed to agents who are in a position to make things right—or at least better. If what is demanded of them is impossible, then the claim is invalid. Wax rightly argues that we lack willful control over automatic thought processes as they occur. However, we do have some control over the circumstances that trigger these processes, and over their effects on conduct. Decision makers can reduce the influence of stereotypes by basing evaluations on clearly defined, objective measures, giving evaluators time to do their jobs properly, not overloading them with too many responsibilities, and holding them accountable for nondiscriminatory judgments.[26] Other evaluation procedures, such as blind reviewing, can also prevent stereotypes from affecting evaluations. Training judgment through exposure to counterstereotypical cases may also eliminate the influence of automatic stereotypes.[27] Most important, since segregation causes stereotypes (§3.1), one way to reduce their formation and activation is to practice integration (§6.3). Since there are many things we can do to reduce the influence of unconscious stereotypes on our conduct, Wax's futility charge fails.

4.3 Arguments for Black Responsibility for Black Segregation and Disadvantage

Conservative commentators on racial inequality tend to attribute the bulk of contemporary black disadvantage to causes for which blacks themselves are responsible. Stephan and Abigail Thernstrom have produced the most important and comprehensive narrative to this effect.[28] In their account, white racism once kept blacks down. However, during the Civil Rights Movement, whites cast off their racism, allowing many blacks to move into the middle class. The ones still mired in poverty, they claim, are there due to pathologies internal to black communities. If only poor blacks would behave responsibly, they would not be disadvantaged. Since black disadvantage is due to blacks' irresponsible behavior, they suggest that state and private institutions have minimal responsibility to help blacks overcome these disadvantages.

Conservatives are not wrong to point to numerous imprudent and harmful activities by blacks in "underclass" communities—especially, involvement in gangs and crime, the dominance of single-parent families, often started by financially insecure youth in unstable relationships, and poor school work—as important proximate causes of black disadvantage. If poor blacks would stay out of legal trouble, delay childbearing until they are financially secure and committed to raising their children with their partners, and study diligently until graduating from high school, they, their children, and their neighbors would be much better off.

These causal claims should not be controversial. Nor should it be controversial that blacks who act in these ways are attributively responsible for their actions. What is controversial is the moral response Americans should take toward these facts. How should substantive responsibility for dealing with the causes and consequences of destructive behavior be allocated among those who act irresponsibly, among the black community (which contains many individuals who are not so acting), and among wider American institutions? Judgments of attributive responsibility do not dictate judgments of substantive responsibility. Even if a group of people habitually engages in self-destructive behavior for which they are attributively responsible, it does not follow that they should be made to bear all of its costs, or denied outside help. Suppose, for example, the habit of smoking in bed prevailed in an immigrant group, and that this habit caused many fires. Although the immigrants who smoke in bed are attributively responsible for the fires, it does not follow that public fire services should be withheld from the immigrant community. To abandon them so would be morally reprehensible—and not only because many innocents, including the immigrants' children and nonsmoking neighbors, would be made to suffer the lethal consequences of others' bad behavior. It would be appalling even with respect to the smokers themselves.

If judgments of causal and attributive responsibility are not sufficient to determine our moral responses to self-destructive behavior, some other factors must be at work. I suggest that our moral responses to self-undermining behaviors within the black community are affected by the interpretive frameworks in which we embed them, which invest these claims with moral meanings that support different assignments of substantive responsibility for helping blacks. Two narrative frameworks suggest different answers to this question. Both make use of the vexed concept of "culture." The "folk anthropological" framework represents culture as a sui generis, autonomous product of a distinctive, self-contained community. "Culture" in this sense is conceived as the immediate expression of the community's fundamental shared values, which are thought to express their social identities. The "economic" framework represents culture as the equilibrium outcome of individuals' strategic responses to each other's conduct, within the constraints of their resources and opportunities. "Culture" in this sense reflects peoples' adaptations to their environments, including other people. These frameworks suggest different moral judgments concerning cultures.

Folk anthropology favors representations that stress cultural diversity and indigenous originality. Anthropology's stress on kinship structures along with cultural distinctiveness encourages the popular conflation of ancestry with culture, suggesting that each ancestral group's culture is the expression of its unique identity. This encourages representations that stress between-group heterogeneity and within-group homogeneity. These features discourage causal inquiries that explain cultures in terms of human universals, or in any terms external to the culture.

Folk anthropology supports two characteristic moral responses to cultural difference. In conjunction with a background egalitarian orientation, it supports multiculturalism: a celebration of diversity; a tendency to see each community as having a right to live in accordance with its own cultural norms, and to see the community's biological descendants as having a right to be brought up in "their own" culture; support for each community's ethnocentric, self-segregationist impulses; and an impulse toward cultural preservation against outside influences (other cultures, globalization, trade), seen as homogenizing threats to the culture's purity and authenticity.

In conjunction with a background inegalitarian orientation, folk anthropology supports feelings of moral distance and alienation from identity groups to which one does not belong, and hostility toward integration with others, except if the others assimilate to one's own culture. This orientation tends to hold segregated groups wholly responsible for the advantages and disadvantages accruing to their cultures, to evaluate cultural differences moralistically, on a single scale of value—as "pathological" or "worthy," "savage" or "civilized"—and to neglect the causal importance of intergroup relations on outcomes for each group. Each group's boat is a product of its own unique design and sails in its own tub. Hence, each group has only itself to blame if it does not keep its own boat afloat.

The economic framework views cultures as stocks of instrumentally valuable behavioral resources. They are honed in response to the environmental contingencies faced by individuals who interact frequently enough that they arrive at strategies that coordinate their expectations and actions. Economists tend to disfavor explanations of cultural differences in terms of sui generis differences in "tastes" or values. Rather, they postulate background universal needs and interests—for the means of subsistence, power, social esteem, and so forth—and model differences as arising from different endowments, incentives, and environments, including different patterns of interaction within and between groups. In evolutionary game theory, the frequency of a behavioral strategy in a population is a function of its payoffs, which are largely determined by how many individuals adopt it and rival strategies in interacting with one another. In successive rounds of interaction, people adjust their strategies in response to the payoffs they experienced in previous rounds, until an equilibrium is reached.[29]

The economic framework is disinclined to associate identity or ancestral groups with cultures. Observed associations are merely the contingent product of who happens to have regularly interacted with whom. Groups may be detached from ascriptive identities. Individuals may belong to numerous cross-cutting groups, which may or may not coincide with ancestral groups, and adopt different norms of interaction for each group. No identity group has special claims to any particular cultural adaptation; their value lies in their circulation among interacting individuals. Culture is "capital": fungible, alienable, tradable, mobile, adaptable.

The economic framework suggests several moral responses to cultural differences. First, its background universalism and instrumentalism encourages a sense of common humanity and a cosmopolitan, pragmatic orientation to cultural differences. Free trade in culture goes hand-in-hand with free trade in goods. The origin of a cultural norm in a particular identity group makes no more inherent difference to its utility than the national origin of a bale of cotton does to its utility. Others may emulate it and find that it works in their own environment. This orientation is hostile to judgments of "authenticity" or "purity" with respect to culture. Hybridization, modification, tinkering with cultural strategies are all normal. Second, the economic framework is open to representations of within-group heterogeneity. Within a population, the equilibrium state may contain different proportions of people adopting different behavioral strategies. This discourages stereotypes and stigmatizing judgments of group cultures since it calls into question the very idea of a group having a unified "culture." Indeed, it calls into question the idea of "groups," understood as self-contained, homogeneous populations internally united by shared values and externally differentiated by distinct values. Cross-cutting groups interact and generate varied repertoires of norms for different situations, depending on the parties to the interaction. Finally and most important, game-theoretic models of culture are open to the possibility that groups may be trapped in collectively dysfunctional norms, as in prisoner's dilemmas. In such cases, it is futile to exhort individuals to change their ways one by one. If the group is short on social capital, it may need the help of collective action by a more encompassing group to achieve a more functional equilibrium.

Economic interpretations of culture offer a natural fit with the theory of segregation presented in the last three chapters. If norms arise from regular interaction, then segregation defines the populations within which regular interactions, and hence distinctive norms, are liable to arise. Segregation theorists trace the rise of dysfunctional, self-destructive norms to the features of disadvantaged segregated communities: not poverty alone, but *concentrated* disadvantage, focused especially on marginalization (high levels of chronic unemployment) and deprivations of access to public goods and social and cultural capital. Thus, segregation theorists reject conservatives' claims that cultural explanations of black disadvantage displace external explanations.[30] They fault conservatives for offering an incomplete explanation of dysfunctional norms, which stops at causes internal to disadvantaged communities. This leaves conservatives with nothing more than "bad values" as an explanation of disadvantage. Rather, segregation theories incorporate dysfunctional cultural norms into their accounts of group inequality, showing how they arise from segregation. Dysfunctional behavior is the product of visibly constrained options. Early motherhood looks a lot more attractive to teenagers who see that their sisters were no better off economically for waiting to have children,[31] and who live in neighborhoods with such alarmingly low levels of social capital that the only person they can count on to love, and love them back, is a child of their own.[32] Single motherhood looks a lot more attractive for very poor young women, given the small pool of men available who meet the most minimal standards of eligibility for marriage: steady employment at a job capable of supporting a family, no criminal involvement or drug problem, and sexual fidelity.[33]

Consider also Elijah Anderson's account of the contest between "decent" and "street" values in ghetto neighborhoods (§2.3).[34] Anderson reports that most ghetto residents favor "decent" values of hard work, obeying the law, and taking care of kin. Game theoretic analysis shows that norms can change in the face of concerted challenges by a few. Consider a community governed by norms of civility. Strangers meeting at random confidently expect that the other will treat them with respect, recognize their rights, and interact on terms of mutual consent. Trust and cordiality prevail. The members of such a community enjoy an economy of esteem at a favorable equilibrium, in which everyone can bask in the glow of everyone else's civility. Now suppose that the community is segregated from mainstream opportunities, leading to concentrated poverty, unemployment, and withdrawal of public services. Even if the vast majority of community members continue to value cooperation, civility, and the law, a few chronically unemployed, frustrated individuals take an alienated view of their society and seek alternative means of self-satisfaction. Suppose they regularly harass and abuse others. Police never seem able or willing to stop them. Everyone else would much prefer to live in accordance with civil norms. But the presence of a few violent individuals can be enough to spread fear and mistrust in the community. One can never be sure whether the next person one meets on the street will be civil or violent. Because the costs of encountering a violent person are so high, people who value civility must now prepare themselves for that contingency in all chance encounters. To protect themselves against violence, they must be prepared to act violently and adopt a threatening appearance to ward off attacks. Because the violent ones interpret civil behavior as a sign of weakness, marking one as a likely prey, decent individuals must hide their impulses toward civil behavior behind a mask of aggression—the game face.

This individually rational response to the threat of victimization undermines trust because no one can afford to signal their willingness to reciprocate others' civility. Despite the values of the majority in the community, people are trapped in a highly unfavorable equilibrium. The economy of esteem now operates on disadvantageous terms: respect is in very short supply because to show it is a mark of inferiority and an admission of vulnerability. Exchanges in the currency of esteem become a zero-sum game: one gains esteem by "dissing" others. Even those who would rather not play this game have little choice, lest they be marked as permanent victims. This makes people touchy and distrustful, prone to detect disrespect even when it is not there, and to display their determination not to get pushed around by pushing others around. In an atmosphere of pervasive mistrust and dissembling, people must constantly test and probe others, so they can acquire the information about their underlying dispositions. The ever-present threat of violence also drives youths into gangs.[35] Acquiring friends who will stand up for oneself if one is "rolled" is a survival strategy in a world where police fail to offer reliable protection.

This economic account of the connections between race and crime suggests several moral responses. First, it highlights the roles segregation plays in narrowing the opportunities available to residents of marginalized neighborhoods. Without segregation and its attendant concentration of unemployment, poverty, and deprivations of social capital, many residents who are currently choosing a life of crime would have chosen better options. While this fact does not excuse those who choose to commit crimes, it extends some responsibility for the problem to the agents of segregation.[36] Second, the economic account reminds us that without segregation, the disadvantaged would enjoy more effective police protection and thereby avoid the invasion of civil society by norms of incivility. The innocent victims are not just those who have been victimized by specific crimes against their persons, but everyone who must live with the fear, humiliation, and distrust that pervades neighborhoods where public norms have switched from "decent" to "street." These innocents are made to pay a severe price, not just in prospects of criminal victimization, but in stigmatization of their race by the highly publicized acts of same-race criminals. Third, the economic account sympathetically situates those who are caught in the prisoner's dilemma of aggression signals. Conformity to signaling norms needed for individual survival within high-crime neigh-borhoods is both collectively dysfunctional in those neighborhoods and individually dysfunctional outside them. Yet it is both unfair and futile to ask those who are prepared to behave cooperatively but intimidated into self-defensive threat displays to simply change their signaling behavior. The penalty they would have to suffer from this is too high. Agents in the wider society should do their part by becoming more "streetwise"—acquiring the cultural capital needed to distinguish the unconditional threats of hardened criminals from the conditional threats of the decent who seek cooperative relations with others but are forced to signal a willingness to do violence to aggressors.

The economic approach, by situating the predicament of segregated blacks in a wider causal context, supplies a richer causal analysis and consequently a more far-reaching and feasible set of responsibility as-signments and policy prescriptions than conservative approaches to race. Contrast this with what conservatives Stephan and Abigail Thernstrom have to offer: "If the African-American crime rate suddenly dropped to the current level of the white crime rate, we would eliminate a major force that is driving blacks and whites apart and is destroying the fabric of black urban life."[37] This remark expresses the view that only blacks need to change to solve their problems. This amounts to a decision to hold blacks alone substantively responsible for all of the costs of a strate-gic trap induced by decades of deliberate racial segregation.

Consider next how folk anthropological and economic explanations of depressed academic motivation among blacks affect our moral responses. One theory of the black-white racial gap in school achievement claims that black students' academic motivation is depressed by an "opposi-tional culture" among black youth that identifies academic achievement with "acting white."[38] As originally formulated, oppositional culture theory lies within the economic framework. Young blacks' disapproval of peers who seek to advance through education is not an autochtho-nous expression of an ideal of "blackness" as anti-intellectual, but rather an adaptation to centuries of white discrimination. Historically, it has been *whites* who identify superior school achievement with "whiteness," justifying their denial of educational opportunities to blacks in terms of their innate intellectual inferiority, and refusing to reward black educa-tional achievement with commensurate employment opportunities. Faced with such an unjust opportunity and incentive structure, blacks respond by stressing the importance of group solidarity in opposition to what whites define as their culture and seek an alternative source of black self-esteem in such opposition. According to the theory, black students who choose individual academic striving over loyalty to their community are therefore rejected by their peers for "acting white." This depresses black students' motivation to achieve in school. Consistent with the economic framework, which explains norms in terms of adaptations to specific environments and is sensitive to within-group variation in responsiveness to norms, researchers investigating the oppositional culture hypothesis have sought evidence that other minority groups whose identities were shaped by a history of discrimination respond similarly to academic challenges,[39] and that some American blacks adopt alternative strategies to reconcile their academic ambitions with peer group pressures.

The original advocates of the oppositional culture hypothesis do not absolve blacks of substantive responsibility for their norms. They urge the black community to "provide visible and concrete evidence for black youths that the community appreciates and encourages academic effort and success" so as to counteract the disabling identification of black identity with rejection of schooling. Their causal analysis implies, however, that such efforts will not succeed unless the wider society also visibly improves the opportunities open to blacks, so that black youths perceive that academic effort makes a significant difference to their economic prospects.[40]

Conservatives have embraced oppositional culture theory. But they reinterpret it through the folk anthropological framework. They use the "acting white" hypothesis to draw invidious comparisons between blacks and purportedly similarly situated but culturally superior Asian immigrants.[41] This leads economically successful whites and Asians to attribute racial inequality to vast inherent differences in values between blacks and themselves. "We" have superior values; "they" have inferior ones; hence "they" deserve their disadvantages. Conservatives strip the idea of "acting white" from its context in unjust intergroup relations and opportunity structures and treat it as a problem internal and specific to black culture. According to John McWhorter, for example, it reflects blacks' anti-intellectualism and attachment to "victimology."[42] This reduces blacks' educational difficulties to the thought that blacks just don't value education. Given a framework that views each culture as autonomously generating its own norms, there is little left to do but to exhort blacks to change their dysfunctional values.

Despite the popularity of oppositional culture theory in conservative intellectual circles, it has not fared well in empirical tests.[43] Theories of academic achievement gaps that stress inequalities in human, social, and cultural capital and access to public goods (§§2.3–2.4), and stigmatization effects (§3.4), enjoy better empirical support. Viewing education as capital turns our thoughts in more productive directions than folk anthropology. We would hardly explain poverty in terms of people placing a low value on financial capital. It is more credible to argue that it takes capital to make more capital, so that deficiencies in initial capital endowments tend to depress one's economic prospects. The same argument applies to human capital.

Conservatives have two main strategies for replying to structural accounts of dysfunctional norms. One is a moral argument: that explanations of black disadvantage that trace it to external causes wrongly exculpate bad behavior and thereby reinforce the very conduct that keeps the black community down. This charge is false. Substantive responsibility for dealing with problems can be extended to additional agents without letting those engaged in dysfunctional behavior entirely off the hook. The second is a causal argument: that similarly poor, uneducated, and despised Asian immigrants have moved ahead, so black disadvantage must be due to defective black cultural values. Yet Asian immigrants are not similarly situated to blacks, either in economic circumstance or in whites' attitudes toward them (§§2.1–2.2).[44] Whites are far more willing to employ them, marry them, and accept them into their neighborhoods.

Two comparisons support the view that concentrated disadvantage, rather than racially specific cultural values, explains the rise of dysfunctional norms in segregated ghetto communities. The first is historical. The dysfunctions of the ghetto—high rates of poverty, crime, and single parenthood concentrated in segregated neighborhoods—arose only after work "disappeared" from the inner cities.[45] If steady jobs capable of supporting a family were still readily available to young blacks, it would be hard to see why they suddenly embraced a set of values disqualifying them for such jobs, when their grandparents upheld these values. The second is international. The same dysfunctional norms appear wherever work disappears from communities in advanced capitalist economies, regardless of their racial composition. Wythenshawe, England, contains neighborhoods of concentrated poverty much like American ghettos. Nearly a third of the residents in the public housing projects are out of the labor force. Truancy, dropping out, early sexual activity, binge drinking, drugs, crime, and gangs are common among youth. Fathers are often absent and mothers are often on welfare. Impoverished relationships with adults leave young people with little of the cultural capital they need to advance. Police are unable or unwilling to control youth harassment of neighbors. A majority of children are crime victims. Yet Wythenshawe is 95 percent white.[46]

If the dysfunctional norms prevalent in black underclass neighborhoods were the autonomous expression of a specifically black culture, Wythenshawe youths' adoption of the same norms would be inexplicable. They become explicable when situated in a causal account that stresses the effects of segregation—of concentrated exclusion from work opportunities. My argument is not only causal, but moral. When dysfunctional behaviors of the disadvantaged are represented as the autonomous product of alien, pathological cultures, value systems, and identities, the advantaged are likely to respond with neglect at best and punitive measures at worst. When we see them as the outcome of universal human dispositions in disadvantageous circumstances, we recognize our common humanity. When we recognize these circumstances as imposed by the advantaged, no one escapes substantive responsibility for remedying the problems of the disadvantaged.

4.4 The Injustice of the Condition and Effects of Segregation

So far I have argued that current racial inequalities are unjust because they are caused by unjust intergroup processes. Here I shall argue that even if current patterns of racial segregation and resulting race-based disadvantage had been produced through innocent processes, they would still be unjust. They can be unjust if they *cause* or *embody* unjust intergroup relations (§1.5).

A pattern of de facto segregation may embody unjust intergroup relations by expressing stigmatizing meanings. If segregation signifies that the excluded group is regarded as inferior, then segregation constitutes an expressive harm to the excluded. In the standard case, de facto segregation would carry this meaning because it came about by systematic discrimination. However, we could imagine a case in which two groups of citizens were originally segregated by innocent causes—say, continental and island dwellers, who arrived in their ancestral locations by chance. If they *remain* apart due to stigmatizing ideas about one of the groups, then de facto spatial segregation acquires a stigmatizing meaning. For example, continent dwellers may regard the island dwellers as impure and hence make them unwelcome on the continent, and the island dwellers in response may perpetuate once-innocent segregation by avoiding the continent.

Current de facto segregation embodies a similar dignitary harm to blacks. This harm is partly due to the legacy of past deliberate segregation, the point of which was to constitute blacks as an untouchable caste. The most extreme of these meanings have dwindled in many public spaces. Blacks and whites now often swim together in public pools. Yet the taint of racial stigma still clings to segregated black neighborhoods. To be sure, de facto segregation cannot carry these meanings unless its persistence can be causally traced to racially stigmatizing ideas. My point is that the condition of segregation can be harmful and unjust in itself, apart from further inequalities, say, in access to material goods. Separate but equal is inherently unequal, even if the original cause of separation was innocent, so long as group stigma maintains the separation today.

Of course, segregation also causes numerous racial inequalities in access to material goods. These inequalities are unjust if they impair the ability of members of the less advantaged group to stand in relations of equality with others. This can happen if the inequalities are so severe as to oppress the disadvantaged group, or if they impair fair access to opportunities to develop talents and compete for offices (§1.5).

The analysis in chapters 2 and 3 shows that black-white segregation in the United States causes four of the kinds of oppressive intergroup relations identified in §1.4. Hypersegregation causes marginalization—extraordinarily high rates of unemployment in black ghetto communities. It deprives these communities of the resources—tax revenues, social and cultural capital—they need to support the education of their youth. This tends to confine ghetto residents to menial jobs and makes them vulnerable to exploitation. The condition of lacking adequate public resources and social and cultural capital is also a condition of powerlessness. It deprives ghetto residents of influence over the decisions by institutions—government and firms—that profoundly affect their prospects. Finally, segregation causes group stigmatization (§3.1). Blacks' dishonored public image in turn inspires a politics of racial resentment and punitive policies toward blacks and disadvantaged groups and places perceived to be tainted by "blackness" (§3.2, §3.6).

Marginalization, exploitation, and powerlessness are extreme cases of group inequality suffered by residents of impoverished ghetto communities but arguably not by the black middle class. Yet the black middle class is also segregated. They also have sound complaints that their segregation causes unjust intergroup relations. Although the stigmatizing images of blacks that inform stereotypes, attribution biases, and public representations of blacks in the mass media and political discourse mostly reflect ideas about underclass black residents of inner city ghettos, these images undermine the standing of blacks of all economic classes. Moreover, black segregation and stigmatization undermine blacks' access to fair opportunities to develop their talents and compete on fair terms for offices.

This last claim can be justified even on a narrow principle of fair opportunity, according to which an individual's access to opportunities should not be undermined by (1) racial prejudice, (2) racial stigmatization, (3) ethnocentric conduct facilitated by state law, or (4) ethnocentric conduct contrary to antidiscrimination principles that govern regulable institutions of civil society (§1.5). We have seen that racial prejudice and stigmatization, embodied in conscious or unconscious affective and cognitive biases, undermine blacks' opportunities to develop their talents and compete on fair terms in numerous ways. These biases cause unjust discrimination (§3.5). Mere awareness of racial stigma causes the nonstigmatized to be uncomfortable and awkward in interracial interaction and gives rise to humiliating norms of interracial interaction. These impair blacks' access to opportunities for cooperation and advancement (§2.3, §3.3, §3.5). Blacks' awareness of their stigmatized status undermines their educational achievement (§3.4). Ethnocentrism, too, while not categorically unjust, becomes so when state power is used to facilitate opportunity hoarding, as when municipal lines are drawn in racially exclusionary ways, or zoning laws are enacted (consciously or unconsciously) to keep blacks from moving in (§4.1). These state-mediated processes pose unjust obstacles to blacks' access to opportunities to develop their talents, especially by confining them to inferior schools (§2.4), limiting their access to financial, social, and cultural capital, and informal sources of human capital (§2.3), and limiting their access to jobs (§2.2). Ethnocentric conduct is also unjust when it becomes the basis for the allocation of opportunities for hiring, promotion, and training within firms (§2.3).

The principle of fair opportunity just articulated is broader than that embodied in antidiscrimination law since it condemns self-undermining effects of stigmatization that are not mediated by others' discriminatory conduct and covers domains of interaction that are not and should not be directly regulated by the law. (Our current object is to identify injustice, not to fashion legal remedies.) Yet it follows an important insight of antidiscrimination law. Title VII of the Civil Rights Act of 1964 prohibits both purposeful racial discrimination and employment practices that have a differential racial impact and cannot be otherwise justified. The law finds an unequal racial outcome unjust if it is causally linked to an unjust process connected to intergroup relations. It acknowledges that the range of unjust processes is wider than purposeful discrimination. Policies (such as word-of-mouth advertising for jobs, §2.3) that negligently permit de facto segregation and employee ethnocentrism to generate unequal employment opportunities for different racial groups are unjust.

Segregation causes numerous racial inequalities by varied causal paths (chapters 2, 3). Group inequalities are unjust if they are caused by, embody, or cause unjust intergroup relations. Current patterns of racial segregation were caused by massive racial discrimination by the state and private actors and are maintained by illegal private discrimination and racial avoidance stimulated by unjust racial stigmatization. Segregation embodies a dignitary harm to blacks and causes unjust intergroup relations by reducing hypersegregated blacks in poor inner-city neighborhoods to a marginalized, powerless, and exploited class, and blacks of all classes to a stigmatized race. It stimulates racial prejudice, stereotypes, and discrimination. It generates a public image of blacks that undermines their political influence by inflaming a politics of white racial resentment and ethnocentrism. It impairs black access to fair opportunities for the development of their talents.

Conservatives claim that systematic racial injustice has ended, and that the current causes of black disadvantage are either morally innocent or due to self-destructive behavior for which blacks are responsible. To support the claim of moral innocence, they suggest that current segregation may be due to voluntary black self-segregation, class-based ethnocentrism, or innocent white ethnocentrism. These explanations fail to account for the facts that much black self-segregation is a response to perceived white hostility, that race swamps class as a factor explaining segregation, and that whites avoid neighborhoods with concentrations of blacks too low to interfere with white preferences for same-race affiliation and do not avoid neighborhoods with much higher concentrations of Asians. Some conservatives claim that unconscious racial stereotyping and consequent discrimination is morally innocent, because it is not based on consciously endorsed racial prejudice, and that it is unfair to hold people responsible for it because it is uncontrollable. The first claim confuses an evil will with injustice. Blacks have a just complaint against processes that judge and treat them unfairly, even if they are unintended and not evil. The second claim disregards evidence that we can arrange institutions to block unconscious stereotypes and biases. It is also morally confused. People can be attributively responsible for mental processes not under willful control. There is also no injustice in holding people substantively responsible for the costs of their uncontrollable mental processes since someone not in control must bear these costs.

Conservatives are right to argue that dysfunctional norms in the black community are significant causes of black disadvantage, and that blacks bear some responsibility for them. However, their analysis of these norms is impaired, both causally and morally, by their implicit adoption of a folk anthropological interpretation of their origins, as if they were the autonomous creation and expression of a self-contained black community. This interpretive framework wrongly supposes that cultural explanations of black disadvantage displace explanations in terms of segregation and discrimination, and it stops causal analysis just before agents outside the black community would be implicated in the generation of these norms. It also unsympathetically represents blacks as an alien race with pathological values. The relational theory of inequality advanced in this book adopts an economic interpretation of norms that incorporates an account of dysfunctional norms in segregated communities. Economic approaches show how collectively disadvantageous norms arise in segregated communities from universal human motives and individually rational actions, thereby highlighting our common humanity with the disadvantaged. They help us see how people can be trapped in dysfunctional equilibriums, how a few bad agents can force innocents to behave in ways that expose them to unjust stigmatization, and how segregation and stigmatization by the wider society create conditions that encourage the generation of dysfunctional norms. A causally sophisticated approach to dysfunctional norms thereby encourages responses from the wider society that are both more morally responsible and more causally effective.

·FIVE·

DEMOCRATIC IDEALS AND SEGREGATION

5.1 Democracy as Membership, Civil Society, and Governance

Throughout this book, I have been alluding to an ideal of democracy as a basis for evaluating racial segregation. This ideal needs deeper articulation. Democracy is a way of life that can be understood on three levels: as a membership organization, a mode of government, and a culture. As a membership organization, democracy involves universal and equal citizenship of all the permanent members of a society who live under a state's jurisdiction. As a mode of government, democracy is government by the people, carried out by discussion among equals. As a culture, democracy consists in the free, cooperative interaction of citizens from all walks of life on terms of equality in civil society. These three levels work together. Democracy as a mode of government cannot be fully achieved apart from a democratic culture and membership organization. Yet the point of a democratic culture is not simply to make democratic government work. Democratic government is an expression of democratic culture. Its point is to serve the democratic community, and to realize its promise of universal and equal standing.

In stressing the cultural dimension of democracy, I oppose conceptions of democracy that focus on its governance structures alone: a universal franchise, periodic elections, majority rule, transparent government, the rule of law. Such conceptions foster the illusion that laws alone make a democracy, even in the absence of interaction among citizens across group lines. It tends to stress a decision rule, handing victory to the majority, at the expense of norms of equality that form the essential background condition for majority decision making to fulfill democratic ideals.

Rather than develop these points abstractly, let us examine what the struggle of blacks to participate in democracy teaches us about its requirements. Consider first the idea of democracy as a membership organization. In the notorious *Dred Scott* case, the Supreme Court declared that blacks were not citizens of the United States. It made plain the symbolic and political import of denying citizenship. In an earlier case, the Court had declared that "citizenship is the charter of equality." It contrasted citizenship with the feudal order in which individuals owed allegiance to particular persons, a condition—akin to slavery itself—that was a "badge of inferiority" and a state of "servitude."[1] Given that understanding, the *Dred Scott* Court declared that blacks could not be citizens because the Constitution, as understood by its framers, deemed them "beings of an inferior order, and altogether unfit to associate with the white race, either in social or political relations, and so far inferior that they had no rights which the white man was bound to respect."[2] It took a civil war, and passage of the Fourteenth Amendment to the U.S. Constitution, to establish the principle of universal citizenship. Without universal citizenship, a society cannot be a democracy, but only a tyranny of one part of the people over the other.

Once blacks won citizenship, opponents of black equality attempted to narrow the meaning and value of what they had won. The *Dred Scott* Court had taken for granted that citizenship entailed being regarded as an equal, fit for association with fellow citizens, and entitled to an expansive set of rights. What rights were at issue in the claim to citizenship? The dominant nineteenth-century understanding divided rights into "civil," "political," and "social" rights. Civil rights pertain to the legally enforceable rights of persons as free economic agents: to buy, sell, and lease property, make contracts, sue and be sued for enforcement of contracts, and testify in court. Political rights pertain to the rights of citizens to participate in governance: to vote, assemble for political purposes, hold political office, and serve on juries. Social rights are the rights of citizens to associate on terms of equality with others in civil society: to share a meal in a restaurant, sit together in a rail car, attend the same schools, work together as colleagues (not only as master and servant), marry and live together.[3] Immediately after the Civil War, a majority of northerners, although they advocated abolition of slavery and universal citizenship, thought that citizenship for blacks should be limited to civil rights, without granting blacks the full range of social or political rights, including the vote.[4] The conjunction of the franchise with adult citizenship, so obvious today, was not so obvious in nineteenth-century America, which accepted voting restrictions on the basis of gender, property, literacy, and other qualifications. Referenda to grant blacks the right to vote were defeated in several northern states in 1865.[5]

The attempt to separate civil, political, and social rights, and to define citizenship narrowly to entail only a subset of these rights, failed. The reasons why it failed yield insights into the nature of democracy as a mode of governance and a culture. The first lesson Americans learned was the folly of claiming to secure civil rights for blacks without granting them political rights. This was attempted under the Reconstruction program administered by President Andrew Johnson in 1865. Johnson opposed black enfranchisement and left the government of the southern states to unreconstructed white supremacists. They enacted the Black Codes, which attempted to virtually reenslave freedmen and free blacks. Blacks were required to sign year-long labor contracts with planters, which included provisions empowering the planters to govern blacks' private lives. They would forfeit an entire year's wages if they left the plantation. Employers were forbidden from offering higher wages to blacks already under contract. Blacks could be bound over in service for "vagrancy," a vague crime that included spending their incomes in ways of which whites disapproved. Northern outrage against the Black Codes, rightly seen as attempting to negate emancipation, along with the recognition that blacks could never count on the enforcement of their civil rights if they had no hand in selecting state officials responsible for upholding the law, led to the demand for black voting rights.[6]

Could blacks' claims to equal citizenship rest only on equality of civil and political rights, and not also of social rights? Many Americans thought so. The Radical Republicans did not. Senator Charles Sumner, a leader of the Radicals, introduced a bill, eventually to be passed as the Civil Rights Act of 1875, to guarantee the social rights of blacks by prohibiting discrimination and segregation in public accommodations. Its first draft also included a ban on segregated schools. Defenders of the bill cited two lines of argument. One justified the bill as an enforcement of the common law obligation of operators of public accommodations and common carriers to serve all customers on equal terms.[7] This rationale stresses the economic injustice of segregation. The second justified the bill as a requirement of republican government. William Forton, secretary of the Pennsylvania Equal Rights League, submitted a petition to Sumner urging the passage of the Civil Rights Act so "that our government may in fact be a true republic."[8]

Radical Republicans linked social rights of interracial association in civil society to republican government through two arguments: one based on status equality, the other on the consequences of association. The status equality argument observed that the segregation of public facilities enforced a caste system. It stressed the incompatibility of republican principles with any kind of caste or inherited inequality. Discrimination in public accommodations is a "degradation to republican institutions" because, in violating the principle of equal rights, it is also a violation of the republican requirement that "just government stands only on the consent of the governed."[9] Against this claim, opponents argued that discrimination by privately owned public accommodations cannot impugn the republican character of government. Only state action can do this. Republicans replied by arguing that these accommodations are regulated by law to ensure that they fulfill a public purpose of realizing individual liberty. Such regulations must secure the benefits of regulation equally to all classes of people. Hence, a nondiscrimination requirement for regulated institutions open to the public is built in to the republican requirement that government afford equal protection of the laws to all.[10] Why did "separate but equal" accommodations fail to satisfy the requirements of equality? The segregation of public facilities "is an indignity to the colored race, instinct with the spirit of Slavery."[11] It inflicts an expressive injury on blacks, making them an untouchable caste, which is incompatible with recognizing them as equal citizens.

Sumner's republican argument claims that racial segregation could not be based on the consent of the governed. Yet at that time, a majority of citizens supported segregation of some public facilities. Hence, Sumner's argument implicitly—and soundly—rejects a standard definition of democratic governance in terms of majority rule. Many laws enacted with majority approval can subvert democracy. A majority decision to disenfranchise a minority and forbid its members from assembling, publishing newspapers, petitioning government, or running for office is plainly tyrannical and undemocratic.[12] So is any law that denies citizens equal status in civil society, or any system of regulation that permits private individuals entrusted with operating services for the public good to deny citizens equal access to those services on the basis of race.

Sumner's consent argument appeals to a conception of democracy not as majority rule, but as government "by the people": a form of collective self-determination whereby those subject to the laws are also in a relevant sense the authors of the laws. Equal rights are a prerequisite for any group of people to constitute a collective able to authorize laws for all. For one part of the people to impose an inferior, castelike status on another amounts to an "oligarchy," not a democracy.[13] To constitute a collective capable of consent *as a body*, all members must be secure in their equal rights. Without civic equality, the people as a body have not consented to anything. Rather, the dominant class has tyrannically imposed its will on the subordinate classes.

Sumner did not believe that adding bare equality of citizens before the law to majority rule was sufficient to constitute citizens as a collectively self-determining body. If some class of citizens could regularly settle public issues by discussing them only among themselves, excluding other classes from their discussions, or ignoring what they say, they would constitute an arbitrary ruling class with respect to the others. Democracy requires that citizens from all walks of life discuss matters of public interest *together*, as equals. So long as the citizens were divided into distinct noninteracting groups, the aggregation of their opinions would still not amount to the consent of a unified body of citizens. For their sentiments would not be attuned to the interests of the whole public, in which each is regarded as an equal to the others. This is the second reason—besides its inherent status degradation—that racial segregation of public accommodations and state-run institutions contradicts republican principles.

Arguing before the Massachusetts Supreme Court against the constitutionality (under state law) of racially segregated schools, Sumner set many of the terms of the modern democratic argument for integration. When public schools are segregated, they become "schools of prejudice and uncharitableness."[14] White children educated in such schools are "nursed in the sentiments of Caste . . . their characters are debased, and they become less fit for the duties of citizenship."[15] If the state had the power to segregate schools by race, it could segregate by any other distinctions, as of ethnicity or class. Then

> the grand fabric of our Common Schools . . . where, at the feet of the teacher, innocent childhood should come, unconscious of all distinctions of birth,—where the Equality of the Constitution and of Christianity should be inculcated by constant precept and example,—will be converted into a heathen system of proscription and Caste. We shall then have many different schools, representatives of as many different classes, opinions, and prejudices; but we shall look in vain for the true Common School.[16]

So far, the argument could be read as undermining de jure segregation only, without necessarily supporting de facto integration. Sumner sought actual integration. "The law contemplates not only that all shall be taught, but that *all* shall be taught *together*."[17] For public schools must be sites for the cultivation of the republican virtues and sentiments needed for citizens to be self-determining. Hence, schools

> must cherish and develop the virtues and the sympathies needed in the larger world. And since, according to our institutions, all classes, without distinction of color, meet in the performance of civil duties, so should they all, without distinction of color, meet in the school, beginning there those relations of Equality which the Constitution and Laws promise to all.[18]

The promise of political equality is a sham without social equality in the institutions of civil society. Political equality in the realm of governance cannot be realized without a democratic *culture* pervading civil society. This is not a matter of mere legal equality, but of habits and sentiments of association on terms of equality:

> As the State derives strength from the unity and solidarity of its citizens without distinction of class, so the school derives strength from the unity and solidarity of all classes beneath its roof.[19]
>
> Prejudice is the child of ignorance. It is sure to prevail, where people do not know each other. Society and intercourse . . . remove antipathies,

promote mutual adaptation and conciliation, and establish relations of reciprocal regard.[20]

I take these points about "solidarity" and "reciprocal regard" to be tightly joined in a democratic culture. Solidarity without mutual regard implies the subsumption of every individual under some collective purpose, without that purpose necessarily serving the interests of the individuals so joined. It could express the solidarity of soldiers on a mission of imperial conquest, for reasons of state. Mutual regard signifies that the common purposes around which citizens are joined have been constructed with due regard for each citizen's interests. No subgroup, not even a majority, is entitled to simply design a public policy that ignores the interests of others and impose it by majority vote. Rather, in a fully democratic culture, public purposes must be shaped by "mutual adaptation and conciliation," to different individuals' interests. This cannot happen without "society and intercourse." Citizens can adjust their sense of the common purpose to others' interests only through discussion and cooperative engagement with other citizens from all walks of life on terms of equal regard. This is what a democratic culture consists in. Its site is civil society. It includes not only the spaces recognized as "public forums"—such as public streets, parks, and auditoriums—but all domains in which diverse citizens may interact and cooperate. This includes public accommodations, stores, shopping malls, places of employment, civic organizations, and nonprofit organizations. Civil society occupies a middle ground between the formal institutions of government and domains of private life, including families, friendships, churches, and private clubs.

Sumner showed how civil, political, and social rights must be joined to realize a republican order, and how democratic governance requires a democratic culture of free interaction on terms of equality of citizens in fully integrated institutions of civil society. His country was not prepared to go along with that vision. In the *Civil Rights Cases*, the Supreme Court struck down the Civil Rights Act of 1875 for exceeding the powers of Congress under the Thirteenth and Fourteenth Amendments.[21] The federal government was in any event unwilling to enforce blacks' social rights to equal access in public accommodations. No case of discrimination was prosecuted under the Civil Rights Act before it was overturned in 1883. Shortly thereafter, the Court upheld the right of states to prohibit the association of whites and blacks in public accommodations.[22] According to the Court, citizenship no longer signified that one was fit for association with other citizens. It would not repudiate the separation of social from civil and political rights until *Brown v. Board of Education* in 1954.

This sketch of democratic lessons learned in the struggle for racial equality highlights some of the essential features of a democratic society, understood as a membership organization, a mode of governance, and a culture. We glimpse within it the importance of integration to democracy, and a vision of what integration entails: the free interaction of citizens from all walks of life on terms of equality and mutual regard in all institutions of civil society, and on voluntary terms in the intimate associations of private life. To fully grasp the importance of integration to democracy, we need to further develop three great themes in democratic theory: collective inquiry, accountability, and equality.

5.2 Democracy as a Mode of Collective Inquiry

In April 1963 blacks in Birmingham, Alabama, began a carefully planned series of daily demonstrations, demanding that the white business elite end their practices of segregation and discrimination. At first, the demonstrations were subdued. Small groups of blacks picketed segregated stores. Others marched to pray at City Hall. Every day police arrested the demonstrators and blocked the prayer marchers. Protesters began to fill up the jails. The Southern Christian Leadership Conference distributed thousands of leaflets in black churches, urging their members to join the demonstrations, and trained volunteers in methods of nonviolent protest. The protests escalated as blacks organized a massive boycott of downtown stores and paralyzed downtown traffic by putting thousands of people on the streets. Commissioner of Public Safety "Bull" Connor set dogs and fire hoses against the demonstrators. White shoppers, afraid of getting caught up in confrontations between police and protesters, avoided downtown, thereby inadvertently putting additional pressure on the white business elite to settle the dispute. Business leaders arranged secret meetings with Martin Luther King, Jr., and other leaders of the boycott to negotiate an end to segregated facilities and employment discrimination. On May 10 they announced an agreement that granted blacks their demands. The white political elite tried to destroy the settlement by bombing King's Birmingham headquarters and his brother's house. They hoped to provoke a riot that would provide the pretext for hundreds of state troopers who had been sent to the city to unleash violence on the black community. Their gambit failed when Civil Rights Movement leaders urged blacks to stay calm while President Kennedy mobilized the National Guard to keep the peace.[23]

The 1963 Birmingham demonstration was the first mass civil rights protest broadcast live on television nationwide. Northern whites were shocked to see violent assaults against peaceful black protesters. They became vividly aware of the brutality underpinning the system of white supremacy that they had complacently allowed to rule the South for generations. This was a turning point in the Civil Rights Movement. As movement leaders had planned, their protests forced whites nationwide to face up to the injustices of white supremacy and led them to throw their support behind the Civil Rights Act of 1964, which enacted as national law the core demands put before Birmingham's white business elite that May. The act prohibited segregation of privately owned public accommodations, thereby fulfilling the lost promise of the Civil Rights Act of 1875, and banned employment discrimination.

Reflecting on the Birmingham demonstrations twenty-five years later, Andrew Young, one of its organizers, said in a roundtable discussion: "[A]lthough I never wrote so much as a memo or made a speech or took part in a consultation on the 1964 or 1965 Civil Rights Acts, yet we were very consciously writing those bills. The demonstrations in Birmingham were specifically designed as measures to educate the United States on the dynamics of race relations and racial segregation."[24]

Let us take Young's remarks seriously and consider the Birmingham protests as *educative* acts, yielding a practical lesson embodied in the Civil Rights Act of 1964. From this perspective, democratic action is a mode of collective teaching and learning by which we discern and define problems of public interest and experiment with solutions to these problems. It is practical intelligence exercised by the body of citizens interacting with one another in civil society and governing institutions.

We owe this perspective to John Dewey. He argued that practical intelligence is the application of experimental methods to value judgments and practical precepts.[25] We test our value judgments by living in accordance with them and seeing whether doing so is satisfactory—whether it can provide satisfactory answers to questions like this: Does action in accordance with the value judgment solve the problem it was intended to solve? Does it bring about worse problems? Does it give rise to complaints from others that need to be addressed? Might we do better by adopting different judgments? If we find life in accordance with the value judgment satisfactory, we stick with it; if not, we seek new judgments that can better guide our lives.

The Civil Rights Movement put the value judgments and practical precepts of whites regarding the management of race relations to the test. Southern whites had long understood their problem to be how to secure their supremacy over blacks, conceived as an alien and inferior race. Their solution was to constitute blacks as an untouchable caste, through systematic segregation and discrimination. Blacks put this solution to the test in Birmingham in 1963, and in many other places across the South, teaching whites that they would no longer put up with such treatment, that whites' lives could no longer proceed unhampered on such terms. Northern whites had, in the post-Reconstruction era, conceived their problem to be how to reconstitute the Union in the face of violent white resistance to black empowerment during Reconstruction. Their solution was to forge a reconciliation between northern and southern whites by allowing the latter to have their way with blacks, under the banner of states' rights. Blacks put this solution to the test, too, repeatedly demonstrating the contradictions between this policy and moral and constitutional principles to which northern whites found themselves more committed.

The exercise of practical intelligence in testing value judgments is not only instrumental (§1.2). It would be too cynical to say that the Civil Rights Movement merely forced an alteration in the means—from overtly racist to formally race-neutral and covert—to a fixed end of maintaining white supremacy. The Civil Rights Movement forced a change in ends as well, by changing whites' understanding of the problem. It could no longer be understood in terms of managing relations with a group conceived to be entitled, at most, to only a minimal set of civil rights, without political and social rights. To be recognized as the rightful bearer of political and social rights is no merely instrumental change. To exercise the right to vote, to no longer be driven to the curb by a menacing hate stare—a portent of whites' readiness to inflict violence on blacks—and to be able to enjoy integrated public accommodations are huge moral achievements, signifying a profound alteration in race relations. The power of democratic methods to promote learning, at least in the long haul, is demonstrated in the successive lessons of blacks' struggle for equality: that there can be no republic without universal citizenship founded on equal rights, no civil rights without political rights, and no political rights without social rights.

Yet it would be naive to suppose that whites have stopped practices of social closure and opportunity hoarding that maintain racial inequality. These continue in modified forms (chapters 2–4). There is also considerable distance between most people's self-image as racially just, and their actual attitudes and conduct, which reflect the continuing power of racial stigmatization—just as there is slippage between the ideologies of color blindness and multiculturalism and the continuing public status of stigmatizing images of blacks (§3.3). Moral transformation in light of experience is real. But it is far messier and less complete than its subjects would like to think.

The struggle for black equality was thus a collective exercise in practical intelligence, achieved through democratic methods—free speech, public assembly, protests, petitions of grievance to officials, testimony before Congress and publicity of complaints through a free press, mobilization of supporters, and voting. Democratic means are a society's way of exercising practical intelligence as a body to articulate problems of public interest and devise and test solutions to those problems. They are, as Andrew Young claimed, means by which different members of the public *educate* one another about public problems and policies.

The epistemic powers of democratic practices are best understood in light of three features: diversity, communication, and feedback.[26] Consider first diversity. Public problems and policies have asymmetric effects on different parts of the population. Those most familiar with these effects tend to be those most affected by them. This entails that knowledge relevant to the articulation and solution of public problems is asymmetrically distributed. Citizens are therefore epistemically diverse. To understand and solve problems of public interest requires that information held by diverse citizens from different walks of life be brought to the attention of decision makers—to voters at large, their representatives, and other government officials.

In democratic theory, public communication of information relevant to articulating and solving public problems is often called "deliberation." That term may unduly narrow our conception of democratic communication to the kinds of relatively sober talk that take place in a congressional hearing or around a negotiating table. Such discussions are essential to democratic inquiry. Often, however, bringing matters to the attention of the public requires communicating with loud voices, in large numbers, with theater, drama, and symbolism. It may require disrupting the normal routines of citizens so that they sit up and listen. This is why the right to mass public assemblies and demonstrations is such a critical feature of democracies.

Restricting communication to quiet rooms governed by norms of subdued and polite conversation can be a means the powerful use to suppress the communication of grievances. Consider the difficulties blacks encountered in North Carolina. White elites in North Carolina prided themselves in upholding a kinder, gentler style of white supremacy than in the Deep South. They saw the unequal race relations they enforced as amicable, grounded in norms of civility. But they rigged the rules of civility to block any polite way for blacks to express their legitimate demands. They characterized blacks who demanded desegregation as rude, unruly, and irresponsible. They selected, as purported spokesmen for the black community, "responsible" blacks whose economic dependence on white employers made them reluctant to challenge segregation. "Credible" blacks had to express their claims in such mild, indirect, and apologetic terms that whites could represent their own neglect of black interests as an accommodation of black claims. Civility provided excuses for endless stonewalling. Time and again, North Carolina's activists had to resort to sit-ins, strikes, and demonstrations to force white elites to pay attention to their demands.[27]

The necessity of disruptive communication is closely connected to the epistemic consequences of segregation. When advantaged groups are able to segregate themselves from the disadvantaged, they lose personal contact with the problems of the disadvantaged. They become ignorant. Enclosed in secure enclaves, insulated from the problems their segregative practices impose on others, they become complacent and insular: *those* people's problems are not *ours*. Disruptive demonstrations are needed to break through these walls of complacency, insularity, and ignorance. They prevent the advantaged from continuing their everyday routines. They make "those" people's problems *everyone's* problems. Only so will the advantaged sit up and listen, and thereby learn from those from whom they have closed themselves off.

Thus, disruptive communication can force people to listen. But because it is episodic and nondeliberative, it cannot by itself forge lasting solutions to the problems the demonstrators articulate. It must work with negotiation and deliberation, which are needed to forge agreements and work out the details of plans to implement them. Negotiation and deliberation, in turn, require integration. If insular elites are allowed to work out "solutions" for themselves, without having to consult excluded groups, their answers will neglect the interests of the excluded.

The value of solutions is rarely settled once and for all. Agreed policies no less than traditional practices must be tested in experience. Effective testing requires feedback on the consequences of policies. Some of these mechanisms, such as the U.S. Inspector General offices and the Government Accountability Office, are internal to the governance structure of democracies. However, most feedback mechanisms, such as periodic elections, a vigilant press, petitions to government, and public commentary on proposed administrative regulations, lie at the intersection between civil society and governing institutions. Disruptive demonstrations and legal action are also needed to provide feedback with respect to serious grievances. All such practices can be viewed epistemically, as mechanisms designed to facilitate collective critical inquiry into problems of public interest, and public policy solutions to such problems.

5.3 Democracy as a System of Accountability

This epistemic account of democratic practices might seem too intellectual, too detached from the content of much democratic communication. Demonstrators and petitioners do not present objective scientific reports on social conditions. They express complaints and make demands, often with great passion and drama. They display their numbers, unity, determination, and virtue. Can communications couched in such terms truly count as *educative*?

They can. To see this, we need to go beyond a conventional account of knowledge as essentially generated from a third-person perspective, the kind of knowledge that can be detached from the identities of the communicator and addressee. Complaints and demands are expressed from an essentially *second-person* perspective: they are addressed by specific grievants to individuals whom they hold accountable for resolving the complaints and meeting the demands. They thus embody normative claims of right, justice, or entitlement.[28] Is it possible to teach, and to learn, not just that such claims are being made, but that they are normatively valid?

Cynics might deny this. Plato's Thrasymachus asserted that justice is nothing more than the advantage of the stronger.[29] Many southern whites, too, felt that the civil rights demonstrations showed only that blacks were a force that had to be reckoned with, not that they had legitimate claims. They saw themselves as bullied by the demonstrators. (Few subjected their own practices to critical scrutiny.)

Yet even some determined racists were capable of being stirred to moral recognition in the right circumstances. In the public memory, the leading image of the 1963 Birmingham protests was that of "Bull" Connor sending dogs to attack peaceful demonstrators. Yet a more morally significant event took place on May 5, as prayer marchers, heading for City Hall, encountered Connor's men. Connor ordered his men to turn fire hoses on the crowd. The Reverend Charles Billups, who was leading his marchers, realized the imminent danger and called upon them to get down on their knees and pray. The prayer filled them with a sense of determination and courage. Upon completing the prayer, Billups told Connor's men that the demonstrators would stand their ground, regardless of the hoses and dogs. Connor shouted to his men to stop the marchers. Awestruck, the men dropped their hoses instead, fell back, and let the marchers move past them to City Hall.[30]

What happened that day was a moment of moral accountability. Connor's men were being held accountable by conflicting claims of opposed authorities: Connor and the prayer marchers. They needed to judge which of these claims was authoritative. We know from the Milgram experiments that most people cave in to the demands of whoever bears the official marks of command, even when these demands are grossly immoral.[31] All the more would we expect this in the case of men who not only could be punished for disobedience, but who identified with the cause of white supremacy. What could the prayer marchers show against the combined force of such powerful motives? Nothing but a set of moral claims, and a show of moral authority. First, they claimed the right to pray without interference. This claim was addressed to Connor's men as fellow Christians, appealing to their inchoate recognition that, however inferior blacks were in the eyes of white men, in the eyes of Christians they had the right to pray. Second, they claimed the right to live. The demonstrators, in showing their determination to stand their ground, dramatically raised the moral stakes attached to obeying Connor's orders. It was one thing to use hoses to disperse a rabble. It was another to look others in the eye, knowing that one would become guilty of murder by turning the hoses on them.

These powerful moral claims were backed up with demonstrations that their makers possessed moral authority. This was the genius of King's method of nonviolence. Democratic social movements that make claims on public authorities try to display what Charles Tilly calls "WUNC": worthiness, unity, numbers, and commitment to their cause.[32] The prayer marchers demonstrated worthiness, and hence authority, by presenting themselves as dignified, pious, nonviolent, and sympathetic (most were youthful students). They demonstrated their unity by not breaking ranks; and they turned out in substantial numbers. Their commitment was evident in their credible announcement of willingness to die for their cause.

The power of WUNC is due to the fact that we count these factors as evidence of the moral authority of the claims made by a social movement. That the claims are made by demonstrably worthy people bolsters their authority. When a movement is divided, this casts doubt on the validity of their claims. If even the movement cannot agree on which claims are right, why should those to whom the claims are addressed concede their validity? Large numbers prove that the claim is general, not idiosyncratic. Commitment counts, too: if members of a movement lack the courage of their own convictions, how can they persuade doubters? Commitment also plays on the difference between force and coercion. Force physically blocks others from achieving their ends; coercion bends them to one's will through threats and intimidation. Coercion, because it works through the wills of the coerced, extracts a recognition from them of at least the de facto authority of the coercing party. The need to publicly resort to force, because intimidation no longer works, strips the violent of that recognition of authority.

In demonstrating WUNC, democratic social movements express their commitment to demonstrating the legitimacy of their claims to those whom they hold accountable for respecting them. Claim-making, accountability, and normative inquiry—not only arguments, but compelling narratives and dramas highlighting the normative force of claims—go hand in hand. This contrasts with other types of political movement, such as terrorist groups, which merely aim to do whatever it takes to achieve their objectives. Such groups do not address others as moral agents entitled and obligated to judge the normative authority of claims and capable of moral learning.

Mass demonstrations of WUNC are not the only ways of tying accountability to normative inquiry through democratic means. Because demonstrations are episodic and hard to organize, their functions are limited. Everyday accountability of decision makers requires the institutionalization of mechanisms for raising claims and judging their worth. The institutionalized feedback mechanisms of democracy cited in §5.2—periodic elections, a free press, petitions to government, and so forth—serve both epistemic and accountability functions on a regularized basis. Yet even these mechanisms may often lack an important feature of effective accountability mechanisms: face-to-face interaction between those who make claims and those who are held accountable for meeting them.

The process of making claims is essentially interpersonal. While it can take place through impersonal media of communication—letters, news reports, and the like—it is all too easy for those being held accountable to wall themselves off from such communications. Elites—those with official decision-making power over others—can ignore letters and decide to view only news media that favor them. However, given democratic norms of interpersonal address, elites cannot wholly duck the implications of face-to-face communication. Here lies the democratic import of integration. There is nothing like direct confrontation between claimants and the addressees of claims to make the addressees feel the force of accountability. If elites are overwhelmingly composed of a closed social group, segregated from other groups, they effectively escape accountability for the impact of their decisions on those groups. In making insular elites unaccountable, segregation makes them irresponsible.

5.4 Democracy as a Society of Equals

The ideal of democracy essentially involves relations of social equality. As the Supreme Court recognized, democratic "citizenship is the charter of equality."[33] Citizenship entails not only equality of legal rights, but public standing as fit for association with fellow citizens. Equality is thus a cultural norm, not only a legal status. Yet the specific content of equality often eludes contemporary political philosophers. Current debates in egalitarian thought tend to focus on equality in the distribution of goods, with barely a nod to how this idea is to be grounded.[34] The normative perspective of this book, by contrast, focuses on justice as a set of relations among people and derives distributive principles from a conception of just social relations (§1.5). The democratic ideal holds that justice requires equality in social relations.

One way to discern the outlines of social equality is to investigate the contours of its opposite: hierarchy. The core mode of hierarchy consists in asymmetrical relations of command and obedience. Thus, to home in on the core types of unjust hierarchy, we must investigate what makes relations of command and obedience unjust. The history of blacks' quest for equality in the United States illuminates this. Here we see a stepwise progression from slavery, to caste, to (under)class, to an ongoing quest for full equality. An examination of the form of command relation rejected at each stage helps define the content of full equality.

Blacks' struggle for equality also reveals the intimate connections between freedom and equality. In contemporary political discourse, freedom and equality are typically portrayed as conflicting. When equality is defined in terms of equal distributions of property, and freedom in terms of individual rights to use and dispose of property in unregulated markets, such a conflict seems inevitable. The fact that blacks' struggle for freedom was also a struggle for equality reveals the superficiality of these definitions. How could freedom be defined in terms of property rights when American slavery was defended in terms of property rights?[35] One person's freedom of property entailed another's subjection. Property is consistent with freedom only if it is limited by reference to a prior substantive conception of freedom. Blacks' quest for equality, too, was not cast in terms of equal distributions of private property. Even the unfulfilled claim of freedmen to "40 acres and a mule" was not a first-order claim to distributive equality, but rather a claim to compensation for the labor stolen from them in slavery.

The history of blacks' pursuit of equality is better understood as a series of challenges to different forms of unjust hierarchy, especially of unjust command relationships. From a relational point of view, social inequality and lack of freedom are one and the same. In the classic republican formula, to be unfree is to be subject to the arbitrary will of another.[36] This is the state of subordination, of inequality. To cast off relations of domination is to live as a free person. The quest for freedom is the quest for a mode of relating to others in which no one is dominated, in which each adult meets every other adult member of society eye to eye, as an equal.

Let us begin our investigation of blacks' pursuit of this goal with their resistance to slavery. Slavery is the ultimate form of unjust command relationship. It combines every mode of oppression: subjection to violence, powerlessness, exploitation, stigmatization, cultural imposition, and marginalization, in the sense of exclusion from social relations outside the master–slave relation. Slaves were not even entitled to maintain kin relations. In principle, slavery puts slaves under the absolute and arbitrary power of their masters. Slaves are thus constituted as nonpersons, without standing to make claims against their masters or anyone else.

It is often suggested that this master–slave relation embodies a contradiction, in that the master tries to exact recognition of his superiority from a slave whose subjection is manifested in the master's denial of any standing to the slave's perspective.[37] Of what worth could recognition in the eyes of the slave have to a master who denies the slave's point of view any authority? That purported contradiction is resolved by the fact that slaveowners sought recognition not from their black slaves, but from fellow whites, by impressing them with the display of total and arbitrary power manifest in the master–slave relationship.[38]

Yet contradiction there was, not in the logic of reciprocal recognition, but in the fact that American slavery was embedded in a legal order that subjected masters to state authority. The state's insistence on defining the relation between master and slave provided an opening for slave resistance to generate recognition of slaves' standing as morally responsible beings. Slave codes defined the crimes, such as running away, that could be committed by slaves against their masters. When courts adjudicated cases of slave resistance, their legal procedures, based on the common law, could not avoid recognizing the moral standing of slaves as responsible beings capable of grasping the authority of claims addressed to them, and as bearers of procedural rights, including the right to testify in court. Southern courts even recognized substantive rights of slaves to self-defense against excessive violence, even against their masters. Claims asserted by resistant slaves limited the masters' power.[39] The first step in the struggle for black equality was thus achieved, albeit in small measure, when blacks' resistance extracted from the slave states a minimal recognition of their standing as beings capable of grasping and making claims.

After emancipation, the Civil Rights Act of 1866 and the Fourteenth Amendment acknowledged blacks' equal rights before the law. This hardly satisfied blacks' quest for equality. Planters and northern whites sought to integrate blacks into the economy as wage laborers, working the plantations under the supervision of white landowners. Blacks resisted this vision because it entailed subjection to the personal domination of white overseers, who sought detailed control over blacks' lives, including how and how much to work, and many aspects of personal life. Blacks insisted on carving out a sphere of personal independence for themselves. They achieved this through the sharecropping system, which brought some freedom from whites' direct command in matters of work, family, and consumption.[40]

The result was far from full freedom and equality. Blacks were mostly excluded from skilled crafts in which they could be free, within an employment setting, to exercise some autonomy. They were excluded from managerial positions that entailed the exercise of command in productive relations over white employees. At the nadir of black power after the turn of the century, they were almost completely excluded from voting and political office. Whites monopolized positions of command in the larger society, relegating blacks to servile positions and second-class citizenship.

Charles Sumner neatly summarized the point: "Once it was Slavery; now it is Caste," a hereditary "Oligarchy of the skin."[41]

In the North, blacks also overwhelmingly occupied subordinate positions in the economy. But they could vote, and they enjoyed more secure protection of their civil rights than in the South. As the sharecropping system declined, blacks voted with their feet, abandoning sharecropping for northern industrial jobs. The move north entailed acceptance of subordination within firms, and hence some loss of the productive autonomy and independence from direct supervision that blacks had as self-employed sharecroppers. On net, however, blacks gained in freedom and equality. They gained civil, political, and social rights, and a chance at greater prosperity. This development marked their advancement from caste to underclass. Still barred from managerial positions in which they might supervise whites, and rarely holding public office, they nevertheless gained a share of command (decision-making power) through the vote.

The culmination of the Civil Rights Movement in the passage of the Civil Rights Act of 1964, barring discrimination in employment and education, can be seen as an attempt to advance the status of blacks from an underclass to an economically mobile group, to whom all class positions are open. Enjoyment of fair and open opportunities for advancement to leadership positions, so that members of a group have a realistic chance of occupying them, is an essential feature of equality of social relations. A group permanently relegated to subordinate ranks does not enjoy equality. For a group to always be commanded, and never to command, in a domain of society is for it to be constituted as an inferior class, its members subordinate to those to whom positions of command are open.

The dominant ideology in America today hopes to reconcile those at the bottom to their subordinate positions by offering the hope of opportunities to move to higher ranks. Yet without substantial constraints on the scope of command, that project is hopeless, no matter how equal opportunities are. Imagine a fair lottery, in which everyone had an equal chance to be a plantation overseer, with the losers relegated to gang labor under the overseers' comprehensive and arbitrary rule. The fairness of the process cannot justify the relations allocated by it.

Liberals have been accused of abandoning the republican ideal of freedom as personal independence for an attenuated conception of market freedom that leaves subordinate workers at the mercy of those to whom they sell their labor.[42] This ignores an alternative mode of realizing republican freedom embodied in the liberal strategies of sphere differentiation and bureaucratization. Liberals do generally suppose that some kind of production hierarchy is necessary for efficiency in at least some domains of production, notably in the services, including law enforcement and defense, provided by the state. Comprehensive workplace democracy is unworkable and inconsistent with democracy at the state level since elected officials, not civil servants or soldiers, must determine the goals of government agencies. Yet this does not require abandonment of the republican ideal. John Locke, the canonical property-rights liberal, explicitly embraced the republican ideal: "freedom of men . . . is . . . not to be subject to the inconstant, uncertain, unknown, arbitrary will of another man."[43] Sphere differentiation helps secure this freedom. While a commander may have authority over subordinates within his narrowly defined domain, he has no authority over his subordinates outside of it. A military officer may "command a soldier to march up to the mouth of a cannon, or stand in a breach where he is almost sure to perish," but may not "seize one jot of his goods" since his soldiers' private property lies outside the domain of his authority. Essential to the strategy of sphere differentiation is a distinction between persons and offices, with powers attaching to offices, not persons. Absent this distinction, essential to the modern bureaucratic state, command relies on systems of personal loyalty, and public services are rendered as favors rendered in return for personal subjection. The bureaucratic principle of instrumental necessity also sets limits to the powers of office: "even absolute power, where it is necessary, is not arbitrary by being absolute, but is still limited by that reason and confined to those ends which required it."[44]

The demand to narrowly tailor the power of command to just those ends that require it was integral to black resistance to white planters' control over their private lives, a resistance that led to the replacement of gang labor by sharecropping. That demand is also present in the pioneering work of black women against sexual harassment in the workplace. Even if economic efficiency requires following the bosses' orders with regard to productive tasks, it does not authorize the boss to turn his employees into sexual playthings. That black women were the plaintiffs in early sexual harassment cases likely reflects the long experience of white masters' and employers' sexual exploitation of black women workers, and their determination to resist this.[45]

We are on the cusp of a positive account of equality in social relations, approached through an examination of types of relation that must be rejected. So far we have the following requirements of equal relations:

1. All parties to the relation have equal rights and equal authority to make claims on one another (the antislavery principle).
2. No one may be consigned to inferior office on the basis of identities or statuses imputed at birth (the anticaste principle).
3. Superior offices (decision-making, supervisory positions) must be open to all qualified persons, and everyone with the potential to acquire competence for such offices is entitled to a realistic

chance to develop their talents and compete on fair terms for them (the anti-underclass, or fair opportunity principle).

4. Superior authority attaches to offices, not persons, and hence may be exercised by persons only within the domain of their office (the principle of sphere differentiation). This entails that no one meeting another outside the domain of office may claim nonreciprocal authority over the other.

5. The powers of office must be narrowly tailored to the ends assigned to it (the instrumental necessity principle).[46]

Still missing from this account is a story of how the ends of office are set. For political office, the democratic answer is clear: the substantive ends of office are set by and for the people, acting through their representatives, who are held accountable to and by the people through the democratic devices noted in §5.3. Political offices are not private privileges whereby officeholders may set their own ends in disregard of the public interest. They are public trusts. Individual citizens constitute themselves as the collective body known as "the people" through communication of concerns they regard as of public interest, on terms of "mutual adaptation . . . conciliation . . . [and] regard" (§5.1). These terms of relating to one another are those by which the people constitute themselves as both free, in the sense of self-governing, and equal.

This conception of equality arises repeatedly in democratic thought. John Stuart Mill characterized a "society between equals" as that which "can only exist on the understanding that the interests of all are to be regarded equally" and "consulted."[47] Dewey put the point more sharply, noting both the importance of asymmetrically distributed information and the pervasiveness of rivalry in a society of equals. As a culture, democracy consists in "free gatherings of neighbors on the street corner to discuss back and forth what is read in uncensored news of the day," and "personal day-by-day working together with others." It

> is the belief that even when needs and ends or consequences are different for each individual, the habit of amicable cooperation—which may include, as in sport, rivalry and competition—is itself a priceless addition to life. To take as far as possible every conflict which arises—and they are bound to arise—out of the atmosphere and medium of force, of violence as a means of settlement into that of discussion and of intelligence is to treat those who disagree—even profoundly—with us as those from whom we may learn, and in so far, as friends.[48]

I would prefer to say "as equals" here, but the point is much the same.

We thus derive an additional egalitarian constraint on social relations:

6. The ends of public offices must be set democratically—that is, by means of mutual consultation among citizens "on the understanding that the interests of all are to be regarded equally." The ends of private offices, while not set collectively by the body of citizens, must nevertheless be consistent with general regulations in the public interest, as for instance those forbidding discrimination in the provision of public accommodations.

The ends of public office are not merely constrained by egalitarian considerations, but determined by egalitarian processes, so that they serve the public interest, not merely the private interest of some subset—even the majority—of the people. For private offices, egalitarian considerations constrain without determining ends. Even here, some sectors, as of health care, may be comprehensively regulated in the public interest. Egalitarian societies thus do not reject hierarchy altogether. They aim to confine hierarchies to offices, tightly constrain the powers of office, and set or constrain the ends of office by egalitarian processes and for the sake of the public.

This last point feeds back into the requirements of fair opportunity. Most discussions of justice in the distribution of opportunities for office consider this question from the point of view of the good that offices are supposed to do for their occupants. Occupants of higher offices enjoy more prestige, autonomy, and decision-making power, exercise a wide variety of challenging and engaging skills, and enjoy greater extrinsic advantages—income, perks, consumption in the course of fulfilling official duties—than do those in subordinate positions. Contemporary discussions of fair opportunity focus on the distribution of these goods. They thus ignore the question of justice in regard to the good that occupants of higher office are supposed to do for those whom they serve.

In an egalitarian society, higher offices exist not to serve their occupants, but to serve the public.[49] How should offices be distributed so as to ensure that they do so? Conventional discussions assume that individualistic meritocratic criteria can determine this, independent of social group membership. This is not so under conditions of group segregation. Segregation causes advantaged groups to form stereotypes and attribution biases that lead to discrimination and public policies founded on stigmatizing representations of the less advantaged (§3.2, §3.5). It deprives advantaged groups of information about the conditions and problems faced by less advantaged groups (§5.2). It makes them less competent in intergroup interaction, due to discontinuities in cultural capital (§2.3) and anxieties and demeaning intergroup norms produced by group stigmatization (§3.3, §3.5). To the extent that higher offices are monopolized by segregated advantaged groups, these cognitive deficiencies will pervade the occupants of higher office, making them less competent to serve groups other than those represented in higher office. De facto group segregation of the occupants of higher office also insulates them from the face-to-face accountability mechanisms needed to ensure their responsiveness to others (§5.3).

It follows that, in societies marked by group segregation, ensuring the competence and accountability of officeholders to serve the interests of the whole public, and not just segregated segments of it, requires that offices be occupied by members of the different groups, who must work *together* to share their asymmetrical knowledge, forge mutually respectful norms of intergroup communication and interaction, and fill out and implement the ends of office in ways that serve the interests of all. Call "elites" the occupants of higher office. In conditions of group segregation, a competent elite must be composed of people from all walks of life, including all significantly segregated groups.

This argument rejects an excessively individualistic conception of qualification for offices, according to which merit is exclusively a property of individuals in isolation, and the merits of a group are the aggregate of the merits of its individual members. Other researchers have undermined this conception of merit on both empirical and theoretical grounds. They have shown that groups that are diverse in information, cognitive styles, and puzzle-solving strategies are better at solving complex problems than are any collection of individually most able puzzle-solvers.[50] My argument does not rely on any ideas about racial differences in cognitive styles. It relies on the idea that segregated racial groups will have direct (first-person, experiential) access to different information about the conditions in which they live and the problems they face. It also claims that certain vital forms of knowledge cannot be known by groups in isolation but are essentially the product of people from different groups working together. Knowledge of the public interest is essentially constructed in this way. So is practical knowledge of how members of different groups can interact on terms of mutual respect. This requires the construction of shared norms of communication and cooperation that, under conditions of segregation, tend to drift apart (§2.3).

"Cultural capital" thus acquires a new sense in the context of democratic theory. Sociologists use the term to refer to the informal norms individuals need to master to attain elite positions. In democratic theory, "cultural capital" refers to the norms elites must master to serve a diverse public. These include nonstigmatizing norms of intergroup communication and cooperation, norms that cannot be unilaterally imposed by one group, but can only be constructed by integrated groups working together democratically.

My argument does not depend on any first-order claim that racial groups as such are entitled to proportional representation in office. It does not accord political standing to "identities," understood as group-based self-definitions and loyalties. It has no truck with identity politics, understood as a kind of group-based spoils system or democratic ethnocentrism, in which each group gets a fair share of the pie of public goods, which it consumes in isolation from the others. Far from endorsing such group self-segregation, the point of the argument is to demonstrate the importance for democracy of integration, of cooperation and communication *across group lines*, for the purposes of forging *shared* norms and goals of the democratic polity as a whole, and to that extent forging a shared identity of citizens. It is not about the celebration of group difference. Nor is it about the effacement of group difference in the name of assimilation to the norms of the dominant group. Rather, to the extent that these norms incorporate stigmatizing representations of subordinate groups and adaptations to group inequality, it is precisely these norms that integration aims to change.

This argument does not depend on any suggestion that racial groups have essentially or intrinsically different ways of thinking or cultural styles. In affirming the importance of cross-group communication for democracy, it repudiates the thought that certain ideas possessed by one group are inherently ineffable to another. It does insist, however, that under conditions of racial segregation, elites composed overwhelmingly of whites cannot be trusted to formulate policies concerning blacks (or any other racially isolated group) that are based on accurate representations of their problems, or that are equally responsive to their interests, however well-meaning they may be. *This is entirely a contingent function of segregation.* It has nothing to do with skin color, ancestry, or genetic or cultural attributes purportedly transmitted through ancestry. Since stigmatizing ideas about the disadvantaged may be propagated independently of racist intent, simply as an effect of segregation, the argument is also not based on the thought that whites are racist. In fact, the argument thus has nothing to do with race as such. It applies to all segregated groups, whatever the basis of their segregation, whether that be race, ethnicity, religion, caste, class, gender, or some other categorical basis of group closure.

I conclude that, under conditions of group segregation, democratic equality requires not just that offices be realistically open on fair terms to all groups (the fair opportunity principle), but that they actually be filled by members of all the relevant groups, such that offices are fully integrated, with members of different groups working together on terms of equality.

Democracy can be understood as a membership organization, a mode of governance, and a culture. As a membership organization, it consists in equal, universal citizenship of all persons subject to the permanent jurisdiction of a state. As a mode of governance, it is government by the people, conducted through discussion among equal citizens from all walks of life. As a culture, it consists in the free cooperation and communication of citizens from all walks of life on terms of equality in civil society. To realize democracy on all of these levels requires comprehensive integration of significant social groups in civil society and the state. Segregation impedes the intergroup communication needed for democratic institutions to gather and use widely dispersed information about problems and policies of public interest. It blocks the mechanisms needed to hold officeholders democratically accountable to all the people. It embodies demeaning group relations incompatible with equal citizenship. It makes elites insular, clubby, ignorant, unaccountable, and irresponsible. The history of American blacks' struggle for equal citizenship, for inclusion as an equal in a democratic society, teaches us many lessons about the requirements of democracy. Blacks have taught us the folly of attempting to secure civil and political rights for citizens without rights to integration—to association as equals with fellow citizens in civil society. They have taught us the importance of disruptive communication to educating insular elites about the problems and claims of the disadvantaged, and to making elites accountable to the whole public. They have taught us the multiple ways in which the quest for equality is at the same time a quest for freedom. These vital lessons would not have been learned in the absence of episodes of genuine integration, in which blacks achieved, at least for a moment, recognition as equals and changed America as a result. The task before us is to move beyond fitful episodes of integration to a sustained culture of integration, in which all citizens take for granted that all institutions of civil society, including elite offices, will be integrated, and in which their interactions are governed by shared norms of mutual respect forged together.

· SIX ·

THE IMPERATIVE OF INTEGRATION

6.1 Racial Integration as a Requirement of Justice

The previous chapters have documented the myriad injustices of racial segregation. It is caused by unjust race relations (§4.1). It expresses racially stigmatizing ideas (§3.3, §4.4, §5.1). It unjustly deprives blacks of access to jobs, public goods, consumer goods and services, and financial, social, cultural, and human capital (§§2.2–2.4). It causes stigmatizing racial stereotypes, prejudice, and discrimination (§3.1, §3.5). It undermines democracy by embodying race-based status inequality, fostering divisive politics and punitive policies toward the disadvantaged, undermining intergroup communication and cooperation, blocking fair access to opportunities, and promoting an insular, unaccountable elite that lacks the competence and disposition to serve members of all racial groups equally (§3.6, §§5.1–5.4).

If racial segregation is the problem, it stands to reason that racial integration is the remedy. Since the problem is an injustice, the remedy is an imperative of justice. Yet we still need a fuller account of integration and the policies that could realize it. Moreover, nonideal theory demands that we put integration to the test by investigating its consequences in practice (§1.2). Does integration really help solve the problems caused by segregation? Does it bring about worse problems? This chapter examines various integrative policies and considers whether their intended effects have been brought about. (I postpone to §9.1 a discussion of the unintended side-effects of integration.)

Let us put the ideal of integration into sharper perspective. Segregation has two faces: (1) structures and norms of spatial and social separation, to prevent contact between members of different groups, and (2) hierarchical role segregation, to ensure that where contact occurs, it is on terms of domination and subordination. Integration is the negation of segregation: it consists in comprehensive intergroup association on terms of equality. This requires the full inclusion and participation as equals of members of all races in all social domains, especially in the main institutions of society that define its opportunities for recognition, educational and economic advancement, access to public goods, and political influence.

Integration may be contrasted with three other ideas: desegregation, color blindness, and assimilation. Desegregation consists in the abolition of legal barriers to intergroup contact, such as legally segregated public facilities and antimiscegenation laws, plus enforcement of antidiscrimination laws in public accommodations and employment. Desegregation is a necessary but far from sufficient step toward integration. It does not disturb prevailing patterns of neighborhood segregation and consequent inequalities in access to public and private goods, forms of capital, and job opportunities. It leaves intact the conditions for group stigmatization, incompetence and awkwardness in intergroup interaction, and ethnocentric and bigoted politics.

Color blindness can be conceived as an ideal or as policy. As an ideal, it consists in the abolition of racial identities. If everyone ceased to think in racial terms and ended all race-responsive behaviors, including racial stigmatization and ethnocentric opportunity hoarding, then integration of individuals formerly classified as racially distinct would occur, and race-based inequality would end. The color-blind ideal can thus be seen as one way in which an integrated society might be realized. As a policy, color blindness consists in the legal prohibition of state and business policies involving explicit racial classification, whether they aim at segregation or integration, racial hierarchy or racial equality. I shall discuss color-blind policies in chapter 8. For now it is enough to observe that color-blind policy is far from sufficient to achieve the color-blind ideal. It does *nothing* to dismantle entrenched patterns of racial segregation, undermine unconscious racial stigmatization and discrimination, challenge informal practices of racial avoidance such as white flight, end coded racial appeals in politics, avoid negligence of disadvantaged racial groups in public policy, or prevent race-neutral policies with differential racial impact from being based on racially stigmatizing ideas.

The ideal of integration, by contrast, aims at the abolition of racial segregation and its attendant inequalities, not of racial identities. It permits the use of race-conscious policies to achieve racial integration and equality and accepts that some degree of racial solidarity and affiliation on the part of the racially stigmatized is needed to spur integrative policies and cope with the stresses of integration. Thus, integration should also not be confused with the dissolution of black institutions or with the absence of racial clustering in neighborhoods.[1] It consists in the full participation on terms of equality of socially significant groups in all domains of society. American Jews have achieved integration in this sense. This has not required the dissolution of Jewish religious organizations, Jewish clubs, or neighborhoods with higher than average concentrations of Jews. The ideal of integration takes no stand on the desirability of the continuation of racial identification once racial equality is achieved. Racial identities and affiliations can be left to individual choice, without special attempts at preserving them. Integration thus sidesteps both the color-blind ideal, which insists on the abolition of racial identities, and racial identity politics, which insists on their preservation.

The ideal of integration has often been confused with assimilation. Assimilation takes a dominant social group as fixed and demands that other groups join it by abandoning their distinct group identities and conforming to what the dominant group takes to be its defining norms, practices, and virtues. Expressed in relation to national minorities, this often amounts to cultural imposition—the Turks, for example, at one time insisting that the Kurds in Turkey abandon the Kurdish language and other markers of Kurdish identity. Expressed in relation to blacks in the United States, calls for assimilation are disingenuous. In the Turkish case, there is at least the promise that Kurds, if they satisfy the cultural demands, will be accepted as Turks. In the American case, no one seriously proposes to accept blacks as *white*, no matter what they do. The concept of race is essentially tied to ancestry, not culture. Unlike the concept of nationality, it does not admit cases of naturalization.

However, a related ideal of assimilation is sometimes proposed for black-white race relations, in which the reciprocation offered in return for adopting majority cultural norms is status equality. So understood, assimilation largely fails to make contact with the problems at hand. It confuses racial inequalities with cultural differences and fails to critically scrutinize the practices of the dominant group. For the most part, American blacks and whites share a common American culture. Racial inequality arises not from specifically black cultural practices, but from interracial relations, especially practices of racial segregation and stigmatization.

Hence, the ideal of assimilation is largely misguided. Yet it cannot be entirely dismissed. To see where it may have some application, let us distinguish four different types of practice commonly regarded as distinctively black. First are practices causally unconnected to the perpetuation of black disadvantage, such as gospel music and the celebration of Kwanzaa. Such practices are benign. Calls for assimilation in such cases would amount to sheer cultural imposition and do nothing to remove black disadvantage.

Calls for assimilation are most commonly expressed with respect to a second type of purportedly race-based cultural difference: dysfunctional behaviors within segregated underclass black neighborhoods, such as participation in youth gangs and disengagement from school. These practices are not specifically black, since underclass neighborhoods in economically advanced societies display the same dysfunctions regardless of racial composition. Nor are they "cultural" in the sense of reflecting intrinsic value differences between underclass and advantaged groups (§4.3). Rather, they are adaptations to disadvantages brought about by the segregation and opportunity hoarding of dominant groups in society. Such adaptations, while they may enhance individual well-being within disadvantaged communities, are collectively destructive and undermine the individual's chances to succeed in more advantaged settings. Calls for assimilation in such cases reflect a misdiagnosis of the problem, steeped in racial stigmatization, and are futile and disingenuous if not coupled with effective steps by advantaged groups to cease their own practices of segregation, stigmatization, and opportunity hoarding.

The third type of case concerns styles of personal appearance that are seen as "black," such as braids, "gangsta" clothes, and dreadlocks. The causal consequences of these practices are limited to how people interpret their meaning. Individuals of any race who adopt such styles are liable to face discrimination in the mainstream business world. Such discrimination is partly due to the desire of firms to present a public appearance to customers that is not seen as black. Hence, these are cases of second-order racial discrimination (§3.5). Yet to the extent that the message projected by some of these practices, such as wearing low-hanging pants, is a rejection of corporate values, their wearers have no grounds for complaint. Such cases are no different from employment discrimination against those adopting countercultural styles seen as "white," such as tattoos, body piercings, and emo clothes.[2] However issues of racial assimilation in appearance in corporate contexts are treated, they are marginal to the central problems of racial inequality.

The fourth type of case involves norms of communication and comportment that may diverge between segregated communities. These are forms of cultural capital needed for advancement in mainstream society (§2.3). Achieving racial equality requires some convergence in these norms. It is not unreasonable to expect that the construction of shared norms of communication requires all groups to meet one another part way. In practice, however, considerations of inertia and cost call for more change on the part of minority groups, in the direction of assimilation. Assimilation in this case does not stand as an independent ideal. It is merely instrumental to successful integration. It does not require that minority groups give up their norms for in-group communication. In practice, however, it must be acknowledged that black in-group norms of communication are liable to fade as a byproduct of integration.

Unlike the ideal of assimilation, integration does not view disadvantaged communities as the only ones that need to change. Integration aims to transform the habits of dominant groups. It is a tool for breaking down stigmatization, stereotypes, and discrimination. Most important, it aims at constructing a superordinate group identity through which its members regard one another as equals, pool the local knowledge they have acquired in more parochial settings to solve shared problems, and hold one another to account.

Integration takes place in four stages: (1) formal desegregation, (2) spatial integration, (3) formal social integration, and (4) informal social integration. Formal desegregation consists in the abolition of laws and policies enforcing racial separation. Spatial integration consists in the common use on terms of equality of facilities and public spaces by substantial numbers of all races. A spatially integrated neighborhood may yet be socially segregated, if neighbors of different races do not interact in neighborly ways—welcome them to the neighborhood, engage in small talk, do small favors for one another. Similarly, a school may be spatially but not socially integrated if students of different races attend different tracked classes, participate in different school clubs, rarely befriend one another, and inhabit different halls or dormitories. Even when people observe antidiscrimination laws, and so avoid "discrimination in contract," they may still practice "discrimination in contact," which often involves shunning of marginalized groups by avoiding neighborly, collegial, or friendly relationships with them.[3]

Social integration requires intergroup cooperation on terms of equality. Formal social integration occurs when members of different races cooperate in accordance with institutionally defined social roles, and all races occupy all roles in enough numbers that roles are not racially identified. It happens when white privates obey orders issued by black lieutenants, with the same degree of alacrity as they obey orders issued by white lieutenants. It happens when white students and Latino students cooperate as equal lab partners, or as members of the school football team. Informal social integration involves cooperation, ease, welcome, trust, affiliation, and intimacy that go beyond the requirements of organizationally defined roles. It happens when members of different races form friendships, date, marry, bear children or adopt different race children. At school and work, it happens when members of different races share conversations at the lunch table, hobnob over the coffee break, and play together at recess.

I call these "stages" of integration because they reflect the typical temporal order in which a society moves from segregation to full integration. Yet different social domains undertake integration at different rates, with different levels of resistance. In the United States, spatial integration has been most easily achieved for public accommodations such as hotels, restaurants, and buses. The stakes are lower here, since admitting blacks to public accommodations does not require social integration and does not threaten whites' dominant positions in employment, politics, and education. Social integration has advanced most effectively in the workplace, especially government offices, and higher education. Antidiscrimination laws are easier to enforce here than in housing and have produced more dramatic results, in part because affirmative action is an available remedy. The authoritarian structure of the workplace gives people compelling reasons to cooperate with their coworkers regardless of race. That the terms of cooperation are largely dictated by employers also facilitates social interaction among groups unused to it. The rules and goals of interaction are externally fixed, offering guides to those who are anxious about intergroup encounters.[4] In neighborhoods, where intergroup encounters are unstructured and unsupervised, there is more room for stereotypes, anxiety, bigotry, and sheer social incompetence to govern the scene, and hence more potential for interactions to go badly.

The ideal of integration envisions a restructuring of intergroup relations, from alienation, anxiety, awkwardness, and hostility to relaxed, competent civil association and even intimacy; from domination and subordination to cooperation as equals. The previous chapters give us theoretical reasons to predict that integration has positive effects on blacks' material well-being, on people's attitudes and behavior toward blacks, and on the ability of democratic institutions to respond justly to the claims of citizens from all social groups. The rest of this chapter tests the theoretical promise of integration against experience. We consider three types of question. First, does the *condition* of integration help blacks? Evidence can be found by asking whether otherwise similar blacks are better off if they participate in integrated settings, and whether otherwise similar nonblacks have better attitudes and conduct toward blacks if they participate in integrated settings. While the latter questions are easier to answer, the answers may conflate unmeasured differences among people in segregated and integrated settings with the effects of integration. Second, do specific *integrative policies* help blacks? Evidence can be found by asking whether blacks are better off under these policies, and whether nonblacks under these policies have better attitudes and conduct toward blacks, relative to their conditions before the policy and to experimental controls. Answers to these questions may be better able to avoid the conflation problem but may fail to test the value of integration if the policies did not achieve the relevant stage of integration, or if controls achieved comparable levels of integration by other means. Third, do integrated working groups realize democratic values and racial justice better than segregated working groups? This question can also be explored through either observational or experimental studies, with similar caveats as apply to the first and second types of question.

6.2 Integration and Black Opportunity

If the argument of this book is sound, then spatial integration should improve the socioeconomic and physical well-being of groups disadvantaged by segregation by enhancing their access to public and private goods. It is also a necessary but not sufficient condition for social integration. Social integration should improve opportunities by opening up social networks of information and referral to disadvantaged groups, and by enabling them to acquire the cultural capital needed to advance in mainstream institutions. Consider first the effects of policies of spatial integration. Does moving blacks from high-poverty, racially segregated neighborhoods to low-poverty, racially integrated neighborhoods improve their well-being? It might not do so, if blacks from the ghetto lack the qualities needed to take advantage of opportunities in their new neighborhoods, or if whites find ways to continue to exclude them from access to these goods.

A famous study of this question examined the results of the Gautreaux program, a court-ordered housing integration project in the Chicago metropolitan area, following a Supreme Court ruling that government authorities had systematically engaged in unconstitutional racial segregation of public housing.[5] Over twenty-two years, 7,100 poor black families received housing vouchers to move to racially integrated neighborhoods in Chicago and its suburbs. The Gautreaux program dramatically improved the lives of participants who moved to integrated suburbs. Among the long-term unemployed, suburban movers were 50 percent more likely to obtain a job than those who stayed in the city.[6] Their children were one-fifth as likely to drop out of school, and 2.5 times more likely to attend college, than their urban counterparts. They were about twice as likely to have a job, and to be paid benefits, and five times more likely to have a job that paid more than $6.50 per hour.[7]

Qualitative evidence shows that neither skeptical hypothesis—that poor, segregated blacks would lack the dispositions needed to take advantage of spatial integration, and that discrimination would block their progress—obtained. Gautreaux participants did report minor harassment when they first moved into suburban neighborhoods, but this subsided as their neighbors learned to trust them. Gautreaux participants also rapidly acquired the cultural capital needed to take advantage of their new opportunities. Among the most important public goods of low-poverty neighborhoods are norms of orderly conduct and trust, which create safe public spaces and facilitate cooperation. Initially, Gautreaux participants felt constrained by more demanding social norms against loud music, late night partying, and similar disorderly conduct, which were enforced by stricter monitoring of behavior in suburban neighborhoods. But once they adjusted to the stricter norms, they reported great benefits from participating in neighborhood life under them: they feared less for their own and their children's safety because they could trust their neighbors to call the police in case of trouble and watch over their property when they were gone. Because neighborhood adults kept children in line, and gangs were absent, mothers felt freer to let their children play outside. They built reserves of social and cultural capital across race and class lines through reciprocal favors. This enabled them to get rides to work when the car broke down, obtain inexpensive used clothing and toys for their children in garage sales, and be offered informal child care from neighbors. These benefits had been inaccessible in their previous high-poverty housing projects, which suffered from high levels of distrust between neighbors.[8] Youth who moved to the suburbs were also much better able than their urban counterparts to build bridging social capital with white peers.[9] These benefits to adults and children endured. Once participants entered better neighborhoods through government assistance, they continued to live in low-poverty, low-crime, racially integrated neighborhoods through subsequent moves over the long term.[10]

Another famous program, Moving to Opportunity (MTO), tested the effects of socioeconomic integration. It randomly assigned public housing participants across three groups: a treatment group, offered a housing voucher usable only in a low-poverty neighborhood; a Section 8 comparison group, offered a housing voucher usable in any neighborhood; and an in-place control group, which continued to receive public housing in their original neighborhood. From 1994 to 1998, 4,600 families participated in MTO in five cities.[11]

MTO improved participants' well-being in several ways. Those who moved to better neighborhoods enjoyed better-quality housing and superior neighborhood conditions: they were much less likely to live in neighborhoods afflicted by vermin, litter, graffiti, or abandoned buildings, or to observe public drinking, loitering, or drug dealing. They were much less likely to complain that police failed to respond to calls. Many more felt safe in their neighborhoods, especially at night, and fewer were victimized by crime.[12] Superior real and perceived safety significantly improved the mental health of adults and girls in the experimental group. For adults, the effect size was comparable to the most effective known medical treatments for depression.[13] Girls suffered less from depression and risky behaviors and much less from generalized anxiety disorders compared to controls.[14]

Spatial integration of neighborhoods is but one domain and stage of integration. It is not expected to yield all of the benefits of comprehensive integration. In addition, for integration to yield certain benefits, formerly segregated individuals may need access to additional resources. Studies of MTO and less intensive residential mobility programs (similar to the treatment offered to the Section 8 comparison group) bear this out with respect to two dimensions of well-being: children's educational achievement, and employment and income.

Scattered reports on MTO find some improvement in children's academic achievement.[15] However, in the aggregate, educational outcomes did not differ between experimental and control groups.[16] This finding is not surprising given that three quarters of experimental group children attended school in the same school district as before the experiment. Overall, the schools they attended differed little from the schools attended by children in the control group.[17] MTO did not function as a test of the educational effects of school integration.

MTO also had no significant aggregate impact on adult employment or earnings.[18] Participants were largely priced out of neighborhoods near areas of high job growth. One quarter of participants could not take advantage of job opportunities due to disabling chronic illness.[19] Many others lacked access to transportation and child care.[20] MTO spatial integration also did not always lead to social integration. The MTO experimental group still relied on in-group acquaintances, rather than their better-off neighbors, for job information.[21] Most did not establish economically useful social ties to middle-class neighbors.[22] Yet, if acquired, social integration appears to help job seekers. Among youth in a Yonkers residential mobility program, suburban movers reported no more access to information about job opportunities than those who stayed in the city. However, if they added just one white or employed adult to their social network, their perceived access to information dramatically improved.[23] Hence, spatial integration is not enough; to generate economic opportunity, integrative policies must also help participants develop more diverse social networks with people employed in better jobs.[24]

Integration of schools appears to have numerous positive effects on black well-being. Research on this issue was launched by the famous Coleman Report, which found that black students' academic achievement was higher in schools with higher percentages of whites, and that students' achievement was better, the higher the socioeconomic status of their classmates.[25] Coleman's finding for racially integrated schools has been reconfirmed in multiple observational studies.[26] The black-white achievement test score gap is largest in states with the most highly segregated schools, and smallest in states with the most integrated schools.[27] The gap was closing most rapidly during the 1970s and 1980s, as schools were desegregating, and most impressively in the South, which, under court-ordered desegregation, achieved the greatest gains in integration during that time.[28] As the pace of school desegregation slowed in the 1990s, progress in closing the racial test score gap stagnated. Analyses at the school level also find significant connections between integration and black academic achievement.[29]

There are several explanations for this effect. Teachers flee schools with a high proportion of blacks, leaving segregated urban schools with an inexperienced faculty and discontinuities of instruction as teachers leave even in the middle of the school year.[30] Classrooms with more whites, and those that have students with higher socioeconomic status, benefit from superior instructional techniques. Blacks in more integrated schools may therefore do better because they have access to better teachers, who use more effective teaching strategies.[31] Having higher-achieving, economically better off peers also appears to spur achievement, although the mechanisms behind this effect are not well understood.[32]

In contrast with observational studies, which test the effects of the *condition* of integration, studies of busing as an integrative *policy* show much less impressive effects on academic outcomes.[33] Metanalyses of the busing studies generally find that busing black children to white schools modestly improves their reading ability in the early years of school but has little if any impact on their math achievement.[34] Skeptics argue that the substantially higher academic outcomes of black students in integrated schools in the observational studies could be explained by selection effects—the black children in integrated schools have unmeasured individual and family characteristics that lead to higher academic achievement than that experienced by their counterparts in segregated schools.[35]

However, this argument would have us believe that teacher quality has no impact on student achievement—an argument contradicted by other studies.[36] In addition, the busing studies suffer from methodological problems.[37] Busing is a policy instrument, not an outcome. Many schools subject to court-ordered busing resorted to within-school segregation techniques, such as tracking, ability grouping, and disproportionate assignment of black children to special education classes, and thereby continued to reserve important educational opportunities for whites, excluding black students with equal ability.[38] Integration has been implemented in many different ways, some of which are incompetent, others undertaken by defiant school districts uninterested in producing favorable results. The busing studies and metanalyses have not taken these variations into account.[39] Finally, it takes time for even conscientious school districts to learn how to run successful integrated schools. Most busing studies investigated student achievement in the first year or two of implementation, while school districts were still working out how to manage desegregation. These studies also tended to be too small to detect small effects that could accumulate over several years.[40]

These facts make it difficult to estimate the size of the effects of integration on black academic achievement, and they help to explain the wide
variation in effect sizes reported in the literature. Yet we do know that
a conscientious and competent integration policy *can* have spectacular
effects. From 1964 to 1972 elite private academies educated more than
five thousand black students from high-poverty segregated communities
through the A Better Chance program. Despite their deficient academic
backgrounds, these students managed to graduate with a median class
rank in the 47th percentile—on a par with their much more privileged
white counterparts.[41] This performance represents a level of academic
achievement vastly superior to what they could have achieved in the segregated schools they otherwise would have attended, given the inferior
curricula at those schools.

The short-term effects of integration on academic achievement are less
important than the long-term effects of integration. These appear to be
impressive and wide-ranging. After controlling for family background,
economic and educational status, and other variables, blacks who attend
integrated schools are more likely than their segregated peers to graduate
from high school.[42] They are less likely to land in prison.[43] Black students
in desegregated schools have higher and more varied (white collar, professional, private sector) occupational aspirations.[44] They are more likely
to elect educational programs, and pursue job tracks, that prepare them
for their career aspirations than are blacks in segregated schools.[45] There
is some evidence that they earn higher incomes.[46] Of black students who
attend majority-white colleges, those who were educated in more integrated high schools have higher grades—an effect that appears to be related to the greater stress and violence experienced by black students who
came from segregated environments.[47] Attendance and success in such
colleges is important because a degree from them carries a wage premium
over a degree from a historically black college.[48]

Most significantly, blacks who attend integrated K–12 schools lead
more integrated lives after graduation. They are more likely to attend
majority-white colleges, live in integrated neighborhoods, work in integrated firms, and have friends of other races than their counterparts who
attended segregated black schools.[49] Experience with integration helps
blacks overcome anxieties and discomforts over participating in plurality-
white institutions and thereby helps to break the cycle of segregation that
perpetuates numerous bad outcomes for blacks.[50] This is important because, as we have seen, academic achievement—human capital—is only
one of the factors affecting long-term socioeconomic status. School integration is needed to gain access not just to academic resources but to vital
sources of social and cultural capital in mainstream schools and later in
adult life.

6.3 Social Integration, Destigmatization, and Learning to Cooperate

The second main hypothesized effect of integration is improved intergroup relations. Integration should reduce antiblack prejudice, stigmatization, discrimination, and anxiety. This thesis follows Gordon Allport's famous contact hypothesis.[51] Allport argued that four conditions were required for intergroup interaction to reduce prejudice: contact must (1) be frequent enough to lead to personal acquaintance, (2) be cooperative, in pursuit of shared goals, (3) be supported by institutional authorities, and (4) take place among participants of equal status (equal roles within the organization). These conditions are encapsulated in my definition of formal social integration. We should therefore expect that destigmatization is best achieved in formal settings such as employment and education, rather than in unstructured informal settings of spontaneous, irregular contact such as public streets, parks, and malls.[52] Some social psychologists broaden the third condition to include any situation in which norms of amicable cooperation apply, even if they are not backed up by institutional authority. In that interpretation, intergroup friendship should also reduce stigmatization of the groups to which the friends belong.

Why should these contact conditions improve intergroup relations? Recall the plurality of sources of unjust or troublesome intergroup interaction (chapter 3). These include (1) in-group favoritism (ethnocentrism), (2) out-group antipathy (prejudice), (3) stereotypes, attribution errors, and other cognitive biases that generate stigmatizing representations of subordinated groups, (4) anxiety and discomfort over interacting with out-groups, and (5) adaptations to stigma—habits of subordination and interaction rituals that reproduce stigmatization. The *common in-group identity model* of intergroup contact focuses on the fact that repeated cooperative interaction creates a new "we" or in-group, the members of which become targets of in-group favoritism.[53] By expanding the boundaries of "us" to include members of different social groups, integration turns in-group favoritism from an obstacle to a tool of intergroup concord. The *decategorization* or *personalization* model of intergroup contact focuses on the fact that cooperation and frequent, amicable, personal contact motivate the participants to reveal and make use of individuating information about one another. This helps people overcome reliance on group stereotypes, and understand and evaluate out-group members as individuals.[54] Friendly or collegial relations with out-group members also help defuse antipathy against the out-group, as empathy with an out-group friend or colleague will arouse indignation against practices that treat one's friends unfairly.[55] Amicable relations also tend to defuse anxiety about interacting with out-group members.[56]

My analysis of the relations between segregation and stigmatization adds the following considerations. Several cognitive biases that lead to stigmatization under segregation lead to destigmatization under integration (§3.1). Intergroup cooperation on terms of equality requires the construction of shared points of view and mutual perspective-taking. These activities trigger the *shared reality bias*, helping different groups appreciate each other's points of view. Personal acquaintance with many out-group members can also disengage the *illusory correlation bias*, which induces those unfamiliar with subordinated out-groups to mistake unusual and sensational acts by out-group members, such as murders, as typical for the out-group. If members of stigmatized groups occupy the same roles as dominant group members, then the *stereotype incumbency bias* will not take membership in the dominant group as a qualification for occupying leadership roles. And if people get used to integrated institutions, then the *system justification bias* will lead people to think integration and group equality are justified.

My account of stigmatization defines the causal role of authorities in the contact hypothesis. Authorities function as norm entrepreneurs in making public their support for integration and supply incentives to induce subordinates to follow norms of civility in intergroup relations. Such norms undermine the public status of stigmatic representations, as mentionable, default presuppositions (§3.3). This is an essential step toward destigmatization.

My account of democratic culture also clarifies the causal role of equality in the contact hypothesis. Face-to-face intergroup encounters on terms of equality are potent settings for heightening people's sense of accountability to the people their actions are affecting (§5.3). Knowledge that one is accountable for what one says and does to equal-status out-group members who are able to observe and complain about one's conduct to one's face tends to make people more respectful of out-group members and more attentive to their interests.

This accountability effect may make people anxious and awkward. Anxiety may also be spurred by an embarrassing awareness of adaptations to subordination. Formal social integration helps allay these anxieties by providing people with sustained opportunities to practice interaction on terms of equality, and thereby acquire competence and ease in intergroup interaction.

Thus, intergroup contact satisfying Allport's conditions should reduce participants' prejudice against one another. But what induces participants to generalize this lesson beyond the integrated setting, and to out-group members with whom they are not cooperating? This question arises with particular force against the decategorization account of the contact hypothesis. Decategorization supposes that prejudice reduction requires people to be group-blind in representing fellow cooperators. They are to see their colleagues as individuals, not as members of stigmatized groups. But insofar as whites, say, no longer see black coworkers as black, how could reduced prejudice against black colleagues lead to reduced prejudice against blacks in general? Generalization of the lessons learned in integrated settings seems to require awareness of the race of fellow cooperators.[57] The effectiveness of intergroup contact depends on participants remaining aware of the social groups to which their colleagues belong.[58]

The contact hypothesis is one of the most widely tested claims in social psychology. Recent metanalyses of hundreds of studies show strong support for the contact hypothesis as applied to numerous group divisions—including racial groups—and contact settings.[59] Interracial friendship appears to be a particularly potent factor that reduces racial prejudice, although it has more impact on affective than on cognitive dimensions of prejudice.[60] The correlation between friendship and lower prejudice appears not to be the result of selection effects.[61] Moreover, merely knowing that a friend has a friend of another race reduces prejudice.[62]

Formal social integration in the workplace is also an important setting for improving intergroup relations. Racial integration has progressed more in the workplace than in neighborhoods and schools. The presence of a single authority legally accountable for enforcing antidiscrimination norms appears to have played an important role in improving intergroup relations at work. Labor unions, too, have played historically important roles in promoting white acceptance of blacks at work, given that employers long exploited racial divisions to undermine working-class struggles for higher wages and better working conditions.[63] The U.S. Army has also proved to be a powerful setting for improving race relations. It is the most integrated institution in the United States, not just by role but in the ease and comfort with which its members willingly associate across racial lines. Its members report that race relations are much better there than in civilian life.[64] The effectiveness of the army's integration is due to its strong institutional commitment to equal opportunity and equality in race relations, along with a large enough representation of well-trained blacks so that their presence in all ranks is taken for granted. Commanders are under orders to improve race relations whenever a discrimination complaint arises in their unit—even if it turns out to be unsubstantiated.[65]

These positive findings contrast with the mixed findings on the effects of school desegregation policies. One famous early literature review of school desegregation studies found that whites' prejudice against blacks actually *increased* in a majority of studies.[66] Numerous other studies report effects of school desegregation on intergroup relations that range widely in both direction and size.[67] There are several reasons for these disappointing results. Many use a seriously flawed measure of improved intergroup relations that assumes a tradeoff between intragroup and intergroup friends (hence, they recorded a positive effect of desegregation only if students began to *prefer* out-group members over in-group members).[68] Most school desegregation studies were undertaken during a tumultuous period of race relations, in which desegregation was achieved by court order over the heated opposition of white parents, many of whom threw rocks at school buses carrying black students to majority-white schools and engaged in other obstructionist behavior. School authorities often dragged their feet over desegregation orders, practiced resegregation within schools, and undermined the conditions for role equality by placing black students in less demanding academic tracks.[69] Since the conditions for Allport's contact hypothesis—institutional support, frequent cooperative contact with acquaintance potential, and role equality—were often flouted in formally desegregated schools, and since the desegregation studies often had a short time frame, negative results recorded in these contexts hardly count as fair tests of the contact hypothesis.[70]

The school desegregation experience shows that there is a large gap between formal desegregation and spatial integration, on the one hand, and social integration, on the other. Improved intergroup relations are only predicted from social integration. Schools that promote social integration have found positive results. Formal integration of sports teams has strongly positive effects on the racial attitudes of student athletes, with similar effects for integration of other extracurricular activities.[71] To integrate classrooms, schools need to offer challenging curricula to all students. Schools that detrack their classes improve race relations by offering frequent opportunities for interracial interaction under conditions of role equality, and they also improve learning outcomes for all students, including low achievers, and reduce the racial gap in achievement.[72] Interracial friendships are higher in highly diverse schools with untracked classrooms and integrated extracurricular activities.[73] Race relations improve when classroom instruction takes place through racially integrated cooperative learning groups. Many of the tested integrated cooperative learning techniques simultaneously improve race relations and promote academic achievement.[74] The positive effects of such practices on intergroup relations increase when racial out-groups are present in sufficient numbers to avoid tokenism, and when integration begins in the earliest grades.[75]

Although many schools have successfully practiced social integration, the conditions for successful integration are less often met in public schools than in other settings, such as the workplace and the army. High degrees of residential segregation, especially across municipal boundaries, pose formidable obstacles to schools achieving more than token integration—a condition that reduces opportunities for intergroup contact and can actually impair race relations. Because residential segregation tends to depress black economic prospects, it often produces an overlap between race and class in school settings. Such "convergent boundaries" exacerbate racial stigmatization by conflating negative stereotypes of the poor with stereotypes about blacks.[76] Allport's equal status condition may be undermined when cooperative learning groups combine high-achieving white students with low-achieving black students. There are ways to overcome such difficulties—for example, by constructing cooperative groups in which the black students, even if they have lower prior academic achievement than their white work group peers, have salient strengths in other dimensions, such as popularity, leadership skills, or physical attractiveness.[77] Cooperative learning techniques have also been designed that ensure that students with low prior academic achievement have an equal opportunity to make salient contributions to the academic success of the learning group.[78] School desegregation with favorable effects on intergroup relations is possible even under challenging conditions. However, to achieve these effects takes a great deal of work, involving substantial school reorganization and revisions of long-entrenched pedagogical habits.

The most important evidence in favor of the contact hypothesis concerns its long-term effects. We have seen that blacks who had experience with integration earlier in their lives lead more integrated lives as adults (§6.2). The same effect is found for all racial groups.[79] Students who attend more racially integrated colleges lead more integrated lives after graduation: they live in more integrated neighborhoods, work in more integrated firms, and are more likely to have other-race friends than students who attended less racially diverse colleges.[80] Adult graduates of integrated high schools and colleges alike also report that they value their interracial experiences, are more comfortable with interracial interaction, and are better prepared to cope with living in a diverse society.[81] These facts speak to the powerful effect of integration on racial destigmatization. Even if members of unstigmatized groups still harbor negative racial stereotypes of stigmatized groups, integrative experiences positively affect their interracial *behavior*—they less often practice group closure and are more likely to welcome members of other racial groups into their lives.

6.4 Integration and Democracy

The third main type of hypothesized effect of integration is the realization of a more democratic society. From a cultural point of view, the case for this claim is evident since integration is practically constitutive of a democratic culture (§5.1). In this section, I focus on the democratic *consequences* of diverse citizens working together. I count an outcome as more democratic if it is more responsive to the rights, needs, and concerns of diverse citizens rather than catering to the interests or perspectives of one or a very few sections of society, and if it is based on unifying rather than polarizing ("us" vs. "them") conceptions of its value. I count elites as more democratic if they are more responsive and accountable to the just claims of citizens from all walks of life. We expect integrated elites to be more responsive and accountable than homogeneous elites (§§5.2–5.5). They can draw on a more diverse pool of information about the asymmetrical effects of public policies on different citizens, and are more likely to modify decisions in light of this information, than homogeneous elites. Consider some evidence on these points from three domains—criminal justice, public schools, and electoral politics.

The domain of criminal justice exhibits some of the harshest racial disparities in the United States (§2.1). Discrimination against blacks has been found at every stage in the criminal justice process. In some jurisdictions, blacks are more likely to be stopped, interrogated, and searched by police, even after controlling for individual, neighborhood, and race-specific factors predicting suspect criminal activity.[82] New Jersey state highway troopers, for example, have been found to stop and search cars driven by blacks far more often than whites, yielding a "hit rate" (evidence of crime) for blacks only half as high as for whites—putting the lie to the claim that using race as a proxy for criminality is an efficient police method.[83] Once in an encounter with police, blacks are more likely to be subject to improper force.[84] Upon being charged with a crime, blacks are more likely than whites to be detained without bail, more likely to be charged bail even when they have a lower flight risk and assessed higher bail than whites with equivalent characteristics, and less able to make bail.[85] Because this means that blacks are more often detained before trial, they are less able to assist their lawyers in their defense and more vulnerable to coercive plea bargains.[86] Black youth are more likely than white youth with equivalent records and charges to be tried as adults.[87] Blacks are also sentenced more harshly than whites with equivalent records and criminal histories.[88] This disparity appears to be particularly pronounced for black male youth offenders,[89] and for black offenders with darker skin tone and more stereotypically "black" features.[90] After conviction, young male black offenders, even if employed, are more likely than their unemployed white peers to suffer revocation of probation.[91]

The causes of these racial disparities in the criminal justice process are complex and not fully understood. They appear to include various combinations of prejudicial discrimination, statistical discrimination, evaluative discrimination, and second-order discrimination (§3.5), often inspired by narratives that trigger stigmatizing stereotypes of black violence, drug use, irresponsibility, and general criminality.[92] Racial integration improves the ability of citizens to avoid racial injustice in this domain. I illustrate this point in three areas: eyewitness testimony, citizen juries, and police forces.

A recent study of felony convicts exonerated by DNA evidence reveals the following pattern. From 1989 to 2003, of all men convicted of rape, 58 percent were white and 29 percent were black. Of rape convicts exonerated on the basis of DNA evidence, 28 percent were white and 64 percent were black. This is strong evidence that innocent blacks are falsely convicted of felonies at a far higher rate than innocent whites are.[93] Furthermore, although black-on-white rapes are far less than 10 percent of all rapes, *half* of all DNA rape exonerations are of blacks convicted of raping a white victim.[94] Some of this higher false conviction rate is probably due to the fact that black-on-white rape charges evoke narratives long used to arouse racial fears and hatreds that dispose white jurors to convict. Yet few rape trials proceed without an eyewitness identification of the assailant. At the core of most of these false convictions, then, lies a mistaken eyewitness identification. That these mistakes are more common for cross-racial identification than for within-race identification reflects the fact that people are better at identifying same-race than other-race faces.[95] Blacks, however, are as good as whites at identifying white faces. This superior capability is due to the fact that blacks have more exposure to whites than whites have to blacks.[96] If whites led more racially integrated lives, they would be more competent eyewitnesses for crimes involving black offenders and would cause fewer grave miscarriages of justice against blacks.

Juries, too, discriminate against black defendants. White jurors often vote to convict black defendants in cases where they would acquit a white defendant.[97] They grant white defendants the benefit of the doubt in ambiguous cases and follow the judge's instructions to disregard inadmissible evidence, but they favor the prosecution's interpretation of events in ambiguous cases and attend to the inadmissible evidence when the defendant is black.[98] White jurors are also more likely to discriminate against black defendants when race is *not* a salient issue in the case. The theory of "aversive racism" predicts both patterns. According to aversive racism theory, many whites consciously accept antidiscrimination norms and want to be unprejudiced, while harboring unconscious negative stereotypes and aversions against blacks (§3.1). When race is salient, this triggers whites' conscious concern to be nonracist, and they work harder to be fair to blacks, especially in contexts where a decision against them could only be explained by prejudice. But when the context is ambiguous and a decision against a black person could be given a nonracist rationale, whites are off their guard and allow their antiblack biases to influence their decisions.[99] Thus, black defendants often cannot expect a fair trial from an all-white jury.

Racially integrated juries offer greater hope. Experiments with mock juries show that racially integrated juries take more time to deliberate about their case, and that the quality of their deliberation is superior to that of all-white juries. They consider more facts, make fewer inaccurate statements, leave fewer inaccurate statements uncorrected, and more frequently raise questions about "missing" evidence (evidence that would be needed to make the prosecution's case convincing).[100] They are smarter and more conscientious. These are reasons to adopt a general policy to select jurors with the aim of creating racially integrated juries.[101]

What accounts for the superiority of integrated juries? The epistemic diversity hypothesis claims that members of different racial groups will raise different issues for the group to consider and take different approaches to solving the problem. Superior information exchange in a diverse group causes superior performance. Mock jury experiments provide some evidence for this hypothesis: black jurors are more likely than white ones to raise race-related issues.[102]

The accountability hypothesis claims that the presence of racially diverse members in a working group of equals widens the range of people to whom each participant must justify their opinions and conduct and so motivates the participants to think more carefully about what they say and do *from what they anticipate are the perspectives of racial out-group members*. This inspires participants to be more thoughtful, to consider a wider range of information, to take more seriously concerns that would be dismissed in a more homogeneous group. As Samuel Sommers, a leading researcher on racially diverse group deliberation, explains, "Knowing that they would have to justify their judgments to a diverse group may very well have increased Whites' sense of accountability, an experience which previous research suggests would lead to more complex thought processes and affect how individuals weighted the trial evidence."[103]

Several lines of experimental evidence point to the importance of the accountability effect. Outside the jury context, Sommers and colleagues have found that whites who simply *anticipate* having to discuss a racially charged issue with racially diverse others score more highly on a comprehension test of readings relevant to their discussion than whites who know they will be discussing the issue with whites alone. Anticipating disagreement and conflict, they prepare themselves by sharpening their focus on relevant material.[104] They also check their predeliberative inclinations to treat blacks harshly. Whites who know they will deliberate on a jury with blacks indicate before deliberation that they would vote to convict the black defendant far less frequently than whites who know they will sit on an all-white jury.[105] Much of the greater deliberative care in racially integrated juries is due to the initiative of whites, who raise a wider range of issues, take greater care to make accurate statements, and correct errors more often than whites in all-white juries. This shows that blacks affect group deliberation not simply by supplying diverse information, but by inspiring whites to deliberate more responsibly. Racially integrated juries also take racially salient issues seriously, in contrast with all-white juries, which rarely raise the possibility that discrimination or cognitive biases concerning race may have influenced the criminal justice process. In *every* all-white jury Sommers studied, if a racially salient issue—for example, doubts about the reliability of a white eyewitness identification of a black person—was raised, someone objected to its mention, and the jury suppressed discussion of it by changing the subject or marginalizing the person who raised it.[106] Racially integrated juries raised racially salient issues more frequently and actively discussed them. This was not a matter of whites timidly caving in to militant blacks' demands for "politically correct" behavior. To the contrary, members of integrated juries often expressed heated disagreement over such issues.[107] In an integrated context, but not in an all-white context, whites recognized the legitimacy and importance of taking such issues seriously.

These phenomena offer strong support for the nonideal democratic theory of chapter 5. There, I argued that integration of diverse groups in society is essential for a well-functioning democracy. It is necessary to ensure that democratic institutions learn from the epistemic diversity of citizens who, due to different group circumstances, are asymmetrically affected by various social problems and policy responses to those problems (§5.2). It is necessary to ensure that democratic decision makers who hold the fates of others in their hands are, and feel themselves to be, accountable to citizens from all walks of life, so that they take pains to make policies they can justify to all (§5.3). The evidence cited here shows that the disposition of individuals to live up to the demands of democracy is situational. Functioning in integrated, diverse groups enhances individuals' democratic competencies, especially with respect to exercising the primary demand of democratic institutions, to treat all citizens as equals.

The same conclusions apply to racially integrated police forces. Residents of black neighborhoods prefer racially integrated police teams over all-white or all-black police teams, perceiving the former to be less likely to engage in police brutality, more likely to know and foster amicable relations with the community, and better able to embody sound race relations than racially homogeneous police.[108] Evidence on how integrated police forces behave supports these perceptions. The increased diversity of America's police forces by race and gender has undermined the insular culture of police solidarity. Police solidarity went hand in hand with an "us" vs. "them" attitude toward civilians, especially racial out-groups. Less solidaristic integrated police forces are more responsive to community concerns. Biracial police teams use less force against civilians than either all-white or all-black teams. When affirmative action brought black police into formerly all-white police forces, they organized under rival professional associations, which brought the concerns of the black community, notably police use of racial profiling and excessive force, to the attention of their departments. Racially integrated police departments have also fostered better relations with minority community organizations.[109]

Similar improvements in the responsiveness and accountability of organizations to the full range of interests in diverse communities have been found when these organizations integrate their decision-making ranks. Recall that many school districts, forced to racially integrate their schools under court-ordered desegregation plans, found ways to continue white opportunity hoarding through internal segregation (§6.2). Integration of school districts' teaching staffs is strongly associated with reducing the placement of black children in classes for the mentally disabled, reducing excessive punishment, suspension, and expulsion of black students, and increasing their placement in advanced classes. Thus, integration of teaching staff promotes the genuine integration of schools and reduces discrimination against black students.[110]

I conclude with some observations about the relationship of integration to public opinion formation and democratic processes. Survey researchers have long known that the opinions people express are affected by the perceived race of the interviewer. On racially sensitive issues, blacks and whites alike express more moderate and conciliatory views when they believe they are speaking with someone of another race.[111] The standard interpretation of this effect is that subjects are hiding their "true" opinion out of the desire to conform to norms of social desirability. Hence, when racially sensitive issues are the focus of a survey, it is common practice for researchers to match the race of the interviewer with the race of the subject. In this view, an individual's "true" opinion is the belief she would avow in the most private setting, when she is least influenced by others— or least influenced by out-group others.

Lynn Sanders argues that this atomized, individualist view contradicts the democratic ideal of public opinion formation, which holds that opinions entitled to the description "public" should arise in a democracy from the discussions diverse citizens undertake together.[112] As Dewey argued, democracy consists in "free gatherings of neighbors on the street corner to discuss back and forth what is read in uncensored news of the day," and "personal day-by-day working together with others."[113] From this point of view, the moderation of opinion that arises in racially integrated settings, far from reflecting an artificial distortion of people's "true" opinions, represents a more authentically *public* and democratic opinion, properly reflecting the influence of diverse others on individuals' views. Opinions on racially sensitive issues generated in integrated contexts are sensitive to a wider range of relevant considerations. For example, white opinion on affirmative action in segregated settings is insensitive to opinions about blacks' economic circumstances but is responsive to such considerations in integrated settings.[114]

Similar findings hold in nonexperimental settings. The political opinions of whites who have more black neighbors, coworkers, and fellow churchgoers are less influenced by antiblack stereotypes than the opinions of more segregated whites.[115] In general, the more diverse individuals' networks of political discussion are, the better informed they are of the grounds for their own and others' opinions *and* the more tolerant they are of opposed political views.[116] These facts suggest that more racially tolerant opinions generated under conditions of integration do not represent an oft-decried cowardly submission to imperious demands of "political correctness" but reflect a more informed and conscientious thought process in light of a normatively legitimate democratic pressure to form opinions that can be justified to a diverse public.

These considerations should affect how we draw the boundaries of representative districts. The conventional wisdom among civil rights advocates has been that effective black political representation requires the creation of "majority-minority districts," in which a majority of voters identify with a single minority racial group and thereby hold the power to elect representatives of their choice. This policy has led to a dramatic increase in the number of blacks holding elected political office, which in turn has increased black political participation and trust that the political process will respond to their claims.[117] It has also arguably provided the foundation for a black political leadership, which, at least in U.S. House of Representatives races, has fostered a racially integrated, coalitional style of politics—contrary to the stereotype of the militant black officeholder who practices racially polarizing politics.[118] Nevertheless, recent shifts in the willingness of whites to vote for black candidates suggest that the time has come to foster interracial coalitional politics more broadly. This would involve shifting the principle for districting away from the majority-minority formula to one that favors coalitional districts, in which blacks would still have an equal opportunity to elect their preferred candidate, but that candidate cannot be elected without white support.[119] This policy moves away from the idea that each racial group is entitled to a representative who represents *them*, toward the idea that democracy requires mutual engagement across group lines, on the basis of policies and justifications addressed to all. This kind of interracial engagement is unlikely to happen unless blacks are present in large enough numbers that politicians must appeal to them to win elections. But this does not require that they constitute a majority in any district. Packing blacks into majority-minority districts makes the remaining districts overwhelmingly white, insular, and free to promote racially polarizing policies. Racially integrated districts should rather be designed to motivate the largest number of whites to pay attention to the claims of all, and to motivate candidates to frame their campaigns around unifying rather than polarizing themes.

Segregation is a fundamental cause of injustice in three broad domains: socioeconomic opportunity, public recognition, and democratic politics. It stands to reason that integration should help dismantle these injustices. This chapter surveyed some evidence bearing on this question. Integration consists in the participation as equals of all groups in all social domains. It proceeds in four stages: formal desegregation, spatial integration, formal social integration, and informal social integration. Each stage helps dismantle different injustices. Formal desegregation removes the official stamp of state authority from stigmatizing practices that constitute blacks as untouchable, but without undoing spatial and social segregation. Spatial integration provides blacks access to the public goods of socioeconomically more advantaged neighborhoods—better housing, orderly neighborhoods, lower crime and blight—and the psychic and social benefits that follow from these goods, including lower psychological stress and freedom to allow children to play outside. Without social integration, however, it does not provide better access to jobs. Formal social integration at school advances blacks' educational achievement and job opportunities. Sustained formal social integration under moderately favorable conditions, including institutional support and cooperative interaction, reduces prejudice, stigma, and discrimination and increases intergroup comfort in the long term, but not without initial difficulties. Informal social integration, if it rises to the level of genuine friendship, has similar effects. Formal social integration has important democratic effects, especially in enabling agents of government—juries, police, schools—to reduce discrimination and respond more effectively to the claims of the disadvantaged. It works through at least two causal routes—epistemic diversity, whereby members of disadvantaged groups bring relevant considerations to the attention of agents who would otherwise be ignorant of them, and accountability, whereby agents respond to the presence of diverse others by expanding the circle of justification to address them as well as in-group members. This results in a more deliberative, public, and democratic politics.

· SEVEN ·

UNDERSTANDING AFFIRMATIVE ACTION

7.1 Four Models of Affirmative Action

Since the demise of court-ordered busing for school integration, affirmative action has been the most controversial race-conscious policy in the United States. By "affirmative action," I refer to any policy that aims to increase the participation of a disadvantaged social group in mainstream institutions, either through "outreach" (targeting the group for publicity and invitations to participate) or "preference" (using group membership as criteria for selecting participants). In the United States, affirmative action is practiced in three domains: employment, education, and government contracting.

This chapter compares four models of race-based affirmative action in the United States: compensatory, diversity, discrimination-blocking, and integrative. The compensatory model represents racial preferences as a way to compensate for the effects of past discrimination. Since blacks have suffered discrimination, they are entitled to compensation in the form of access to the opportunities that discrimination has unjustly denied them. Compensatory affirmative action is backward looking: it aims to restore justice by undoing wrongs of the past. Its principal legal foundation can be traced to Justice Blackmun's concurring opinion in *United Steelworkers of America v. Weber*, which upheld affirmative action in employment.[1]

The diversity model represents racial preferences as a means to increase the cultural and epistemic diversity of the institution practicing it. In this view, blacks, by virtue of their historical and cultural differences from other groups, have diverse ideas and perspectives from other racial groups. This epistemic diversity enriches the educational mission of schools, the public discourse needed to advance democracy, and the ability of corporations to design and market products and services that appeal to diverse consumers. This is a present-oriented and forward-looking rationale: it views the participation of racially diverse individuals as advancing institutional objectives. The principal legal foundation of this rationale is Justice Powell's opinion in *Regents of the University of California v. Bakke,* supporting race-based affirmative action in college admissions.[2]

The discrimination-blocking model represents affirmative action as a tool for counteracting continuing discrimination. It is founded on the fact that, without pressure on institutions to meet race-conscious goals, antidiscrimination laws fail to produce race-neutral hiring and promotion in the face of entrenched and often unconscious discriminatory habits. This is a present-oriented rationale: hiring goals and timetables are means to force institutions to stop discriminating. The principal legal foundations for this model include a series of executive orders requiring federal agencies and their contractors to comply with antidiscrimination laws, and *Sheet Metal Workers v. EEOC,*[3] which affirmed the power of federal courts to order employers found guilty of discrimination to adopt remedial affirmative action programs.[4]

The integrative model represents racial preferences as a means to racially integrate the main institutions of civil society. Segregation is the linchpin of unjust systematic race-based disadvantage because it blocks blacks' access to public and consumer goods, employment, and financial, human, social, and cultural capital and causes pervasive antiblack racial stigmatization and discrimination (chapters 2 and 3). Integration helps dismantle these underlying causes of race-based injustice (chapter 6). Integration is also needed to advance a democratic culture, by providing opportunities for citizens from all walks of life to communicate on matters of public interest, forge cooperative relationships, and construct an integrated collective identity, and to advance democratic governance, by creating an integrated and thereby more competent and accountable elite, better disposed and able to honor the rights and serve the interests of all members of society, regardless of their group identities (chapters 5 and 6). This is a forward-looking rationale: it views the integration of mainstream institutions as essential to advancing justice and democracy. The principal legal foundation of the integrative rationale for affirmative action can be traced to a line of cases from *Brown v. Board of Education* (prohibiting racial segregation of schools),[5] including *Swann v. Charlotte-Mecklenburg Board of Education* (upholding race-based assignment of students as a means to desegregate schools),[6] and culminating in *Grutter v. Bollinger* (upholding race-based affirmative action admissions at the University of Michigan Law School).[7]

Public discourse about affirmative action is dominated by the compensatory and diversity models. The discrimination-blocking and integrative models are not well understood. I shall argue that the latter models have several virtues not shared by the former: they better fit the practice of affirmative action, do not foster racial myths or lend themselves to stigmatizing interpretations, do a better job explaining the continuing causes of race-based disadvantage, and answer or avoid the objections that undermine the other two models.

Affirmative action enjoys strong elite support. When the constitutionality of affirmative action in higher education was challenged in *Grutter*, sixty-nine amicus briefs were filed on behalf of the university, representing, among many other interested parties, officers in the U.S. military, leading universities, Fortune 500 corporations, major media companies, the American Bar Association, and many states and elected officeholders.[8] Yet affirmative action is in peril. An ongoing campaign to ban it state by state has succeeded in eliminating state-sponsored affirmative action in California, Washington, Michigan, Florida, and Nebraska, with more states on the way. The Supreme Court also threatens affirmative action by severely constraining its freedom to operate.[9] Advancing a better rationale for affirmative action will not by itself overcome popular opposition. The integrationist rationale predicts that opposition will be overcome mainly through practical experience with integration, not through abstract arguments. Nevertheless, a policy under popular assault in a democracy is at additional risk if its practitioners do not fully grasp the principles that make sense of it, if their rationales feed racial myths and stigmas, if they fail to educate the population about the continuing causes of race-based disadvantage, and if they have only weak answers to fundamental objections.

7.2 The Compensatory Model

Every model of race-based affirmative action offers an account of its purpose, which determines (1) which agents may practice affirmative action, (2) who should be a targeted beneficiary, and why, (3) how much weight may be given to group preferences, (4) who should bear the costs of affirmative action, and (5) the meaning and relevance of race to the purpose of affirmative action. In addition, if the model is based on considerations of justice, it also presupposes (6) an account of the causes of race-based injustice.

The compensatory rationale typically draws on an individualized model of compensatory justice.[10] In this model, if a person has suffered from wrongdoing, she is entitled to compensation from the wrongdoer, to the extent of the damages the wrong inflicted on her. This implies that (1) the agents who should practice affirmative action are those who had previously engaged in racial discrimination; (2) the beneficiaries are targeted by virtue of being the victims of past racial discrimination by the agents;

(3) they should be compensated to the extent of the harm they suffered, and (4) the agents who had engaged in discrimination should bear the costs. Membership in a disadvantaged racial group is a relevant basis for targeting beneficiaries for affirmative action, on the assumption that (5) membership serves as an accurate proxy for the morally relevant characteristic of having been victimized by racial discrimination. This model supposes that (6) past racial discrimination is the main cause of current race-based injustice.

Critics object that the practice of affirmative action does not fit the compensatory rationale very well.[11] Schools, government bodies, and employers practice affirmative action even if they have not been found guilty of discrimination. They do not attempt to identify and compensate the victims of their own discrimination but target their benefits to others on the basis of their shared racial identity with those presumed to be victims of their own or others' discrimination. They do not adjust the degree of benefit to any measure of damages that targets suffered from discrimination. Those who bear the costs of the policy are not its practitioners, but innocent whites and Asians who are displaced by racial preferences. Finally, race is an imperfect proxy for victimization-by-discrimination. It is overinclusive, in selecting some individuals in the target groups who have not experienced discrimination, and underinclusive, in excluding individuals outside the targeted groups who have suffered discrimination.

Because affirmative action fails to meet the exacting standards of individualized remedies, the compensatory model is sometimes cast in terms of group compensation.[12] In this view, society is fundamentally divided into racial groups who constitute the relevant units of moral agency and considerability. A discriminatory act by one white constitutes whites as a debtor class, creating a group obligation to compensate that could be discharged by any other white. A discriminatory injury to any black constitutes blacks as a creditor class, creating a group entitlement in which an injury to one black can be made up by a preference to any other. This group model does a better job fitting the practice of affirmative action to a rationale. But it is unacceptable. Individuals, not racial groups, are the relevant units of moral entitlement. In addition, the group rationale advances a divisive conception of society that undermines the democratic aspiration to unite all citizens under a common identity.

The compensatory model must therefore address the objections lodged against it within an individualist conception of justice. Start with the agents practicing affirmative action. Whether an agent has discriminated in the past is relevant only to the question of whether they are *obligated* to compensate, not whether they are *permitted* to do so. There is nothing morally objectionable about an agent compensating for damage caused by others' wrongdoing.[13] Americans committed no wrong in donating money to help the victims of 9/11.

Now consider the targets of affirmative action and the amount of their damages. The individualized ideal of case-by-case adjudication makes little sense where it is known that there are victims, but it is too costly, difficult, or impossible to precisely identify who they are or how much they were damaged. Individuals usually do not know whether a particular agent has discriminated against them because they do not know how that agent has treated others.[14] Moreover, people have a cognitive bias against seeing themselves as victims, even when they know they belong to a group often subject to discrimination.[15] Discriminating agents also may not know who their victims are. A firm notorious for discrimination cannot know who was discouraged from applying for a job because they knew they would get no consideration. A firm that publicizes job openings only to its all-white staff may know that no blacks will learn of its opportunities. But there is no answer to the question of which blacks would have applied, had the firm adopted a nondiscriminatory publicity policy. There are many fair policies it could have adopted, each of which would have led to a different black applicant pool.

In such cases, we know that people have been unjustly disadvantaged because of their race but we cannot identify who they are. Many discriminatory policies inflict their damage probabilistically, like air pollution. In pollution cases, that the causal connection is statistical and not provable in any single instance does not undermine the case for compensation in a class action suit. Racial discrimination often works the same way and is often similarly settled under Title VII of the 1964 Civil Rights Act through class actions that offer affirmative action as a remedy.

The "innocent white" objection to who bears the costs of affirmative action also has little normative force. Some defenders of affirmative action argue that whites enjoy unjust enrichment, in the form of competitive advantages due to past antiblack discrimination, and thus have no valid complaint against affirmative action programs that take this advantage away from them.[16] I am disinclined to press this divisive argument. It is enough to observe that *all* compensatory projects undertaken by corporate bodies place burdens on innocents. Whenever a corporation helps the victims of some wrongdoing, the costs are borne by innocent individuals who are or would like to be associated with it. Firms that offered jobs as compensation to the survivors of 9/11 victims denied these jobs to other innocent job applicants. We observe no protests about such compensatory acts, nor should we.

The "innocent white" objection also neglects the fact that as long as discrimination or its effects persist, there will be innocent victims suffering unjust burdens. The only question is whether these burdens should be borne exclusively by disadvantaged racial groups or more widely shared. There is no injustice in sharing the costs of widespread injustice. A main point of government is to share the costs of injustice by sharing the costs of protection from and punishment of crime. That one has neither committed nor benefited from any crime constitutes no claim against paying the taxes used to help the victims of crime.

These considerations support a compensatory model of race-based affirmative action as a kind of "rough justice."[17] Where the wrongdoing against a group has been pervasive enough, the harm so great that there is little chance that compensation would overshoot the aggregate damages, and individualized compensation is too costly or impossible, then general compensation to the group comes closer to the ideal of compensatory justice than a refusal to compensate without individualized proof.[18] The "rough justice" defense of affirmative action also explains why it is not unjustly underinclusive to focus on affirmative action for blacks and similarly disadvantaged groups, while not targeting groups that have not suffered extensive discrimination.

Thus, the compensatory model of affirmative action can be defended against common objections. Yet it suffers from an inadequate conception of the wrongs its beneficiaries suffer. In focusing on past discrimination, it suggests that discrimination is only in the past, and that current group disadvantage consists only of the inherited effects of past events. This inspires impatience about the continuation of the policy once antidiscrimination laws have been in place for decades since it does not explain why the current beneficiaries of affirmative action have been unable to overcome the legacy of discrimination against their ancestors, unlike many groups, such as Asians and Irish, who have suffered severe discrimination in the past.

The compensatory model also does not offer a satisfactory explanation of why affirmative action, which is practiced only by selective colleges, large corporations, and governments, is an appropriate form of compensation. It benefits only a small proportion of the members of such groups, often the best-off among them—those who already have enough education to handle the work at a selective college, enough qualifications to function in a corporate job, and enough assets to own a business capable of executing government contracts. Rough compensatory justice would be better served if we distributed lump-sum cash reparations to every member of the disadvantaged group, or concentrated compensation on the least well-off within the group.[19]

Finally, the compensatory model offers an inadequate conception of the role of beneficiaries in the institutions practicing affirmative action. They are represented as passive victims of injustice, rather than as active contributors whose participation contributes to the mission of these institutions. This representation feeds stigmatizing thoughts that affirmative action's beneficiaries are not pulling their own weight in these institutions, that they do not deserve to be there, and that they lack real merit.

An adequate, nonstigmatizing conception of the beneficiaries of affirmative action would represent them as meritorious, as contributing to the missions of participating institutions through the roles they occupy. It would explain why, within the targeted classes, affirmative action often prefers the relatively more advantaged—those *least* injured by past discrimination. It would not locate the rationale for affirmative action in fast-receding events of the past, but in present- and future-oriented concerns. The diversity model of affirmative action meets these criteria.

7.3 The Diversity Model

The diversity model represents affirmative action as promoting a "robust exchange of ideas."[20] In this model, (1) the institutions eligible to practice affirmative action are those whose mission would profit from a greater diversity of ideas brought by participants. (2) The targeted beneficiaries should be members of any group that would contribute to the epistemic diversity of the institution. (3) The weight given to preferences for including members from any group should be proportional to the diversity of ideas they bring, and inversely proportional to the degree to which they are already represented. (4) Those who should bear the costs of affirmative action are those whose perspectives and ideas are already well represented in the institution. (5) Race is presumed relevant to diversity because it is viewed as a proxy for possession of ideas distinct from well-represented groups. Finally, (6) individuals are targeted by affirmative action not to remedy injustice, but to advance the missions of the institutions that practice it.

The diversity model answers the surviving objections against the compensatory model. It is future-oriented, locating the point of affirmative action in continuing institutional needs for epistemic diversity rather than in receding events that, over time, lose their claim on how current institutions should be structured. It explains why affirmative action favors the more advantaged members of targeted groups. To effectively contribute to epistemic diversity, the beneficiaries must be otherwise qualified to perform up to the institution's standards. The more advantaged within the targeted groups possess those qualifications to a greater degree. The diversity model offers a nonstigmatizing account of why members of targeted racial groups are preferred: they bring valuable features to the institution—epistemic diversity—that advance the institution's mission.

This is a meritocratic rationale, which represents the targets of affirmative action as contributing, deserving agents rather than as pitiful subjects of an institution's beneficence. It gives other participants positive reasons to value the presence of affirmative action's beneficiaries.

Yet the diversity model, when divorced from the aims of social justice,[21] suffers from several flaws. First, its rationale does not fit the *scope* of the practice. It best suits educational institutions and the award of broadcast licenses. It can be extended to certain jobs that deal with producing new ideas and marketing products and services to diverse populations. It is harder to justify diversity-based affirmative action in employment for routinized blue- and pink-collar jobs that do not ask their occupants to contribute ideas, or for enterprises that produce undifferentiated commodities such as oil and coal, or undifferentiated services such as driving a bus or delivering mail. The diversity model seems inapplicable to much government contracting: it is hard to see how having a diverse set of subcontractors improves a road-building project. It even has a hard time explaining the scope of racial preferences by educational institutions. While it is plausible that the racial diversity of a classroom would enhance discussion of social, political, and cultural subjects by enriching the variety of perspectives, it is hard to see the cognitive relevance of racial diversity to investigations in mathematics, engineering, or the physical sciences. Yet schools extend racial preferences in admission to graduate programs in the latter fields.[22]

Second, the diversity model, when separated from considerations of justice, cannot account for the special *weight* institutions give to race compared to other dimensions of diversity. In principle, race should figure no more than other background factors that affect a person's perspective, such as practicing an unusual religion, having lived abroad, or having grown up on a farm. In practice, schools give race enough weight to produce a "critical mass" of students from disadvantaged racial groups but are satisfied with mere token representation of people with other unusual backgrounds. The special weight given to admitting U.S. citizens from disadvantaged racial groups is even stranger. Blacks in the United States are as American as apple pie: they bring less cultural diversity to American schools than blacks, Asians, and Latinos from abroad and are already more heavily represented than the latter in most schools. Yet schools still place greater weight on admitting American blacks than the latter groups.

Third, the diversity model, when separated from justice concerns, promotes racial myths that may be stigmatizing. In stressing how different African Americans are from other Americans, it potentially primes stereotypes of blacks as alien and blocks recognition of common perspectives and identities. To the extent that it avoids issues of social justice, treats racial groups on a par with cultural groups, and refuses to specify precisely what kind of diversity race brings to the table,[23] the diversity model invites the inference that the diversity represented by race is a matter of racially distinct cultures. Yet "race" denotes an identity group, a social category that has been made the basis of social inequality by means of in-group closure and out-group stigmatization. This is not the same as a cultural group.[24] To suppose otherwise invites several potentially injurious ideas. In searching for the supposedly cultural content of black difference, people are liable to fix on stigmatizing representations of blacks in the folk anthropological account of black disadvantage, attributing such "underclass" behavior as gang membership, criminal conduct, welfare dependence, disdain for "acting white," and single teenage childbearing as cultural values of the black community (§4.3). Blacks who do not conform to these stereotypes may thereby appear to be not "diverse" enough to satisfy the diversity model, while those who behave in ways that trigger these stereotypes (say, in listening to gangsta rap or wearing dreadlocks) may appear to lack the values needed to succeed in mainstream institutions and hence seem unqualified to participate. The multiculturalist account of diversity also suggests that all "cultural" differences ought to be celebrated and preserved. This thought undermines the quest for racial equality insofar as it insists on self-segregation within mainstream institutions for the sake of cultural preservation, and on the preservation of distinct forms of cultural capital, when black advancement requires social integration and the construction of common forms of cultural capital (§2.3, §6.1). Finally, the representation of the difference blacks make to institutions as "cultural" invites the misleading thought that "all blacks think alike."

The last thought misunderstands how the logic of diversity works. Consider the argument that students of ecology, to fully grasp biodiversity, need to study plants not just in temperate regions but in the tropics. This argument, far from supposing that all tropical plants are alike, claims that the class of tropical plants includes a range of diverse characteristics not well represented among temperate plants. Similarly, the diversity defense says not that all blacks think alike, but that blacks have a range of diverse experiences and perspectives not well represented by the range of experiences and perspectives of members in other groups. This claim is hard to square with a cultural representation of the relevance of race. Cultures are understood, at least within folk anthropology, as shared, and hence as bases of in-group homogeneity. What is needed is an account of the difference race makes that is not cultural in this sense.

A fourth objection to the diversity model is that, in treating race as a proxy for relevant features—diversity of ideas and perspectives—it has a hard time explaining why institutions should not select directly for diverse ideas. If all that matters is that the whole range of ideas worth considering should be heard, why care about the racial identities of those who voice them? Schools should simply select students for ideological diversity, rather than using race as a crude proxy for this.[25] Furthermore, if diversity of ideas is all that matters, why do we need the actual presence of racially diverse persons in schools? Why can't instructors and reading assignments represent all the diversity of information and opinion students need?

Finally, the diversity model, when divorced from social justice, raises worries about the justification of racial preferences in terms of institutional goals. If such goals are sufficient to justify racial preferences in favor of disadvantaged groups, why aren't they sufficient to justify discrimination *against* these groups?[26] People in racially heterogeneous groups feel more stress and conflict than when they are in racially homogeneous groups.[27] Yet diversity advocates do not allow that an institution's interest in promoting internal work group harmony by means of racial homogeneity may override its interest in epistemic diversity.

An adequate model of affirmative action would explain the full scope and weight given to race in the institutions that practice it. It would not represent the significance of race in misleading ways that trigger alienating or stigmatizing stereotypes. It would not represent race as a proxy for some independently relevant characteristic that could be directly targeted. It would explain why the presence of blacks is needed in institutions, and not just their ideas. Finally, it would explain why, if the role of racial preferences in affirmative action is instrumental to institutional goals, such goals cannot justify preferences for racial homogeneity.

7.4 The Discrimination-Blocking Model

The discrimination-blocking model of affirmative action focuses on the practical difficulties of stopping current discrimination in a world saturated with stigmatizing stereotypes of disadvantaged groups and structured by entrenched habits that favor advantaged groups. To remedy this problem, merely passing antidiscrimination laws is insufficient to stop discrimination. Affirmative action is needed. In this model (1) the agents eligible to practice affirmative action are any institutions that are still discriminating. (2) The targets of affirmative action are qualified members of disadvantaged groups who would not gain access to opportunities in the absence of affirmative action. (3) Discrimination-blocking programs generally allow only "tie-breaking" preferences for members of disadvantaged groups. (4) The costs to innocents are very small since racial preferences that override meritocratic criteria are generally not involved. (5) Race, in the discrimination-blocking model, helps identify those who, but for affirmative action, would be victims of ongoing discrimination. (6) The discrimination-blocking model represents *current* discrimination as the fundamental cause of unjust race-based disadvantage.

The discrimination-blocking model arose from the experience of administrative agencies charged with enforcing antidiscrimination laws. They found that after the passage of antidiscrimination laws, nothing changed. Employers continued to discriminate, and members of groups suffering from discrimination made virtually no inroads into occupations and businesses that had been excluding them. The complaint remedy, based on an individualized compensation model, proved ineffective in combating this discrimination. Individual victims of discrimination had a hard time identifying themselves and proving discrimination (§7.2). When they managed to do so and filed suit, they still saw little relief. Huge, intractable caseloads overwhelmed the ability of courts and administrative agencies such as the EEOC to handle them in a timely way.[28] Case-by-case litigation imposed enormous costs on plaintiffs and employers alike.

Why does discrimination persist, despite antidiscrimination laws? Whenever the law has attempted to dismantle antiblack segregation and discrimination, it has met with massive resistance from recalcitrant whites. This was true for abolition, voting rights, school desegregation, and housing desegregation. It is true for equal employment opportunity as well. When recalcitrant actors repeatedly refuse to stop discriminating, antidiscrimination law must force outcomes on them that mirror what nondiscriminatory processes would produce.[29]

Several additional mechanisms besides deliberate ethnocentric or prejudicial discrimination continue to operate despite antidiscrimination law. Some reflect entrenched habits formed when overt racial discrimination and segregation were the norms. For example, a firm that advertises job openings through word-of-mouth to a racially homogeneous, segregated workforce will continue to reproduce segregation (§2.3).[30] The stereotype incumbency effect (§3.2) is also resistant to change. This may reflect statistical discrimination: managers worry that individuals who do not fit the demographic stereotypes for their jobs will not work out.[31] Or it may reflect evaluative discrimination: demographically nonstandard candidates may *seem* less able to do the job, even if their qualifications are equivalent (§3.5).[32] The stereotype incumbency effect explains why job segregation declines more slowly in older organizations than in newer ones after enforcement of antidiscrimination laws.[33] Aversive racism—where people discriminate when nondiscriminatory rationales are available (§3.1)—has free rein in hiring practices that rely on subjective assessments such as interviews, which are notoriously unreliable vehicles for measuring merit—in part because of anxiety-based discrimination (§3.5).[34]

Discriminatory habits and unconscious evaluative biases can be somewhat offset by group-blind policies that reduce the scope for such biases to operate.[35] Employers can advertise jobs formally, in places excluded groups regularly consult, abolish interviews, and "blind" job applications. They can formalize objective criteria for hiring, firing, and promotion, and reject subjective criteria that leave room for evaluative bias and aversive discrimination. They can create formal promotion ladders linking jobs. Affirmative action policies typically incorporate such group-blind measures.[36]

Yet such measures are not sufficient to eliminate discrimination, especially if it is unconscious. Race can be inferred from many factors, such as applicants' addresses, association memberships, letters of recommendation, schools attended, and vocal signs recognized over the phone. Internal promotion decisions usually cannot be blinded and often rely on softer criteria that cannot be fully shielded from evaluation biases. Because biases can insinuate themselves at many points, formalized group-conscious measurement of outcomes is needed to ensure that discrimination has really ended. Hence, affirmative action programs typically include regular monitoring of employment practices to check for unexplained group disparities.

Even such group-blind measures combined with group conscious monitoring is not enough to stop discrimination in the absence of pressure to improve outcomes in the face of unexplained group inequalities. Habits and unconscious biases continue to operate to the extent that they are not checked by countervailing motives. Hiring goals and timetables help supply such motives.[37] When a firm adopts an affirmative action plan due to a court order in a class action that found systematic discrimination, because of pressure from the EEOC or the Office of Federal Contract Compliance (OFCC), or in voluntary compliance with Title VII, the goal is to achieve a racial composition of workers in each job that reflects the racial composition of the pool of workers qualified for those jobs in the firm's locality.

Critics of such plans complain that they amount to a racial spoils system, reflecting a divisive conception of society as sorted into racial groups, each entitled to its proportional share of opportunities.[38] Yet these plans do not generally require hiring goals out of line with the background qualifications and employment preferences of individuals in each group, as a "proportional representation" system would. They do not assume that racial groups are subjects of distributive claims. Rather, they assume that if employers stopped discriminating, then the racial composition of workers in their jobs would reflect the local racial composition of the pool of workers qualified for those jobs. Substantial, persistent, unexplained group inequalities should be closed because their most likely cause is ongoing discrimination. Since there is no meritocratic justification for these inequalities, whatever business practices are generating them amount to arbitrary obstacles to equal opportunity. The purpose of hiring goals is thus to block current discrimination that unjustly deprives individuals of equal opportunity.[39]

Critics of discrimination-blocking race-conscious affirmative action goals also complain that they lead to reverse discrimination. Although there are some highly publicized cases—for instance, female firefighters—in which qualifying criteria have been substantially relaxed for traditionally excluded groups—the vast majority of employer-based affirmative action plans apply the same hiring and promotion criteria for members of all groups. Neither the purpose nor the result of affirmative action pressure in most employment contexts has been to override meritocratic criteria.[40] Individuals hired or promoted under affirmative action programs perform as well as other employees.[41] Private, for-profit establishments that employ more blacks do not suffer lower productivity than establishments with fewer black employees.[42] Only a handful of reverse discrimination claims have been found credible in the courts.[43]

A mild racial preference does occur when goals are joined with time-tables. Without timetables, vigorous race-conscious outreach would produce a pool of applicants with a racial composition equal to the racial composition of the local qualified talent pool,[44] and race-neutral procedures combined with race-conscious goals would, without any racial preferences, result in hires from that pool with a similar racial composition.[45] However, timetables introduce pressures to reach goals more quickly than would be brought about through a neutral hiring process. In such cases, group preferences function as tiebreakers.

Can the costs of tie-breaking preferences to innocent whites be justified by a discrimination-blocking rationale? Some have defended tiebreakers, or even somewhat stronger preferences, on the grounds that stereotype threat artificially depresses the test performance of stigmatized candidates (§3.4), and that evaluation bias causes their ability to be underestimated.[46] Yet we cannot suppose that such factors always operate—especially not for timetables applied to jobs for which employers do not care about differences in qualifications past a minimal threshold. To justify the urgency implied by timetables, we need to be more future-oriented. The point of trying to quickly achieve proportional hiring goals would then be to eliminate the underlying causes of discrimination—for example, by eliminating the stereotype incumbency bias—rather than just to oppose continuing causes by countervailing forces.

The discrimination-blocking model is indispensable to understanding how affirmative action operates in employment contexts.[47] It introduces no novel or controversial moral principles. It simply requires recognition of the difficulty of avoiding discrimination in contexts organized around discriminatory habits and pervaded by group stigmatization. In the absence of concerted pressure to produce results, discrimination continues to undermine opportunities for stigmatized groups.[48] Discrimination-blocking affirmative action is simply an application of Aristotle's point that to do the right thing in the face of a contrary inclination, we must drag ourselves in the opposite direction, as an archer must aim against the wind to hit the bull's-eye.[49]

Although indispensable, the discrimination-blocking model offers an incomplete rationale for affirmative action. To justify attaching timetables to goals, a more future-oriented rationale is needed—one that represents affirmative action as dismantling the continuing causes of discrimination, rather than simply opposing it with a countervailing force. The discrimination-blocking model also offers an incomplete account of current obstacles to equal opportunity: it focuses only on current discrimination, not on segregation and the lingering effects of past discrimination. This defect is particularly significant for affirmative action in higher education. Human capital deficits are among the stubborn legacies of historic discrimination, perpetuated by continuing segregation (§2.3). To correct for these deficits, selective educational institutions that practice affirmative action give a weight to race that exceeds what can be justified on a discrimination-blocking model. To justify this weight, we need to resort to compensatory or integrative models of affirmative action.

7.5 The Integrative Model

The integrative model of affirmative action begins with the observation that Americans live in a profoundly racially segregated society. De facto racial segregation unjustly impedes socioeconomic opportunities for disadvantaged racial groups, causes racial stigmatization and discrimination, and is inconsistent with a fully democratic society. To remedy these problems, we need to practice racial integration. In this model, (1) the agents eligible to practice affirmative action are any institutions capable of promoting racial integration. (2) The targets of affirmative action are those individuals best placed to act as agents of racial integration. (3) The weight given to preferences for admitting these targets depends on how much integration is needed for its positive effects to be realized. I shall argue below that this justifies seeking a critical mass of any segregated and stigmatized racial group. (4) Since all citizens have a duty to promote the justice of social arrangements, and integration is instrumental to justice, it is just to expect all citizens to bear their fair share of the costs of integration. (5) Race, in the integrative model, is not a proxy for some other relevant characteristics but directly relevant to the integrative mission of affirmative action. (6) The integrative model represents racial segregation and stigmatization as the fundamental causes of unjust race-based disadvantage, treating discrimination as but one consequence of stigmatization. Affirmative action is a tool for dismantling the continuing causes of unjust race-based disadvantage. It offers a comprehensive defense of affirmative action that fits the practice and meets or avoids the objections against the other three models.

The integrative model solves the scope problem by covering all institutions that practice affirmative action. Institutions may promote integration whether or not they have or are engaged in racial discrimination. The integrative model has wider scope than the diversity model because it affirms that integration plays multiple roles, in addition to epistemic ones, in a just and democratic society. Across all domains of interracial interaction, integrative affirmative action helps people learn to cooperate across racial lines, breaks down racial stigmatization, interracial discomfort, and habits of segregation, makes decision makers more aware of and accountable for the impact of their decisions on all racial groups, and invigorates democratic exchange in civil society (chapter 6).

Integration also has distinct roles to play in particular domains. For professional schools, affirmative action helps remedy the severe deficit residents of segregated neighborhoods suffer in access to professional services (§2.2). Black physicians are far more likely than white physicians to locate in underserved minority neighborhoods and serve far more black, Latino, and Medicaid patients, even after controlling for their location.[50] For routinized, unskilled jobs, affirmative action ensures that blacks are not always in the back of the employment queue for lack of social connections. For government contracting, affirmative action promotes the acquisition of social, cultural, and human capital on the part of business owners from disadvantaged segregated groups, increases employment for racial groups suffering from high rates of unemployment, and provides its beneficiaries with experience working for racially diverse clients. In the case of black-owned businesses, the latter functions are particularly important because of the strong relation between the race of owners and the race of their employees. Fifty-eight percent of white-owned firms in major metropolitan areas where minorities live have no minority employees, whereas 89 percent of black-owned firms have workforces that are at least 75 percent minority. This correlation is not merely a function of firm location. Even among white-owned firms located in black neighborhoods, one third still have *no* minority employees.[51] Government contracting programs that favor black-owned businesses thus have a greater impact on reducing stubbornly high black unemployment rates than race-neutral programs because black-owned businesses open opportunities to the social networks to which blacks have access. Such programs also promote integration, by connecting black-owned businesses to a wider, racially diverse customer base.[52]

The integrative model offers a nonstigmatizing representation of affirmative action's targets. It identifies the proper targets of affirmative action as those who can function as agents of integration and destigmatization. They are not passive recipients of compensation delivered to them as victims, but partners with the practitioners of affirmative action in breaking down the barriers that block segregated groups' access to mainstream opportunities. Justice is part of the mission of all institutions of civil society, and the targets of affirmative action play an active, indispensable role in advancing this mission. They therefore win their places on the merits, by virtue of their capacity to contribute to institutional goals through their performance in their role. The beneficiaries of affirmative action play this role in multiple ways, corresponding to the ways integration breaks down segregation and stigmatization and promotes democracy. The targets of affirmative action remain linked to social networks of family, neighborhood, and friendship that are largely black and typically poorer than they are.[53] They serve as sources of social capital to less advantaged black relatives, acquaintances, and neighbors. They transmit human and cultural capital (including knowledge of how to operate successfully in integrated settings).[54] Through demonstrably successful functioning in their roles, the targets of affirmative action help break down racial stereotypes that underlie stigmatization and discrimination. This effect is not simply a matter of bringing counterstereotypical individuals to the attention of other participants in institutions practicing affirmative action. On a larger scale, affirmative action aims to break the public association of blacks with poverty and associated dysfunctional behaviors by moving blacks to secure middle-class positions, reproduced across generations. This reduces statistical discrimination against blacks and destigmatizes by reducing the usefulness of race as a basis for making inferences about an individual's position in society and conduct correlated with that position.[55] Finally, the targets of affirmative action advance the democratic project of integrating civil society in central sites—schools and workplaces—making information about the asymmetric impacts of policies and other social phenomena on segregated communities more salient to others, and holding decision makers accountable for responding to this information.

The integrative model's representation of beneficiaries of affirmative action as agents of justice explains why affirmative action programs tend to select from within the disadvantaged racial groups those who are likely to be better skilled and more highly educated, who have suffered less from the racial caste system than their peers. These individuals are usually better able to perform their integrative roles since successful integration requires successful functioning in the position to which affirmative action opens access. The integrative model is based on a recognition of the fact that sometimes an effective way to help the disadvantaged is to give opportunities to their more privileged peers, who will then be better situated to help them.[56]

The integrative model explains why affirmative action should give enough weight to race to yield a critical mass of representatives from disadvantaged racial groups, beyond tokenism. Integration of a critical mass of workers from underrepresented groups reduces the salience of social-group membership, enables others to view them as individuals, facilitates meritocratic evaluation, and undermines the stereotype incumbency effect (§3.2, §6.3).[57] A critical mass is also needed to raise the probability that whites will have contact with blacks in large institutions, and thereby learn to interact more competently and comfortably with them.[58]

Race, in the integrative model, does not function fundamentally as a proxy for some other morally relevant property. It is the direct object of moral and instrumental concern. It refers not to a biological classification, but to an identity that has been constituted as a ground of categorical inequality through segregation and stigmatization (§8.2). The causal power of a person's race to break down race-based barriers to opportunity through integration is directly linked to these features. If the problem is racial segregation, then the most direct way to remedy this problem is to practice racial integration. Integration directly opens up hoarded opportunities to the targets of affirmative action and their in-group associates (§6.2). As the contact hypothesis holds, institutionally supported cooperative interaction with members of stigmatized groups on terms of equality reduces stigmatization of and discrimination against them (§6.3). As the accountability effect holds, the presence of members of stigmatized or excluded groups as equals in decision-making bodies reduces discrimination and increases responsible deliberation by decision makers (§6.4).

The integrative model might be thought to use race as a proxy in the case of the epistemic diversity effect (§6.4).[59] In the integrative model, epistemic diversity follows from the ways racial segregation and stigmatization shape individuals' experiences. People who live in disadvantaged, segregated communities have personal knowledge of the conditions of life in such communities, as the stigmatized have personal knowledge of what it is like to be stigmatized. These kinds of knowledge, important for just and democratic decision making, are salient to members of stigmatized, segregated groups, and hence likely to be practically engaged. Members of privileged groups who have grown up in racially isolated, sheltered environments have no such personal knowledge or experience. Even if they learn about such matters in books, such knowledge is less likely to be salient or practically engaged, except in integrated settings, where the accountability effect operates.

Even here, at the integrative model's point of closest contact with the diversity model, the former avoids the problems associated with the latter. It does not treat race as a proxy for cultural difference, but as a proxy for personal knowledge of what it is like to live as and be treated as a member of one's race. This latter relationship is so tight—being treated as a member of one's race is a necessary and nearly always sufficient condition of having personal, firsthand knowledge of what this is like—that calling it a "proxy" relation suggests a misleading contingency. This knowledge is inherently dependent on possession of specific racial identities. The integrative model, by refusing to base the epistemic diversity argument on claims of race-based cultural difference, also does not threaten to trigger feelings of alienation, stigmatizing stereotypes of out-group pathology, or exaggerated perceptions of out-group homogeneity.

The integrative model stresses several effects of affirmative action that require the participation of affirmative action's targets in institutions because they work through interracial interaction rather than mediated information exchange. Interracial cooperation more effectively reduces stigmatization than teaching tolerance in segregated settings.[60] The accountability effect depends on interracial interaction. Integrating social networks requires interracial personal acquaintance. Finally, there is one particular kind of know-how that can only be constructed in integrated groups: knowledge of how to effectively cooperate and communicate on terms of equality across group lines, in a relaxed and comfortable way. This requires the construction of common forms of cultural capital. Here, at the one point where the integrative model alludes to race-based cultural differences, the point is not to preserve such differences but for all sides to overcome their mutual ignorance and construct shared norms of respectful interaction.

Instrumental defenses of racial preferences raise the worry that they could be used to justify segregation, or discrimination in favor of advantaged racial groups, if this is useful for achieving sound institutional goals. The integrative model restricts the use of racial preferences to promoting justice and democracy. Optional institutional goals cannot justify racial segregation.

The compensatory, discrimination-blocking, and integrative models identify justice as the goal of affirmative action. They differ in their conceptions of the injustices that require correction, and their accounts of how affirmative action corrects it. For the compensatory model, the core injustice that affirmative action aims to remedy is past racial discrimination. Its remedy is post hoc: it waits for discrimination to happen and compensates for its effects after the fact. This stance raises questions about how long claims to compensation for long-past acts of discrimination should last. The discrimination-blocking model avoids this challenge by focusing on current discrimination. But it still offers a limited discrimination-based account of the causes of unjust racial disadvantage and only blocks discrimination without attacking its underlying causes. For the integrative model, the core injustices that affirmative action aims to remedy are segregation and stigmatization. Segregation has unjust effects that are not mediated by discrimination (§§2.2–2.4, §3.7). So does stigmatization: it constitutes an expressive harm (§3.3), depresses performance through stereotype threat (§3.4), and promotes public policies that have harsh differential impacts on the stigmatized (§3.6). The integrative model takes a proactive stance toward these injustices: its aim is to *dismantle* the continuing causes of racial injustice.

This chapter has examined four models of affirmative action: compensatory, diversity, discrimination-blocking, and integrative. All but the diversity model aim at correcting race-based injustice. The compensatory model survives the conventional criticisms lodged against it but suffers from a limited account of the causes of current unjust race-based disadvantages, threatens to stigmatize the targets of affirmative action by failing to represent them as meritorious, lacks a clear explanation of why many affirmative action programs target the better-off within target groups, and raises worries about how much longer these programs can be justified. The diversity model avoids or answers these challenges but fails to account for the scope and weight of affirmative action preferences, invites ideas about racial differences that threaten to trigger alienating or stigmatizing stereotypes, and faces difficulties in explaining why, if race is a proxy, the relevant characteristic cannot be directly targeted instead, why people rather than disembodied ideas need to be present, and why, if racial preferences can be justified as instrumental to institutional goals, they cannot be turned against disadvantaged groups. The discrimination-blocking model relies on uncontroversial normative premises, avoids stigmatizing the targets of affirmative action, has a better account than the compensatory model of the causes of current race-based injustice, and explains why affirmative action is still needed today. The minimal weight it gives to racial preferences overcomes conventional meritocratic objections to affirmative action and explains how most affirmative action programs work in employment contexts. It is an indispensable model. But it does not account for the full scope and weight of racial preferences in affirmative action and suffers from an incomplete account of the causes of race-based injustice. The integrative model offers a complete account of the scope and weight of affirmative action preferences and of race-based injustice and answers or avoids the objections to the other models. It is uniquely proactive: instead of waiting for injustice to happen and compensating afterward, or merely blocking discriminatory mechanisms that retain their force, it aims to dismantle the continuing causes of race-based injustice by practicing integration, which is an essential tool for undoing segregation and stigmatization.

· EIGHT ·

THE FOLLY AND INCOHERENCE OF COLOR BLINDNESS

8.1 Color Blindness as Ideal, Policy, and Principle

The preceding defense of race-based affirmative action policies does not address what many critics have thought to be a decisive objection: that they offend the moral requirement of color blindness. This chapter finds this supposed moral requirement to be conceptually confused, empirically misguided, and lacking a morally coherent rationale.

Color blindness can be understood as a moral ideal or a policy. As an ideal, color blindness extols a world in which no one draws racial distinctions. In such a world, race would no longer serve as a basis for social inequality, segregation, or stigmatization. It would also no longer serve as a basis for ethnocentric identification or affiliation, even if this never led to racial inequality.

As a policy, color blindness rejects intentional uses of racial preferences by institutions. Some advocates of color-blind policy reject racial preferences for their purportedly bad consequences: they are divisive, stigmatizing, and inefficient, depress motivation, and harm their intended beneficiaries. These advocates also claim that if only people would stop intentionally discriminating by race, then racial discrimination would end.

Other advocates of color-blind policy reject racial preferences on principle. They claim that formally race-conscious preferences and sometimes also underlying race-conscious purposes are inherently morally objectionable. Various accounts of their supposedly inherent moral flaws include that they mistakenly treat races as really existing, are vengeful or racist, discriminate on irrelevant grounds, violate the principle of merit, depend on unsound collectivist conceptions of justice, regard their intended beneficiaries paternalistically, and offend individuality by evaluating people according to racial stereotypes. To distinguish such grounds for color-blind policy from consequentialist ones, I shall refer to them separately as underwriting a color-blind *principle*.

I shall argue that the color-blind principle is conceptually confused because it conflates several distinct meanings of race. Some do not refer to actual entities, some are morally arbitrary, but others refer to causally and morally significant entities. The concept of race as it figures in the integrative and discrimination-blocking programs discussed in chapters 6–7 is of the last sort.

The color-blind principle is also morally confused. To have standing as a moral principle, it must show that there is something *inherently* morally objectionable in race-conscious policies. Every attempt to expose an inherently illegitimate purpose to race-conscious policies confuses contingent with inherent features. The integrative programs discussed in chapters 6–7 do not fall afoul of the objections purported to be inherent in race-conscious policies.

Color blindness as a policy grounded in consequentialist considerations is empirically misguided. Discrimination cannot be stopped by ending color-conscious policies. Even perfect color-blind enforcement of antidiscrimination laws is inadequate to the task of ending racial segregation, stigmatization, and discrimination. These laws reflect an empirically inadequate account of the mechanisms of discrimination and racial inequality, were designed with loopholes, and often lack serious enforcement power. They are weak tools for ending race-based injustice.

Many advocates of color-blind policy point to bad consequences of race-conscious preferences for the racially stigmatized. Some of these consequences—racial resentment and stigmatization—may be real. But they are predicated on stigmatizing representations of the disadvantaged and should therefore be discounted. Stigma and resentment would exist even in the absence of race-conscious policies, while these policies have the long-term effect of reducing these costs. Hence, these policies should continue notwithstanding their short-term costs.

The ideal of color blindness has genuine moral appeal. It may be a valid ideal. But it has no direct application in our nonideal world. The best way to achieve it may even be to adopt race-conscious integrative policies.

The uses of racial preferences and classifications for the purpose of promoting racial integration, as in the race-conscious integrative policies examined in chapters 6–7, are not undermined by any coherent objection from color blindness, whether this is construed as an ideal, a policy grounded in principle, or a policy grounded in consequentialist considerations. To understand this point, we must distinguish several concepts of race, reason from an empirically adequate conception of the causes of race-based disadvantage, and sort out contingent from inherent moral problems with different uses of racial preferences.

8.2 The Color-Blind Principle Is Conceptually Confused: Multiple Concepts of Race

Several conceptual distinctions must be drawn within the family of concepts expressed by the term "race."[1] All such concepts, to count as "racial," must include the following three elements: (1) real or imagined bodily differences (as of skin color and hair texture), marking their bearers as (2) sharing real or imagined ancestors, who (3) have a real or imagined common geographical origin.[2] Call this concept *minimal race*. In the United States today, dominated by a racial classification system David Hollinger has called the "ethnoracial pentagon,"[3] the continents roughly define the geographical origins of different races' ancestors. Thus, blacks have ancestors from Africa (who were born in Africa after humans settled the other continents, and prior to the European colonialist era); whites, from Europe (and not from any other continent in the same time period); Latinos, from Latin America; Asians, from Asia; Native Americans, from North America.[4] In the nineteenth and early twentieth centuries, racial classifications were more fine-grained because they were attached to ideas of national or ethnic distinction (as of Slavs, Celts, Semites, etc.).

Such minimal racial concepts may lead to, but are not enough to rationalize, out-group stigmatization. There is nothing in the bare ideas of superficial bodily difference or ancestral origins to rationalize contempt, fear, hatred, or ideologies of racial inferiority. For a racial concept to figure in stigmatizing representations, it must add the idea that racial groups (4) differ in normatively significant character traits and talents, as of intelligence, honesty, sobriety, criminality, laziness, and licentiousness, that can be traced to causes intrinsic to the group or its members. Call the concept of race including features 1–4 *character race*. The notion of causes "intrinsic" to the group includes such possibilities as free choice, group culture (in the folk anthropological sense of §4.3), and genetic differences but excludes situational explanations of racial differences, such as a socially imposed differential access to resources. The concept of race in the nineteenth and early twentieth centuries held that different racial groups (5) constitute biologically distinct subspecies, in which genetic differences determine character differences (4). Call the concept of race including features 1–5 *biological race*. Current American folk concepts of race downplay ideas of genetic difference while retaining stigmatizing content (§3.2). They count as species of character but not biological race.

The concept of race that figures in social scientific theories of categorical inequality, and in normative defenses of integration and affirmative action, does not assert any intrinsic connection between race and normatively significant character traits. It recognizes that *ideas* about such connections figure in ideologies that rationalize race-based categorical inequality and processes of stigmatization, segregation, and discrimination. It adds to minimal race the idea that (6) people differentiated by features 1–3 are *represented as* differentially possessing normatively significant character traits and talents for reasons intrinsic to them, in ways that are used to *justify* practices of categorical inequality (segregation, stigmatization, discrimination), and that (7) such representations help *cause* such practices. The concept including features 1–3, 6, and 7 is that of a *racialized* group.[5] Racialized groups stand to character races as demonized people (such as those accused of being witches) stand to evil demons. *Normative* uses of the idea of a racialized group hold (8) that the representations in 6 are false, and that the practices based on them (7) are unjust.

These distinctions help us see that *not all "discrimination on the basis of race" is discrimination on the same basis.* Discrimination on the basis of minimal race is a form of pure unrationalized ethnocentric or prejudicial discrimination. Minimal race grounds an arbitrary notion of social identity, of who "we" are, that triggers in-group favoritism, and perhaps also inarticulate feelings of alienation from groups identified as "not us." Discrimination on the basis of minimal race treats 1–3—common ancestry, a common "homeland," or a vague aesthetic sense attached to "looking like us"—as intrinsically normatively relevant. Discrimination on the basis of character race is manifested in statistical and evaluative discrimination and also figures in prejudicial discrimination, if it is rationalized by racist ideologies. Such discrimination treats 1–3 as proxies for normatively significant intrinsic traits (4)—virtues and vices, talents and incapacities—that warrant favorable or unfavorable treatment and regard. Discrimination on the basis of biological race works the same way. Here, the appeal to genetics (5) secures the claim that the normatively significant traits (4) are intrinsic. Discrimination on the basis of racialization, as it occurs in compensatory, discrimination-blocking, and integrative affirmative action, and in other integrative policies, treats the facts of being unjustly stigmatized (6, 8) and therefore being liable to unjust treatment (7, 8) as normatively relevant features that warrant compensation or inclusion (§7.2, §§7.4–7.5). Such discrimination does not treat ancestry, geographical origins, or biological differences among racialized groups to be normatively relevant, nor does it regard racialized groups as differing intrinsically in any virtue or talent.

Failure to distinguish the different concepts of race has led to misguided criticisms of affirmative action. Justices Stewart and Rehnquist rejected an affirmative action policy on the ground that "[d]istinctions between citizens solely because of their ancestry are by their very nature odious to a free people whose institutions are founded upon the doctrine of equality."[6] They mistakenly assumed that affirmative action discriminates simply on the basis of minimal race. To ward off the thought that the affirmative action program in question took minimal race as a proxy for a normatively relevant feature, Stewart and Rehnquist dogmatically asserted that "The color of a person's skin and the country of his origin are immutable facts that bear no relation to ability, disadvantage, moral culpability, or any other characteristics of constitutionally permissible interest to government."[7] Yet as the judgment of the Court made clear, the program was justified precisely because "the color of a person's skin and the country of his origin" do bear a close, if contingent (nonintrinsic) relation to disadvantage in the United States—in the form of unjust *racialization*. Unjust racialization is plainly a characteristic "of constitutionally permissible interest to government." It was the core concern underlying the Fourteenth Amendment as well as the Thirteenth Amendment's prohibition of all of the "badges and incidents" of slavery.[8]

There are two ways to deny that there is a tight connection between minimal race and unjust racialization. One is to point to the fact that some blacks are financially well off and occupy prestigious jobs. This confuses class disadvantage with racial disadvantage. Poverty is but one consequence of race-based disadvantage. The core features of race-based disadvantage are segregation and stigmatization, which blacks do not escape with higher class status. Blacks' levels of segregation do not decline with higher class standing (§2.1), greatly exceed what blacks would voluntarily choose for themselves, reflect antiblack stigmatization (§§4.1–4.2), and damage the economic opportunities of middle-class and poor blacks alike (chapters 2–3).[9] The mere perception of a black person's race, regardless of class, triggers stigmatizing thoughts, evaluative and anxious discrimination, and demeaning interaction rituals (§3.3, §3.5). The second way to deny a tight connection between minimal race and unjust racialization is to reduce the latter to personal victimization by illegal discrimination. This ignores the fact that discrimination against individual members of a segregated group spreads its injuries to their same-race associates (§3.7). It also ignores the fact that being racially stigmatized is not an individual, private event, but a *public* stamp of dishonor on a racial group. Racial stigmatization imposes an expressive harm on individuals simply by virtue of their group membership (§3.3). Hence, to deny a tight connection between race and unjust race-based disadvantage is empirically deluded.

Which concepts of race figure in the color-blind principle? Plainly, minimal, character, and biological race do. Does the color-blind principle also forbid taking *unjust racialization* as a normatively relevant feature that could justify differential treatment of individuals? If not, it is irrelevant to the debates over the justice of affirmative action, and of all other race-conscious integrative policies that aim to dismantle the causes of unjust racialization.

8.3 The Color-Blind Principle Is Morally Incoherent

Our first task is to consider whether the reasons given by advocates of the color-blind principle against discrimination on the basis of minimal, character, and biological race are also reasons against discrimination on the basis of unjust racialization. Here we are concerned only with arguments that there is something *inherently* objectionable about differential treatment of individuals on the basis of their racialized status. In §8.4 we will consider claims that such discrimination has bad consequences.

Advocates of the color-blind principle have advanced the following reasons for thinking that racial discrimination is inherently wrong: (1) it is *irrational*; (2) race-conscious purposes express illegitimate *racist* attitudes; (3) racial discrimination violates principles of *fairness* and *merit*; (4) it expresses a *racially divisive* conception of the proper relations among racial groups, or (5) it misconceives individuals as mere tokens of their racial type, thereby *offending their claim to be regarded as individuals*. I shall argue that none of these reasons applies to discrimination on the basis of racialized status for discrimination-blocking or integrative purposes, and most also do not apply to such discrimination for compensatory purposes.

Irrationality

Racial discrimination may be thought to be irrational on either of two grounds. First, it is sometimes claimed that races do not exist. Since it is irrational to discriminate between people on the basis of a nonexistent feature, it is irrational to discriminate on the basis of race.

The conceptual distinctions drawn in §8.2 help us assess this claim. Minimal races do exist in a *very* rough way, in the sense that possession of particular physical features is often a sign that a person has ancestors from a particular region. This claim must be qualified, however, because the physical features that define popular racial stereotypes do not all originate from the same regions and hence do not always cluster as the stereotypes prescribe; there is substantial overlap in body features among minimal racial groups and much differentiation in body features within these groups.

Character races, including biological races,[10] do not exist. There are no normatively significant intrinsic character differences among groups picked out by any set of criteria for minimal race. Yet racialized groups do exist in many countries, including the United States. (Compare: that demons don't exist doesn't imply that demonized people don't exist. That it is irrational to discriminate against people on the ground of their purported demonhood doesn't imply that it is irrational to help people on the ground that they have been unjustly demonized.) Thus, the first argument of irrationality does not apply to discrimination on the basis of racialization for purposes of correcting, blocking, or undoing race-based disadvantage.

Second, it is sometimes claimed that racial discrimination is irrational because it is *arbitrary*. The charge of arbitrariness is usually valid as applied to discrimination on the basis of minimal race. Discriminating for or against individuals simply on account of the geographical origins of their ancestors, or the trivial bodily differences associated with this, is usually morally arbitrary. There are some exceptions to this rule—for example, in casting individuals for a play about characters whose body features or minimal race figure in the plot.

The arbitrariness charge has also been made against statistical discrimination. Here the claim is that, because character races do not exist, such discrimination is arbitrary. This objection is weak. The criteria for minimal race, because they are incorporated into the criteria for racialized groups, are correlated with morally relevant criteria such as educational attainment and having a felony conviction (§2.1). Minimal race is typically less costly to detect than the underlying relevant criteria. This can make statistical discrimination on the basis of minimal race instrumentally rational, even if the correlations are not due to character races but to racialization. Moral objections to statistical discrimination must therefore lie elsewhere.[11]

The arbitrariness charge as applied to discrimination on the basis of *unjust racialization* is misguided. Being a past or likely present victim of unjust racialization is a morally relevant characteristic for purposes of compensatory and prophylactic (discrimination-blocking) justice. In these cases, discrimination on behalf of blacks is a form of statistical discrimination, taking minimal race as a proxy for being subject to unjust race-based disadvantage. Given the costs of directly measuring degrees of subjection to race-based disadvantage, and the difficulties of preventing unconscious and recalcitrant unjust discrimination, these kinds of statistical discrimination are rationally related to a just purpose (§7.2, §7.4), and more narrowly tailored to that purpose than any other feasible and cost-effective policy.[12]

Discrimination on the basis of unjust racialization for purposes of integration and destigmatization does not take racialization as a proxy for some other relevant characteristic. Rather, racialized status itself—being a member of a racially segregated and stigmatized group (rather than being a specific victim of discrimination or its effects)—is the relevant feature of interest. Belonging to a racially stigmatized group is the causal factor generating the epistemic diversity and accountability effects of integration that promote a democratic culture and a democratically qualified and responsible elite (§5.2, §5.3, §6.4), as well as the intergroup contact effects that reduce racial stigmatization, stereotyping, and discrimination (§6.3). Belonging to a racially segregated group is the constitutively relevant factor making a person an agent of racial integration. Racial integration is an end required by justice, since racial segregation is a fundamental cause of unjust race-based material and social psychological disadvantages (chapters 2–3), and integration helps dismantle these injustices (chapter 6). Since these purposes are just, and racialized status is directly relevant to achieving them, discrimination by racialized status for these purposes is not morally arbitrary or irrelevant, but instrumentally rational and morally justified.

Racism

Racism, as a psychological phenomenon and moral vice, consists of *prejudice* (consciously endorsed antipathy toward a racial group), *stigmatizing stereotypes* (consciously endorsed representations of the group as meriting such antipathies), or consciously harmful *conduct* toward the group that expresses these antipathies or stereotypes (§3.1). Advocates of the color-blind principle sometimes claim that racial discrimination is wrong because it is racist. This is true of the systematic racial discrimination that characterized slavery and Jim Crow in the United States, and of some racial discrimination today. Yet it does not apply to pure unrationalized ethnocentric discrimination on the basis of minimal race since in-group favoritism is distinct from out-group prejudice (§3.5). And it applies only in an attenuated sense to statistical racial discrimination, which need not be committed to character races and is more cognitive than affective.

This has not stopped advocates of the color-blind principle from attacking race-based affirmative action for manifesting racial prejudice. Sometimes affirmative action is thought to rest on a principle of *hostile retaliation* against whites, conceived as guilty of discrimination.[13] Sometimes the racism charge is expressed in the thought that affirmative action amounts to "discrimination for its own sake" or "naked racial preference."[14] These criticisms are misguided since no form of race-based affirmative action discussed in chapter 7 enacts racial preferences as ends in themselves, and none is grounded in racial antipathy. All regard racial preferences as instrumental to some further legitimate goal—compensation, enhancing education, blocking ongoing discrimination, undoing segregation and stigmatization.

Some critics claim that affirmative action is committed to a kind of racial paternalism, contemptuously representing blacks as innately inferior, unable to succeed on their own and hence in need of special help.[15] This objection misrepresents how affirmative action conceives of its targets. Diversity-based and integrative affirmative action represent their targets as making distinctive meritorious contributions to the institutions that admit them. Discrimination-blocking affirmative action represents its targets as no less qualified than others. Compensatory affirmative action represents its targets as competitively disadvantaged due to extrinsically imposed injustices, not intrinsic defects. Thus, none of the forms of affirmative action discussed in chapter 7 expresses antipathy or contempt toward any racial group.

Violations of Principles of Fairness and Merit

It is sometimes claimed that racial discrimination is unfair because it is based on involuntary, unchosen characteristics. This is not a persuasive explanation of what makes racial discrimination wrong. Rather, the claim to be selected on characteristics that can be affected by the agent applies only to contexts where meritocratic selection is apt, and where the underlying merits are themselves affected by choice, effort, or practice (§3.5). The complaint that racial discrimination is unfair on meritocratic grounds should therefore be based on this narrower claim.

A "merit" is any characteristic of individuals whereby they advance an institution's proper mission through their performance in an institutional role. Promoting justice and democracy are among the proper missions of the institutions that practice affirmative action. Racial integration advances these missions. Membership in a racialized group that is relatively scarce in an institution is a constitutive qualification of individuals who can function as agents of racial integration. Hence, possession of such a racialized identity counts as a merit for institutions practicing integrative affirmative action. It is the basis for the accountability, contact, and destigmatizing effects of integration and is a necessary condition for the epistemic diversity effect of racial integration (§7.5). Diversity-based affirmative action also respects meritocratic standards, although it uses race as looser proxy for a more open-ended notion of epistemic or cultural diversity (§7.3).

Racialized status is not a merit, or a proxy for merit, in the other two types of affirmative action. In discrimination-blocking affirmative action, it is a proxy for liability to unjust underestimation of one's merits or exclusion from meritocratic consideration. Racial preference blocks forms of discrimination that violate meritocratic criteria and thereby helps institutions come closer to reaching meritocratic outcomes.

Matters are more complicated for compensatory affirmative action. To the extent that racialized status is an accurate proxy for subjection to discrimination by the institution practicing affirmative action, compensation tracks the unjust denial of access to a merited opportunity and thus generates what meritocratic evaluation would have produced. Usually, however, there is not such a tight fit between benefiting from affirmative action and subjection to prior discrimination. Rather, compensation is for the more diffuse *effects* of discrimination on the racialized group targeted for preferential treatment. These include competitive disadvantages due to a relative lack of opportunity to develop human capital in decent schools, on the job, and from well-placed social connections (§2.3). Insofar as this is true, members of unjustly racialized groups manifest a greater gap between actual achievements and underlying potential than others. This supports the view that ex ante achievements are not a fair way to measure merit or desert.

Whether an opportunity was deserved can be vindicated instead on the basis of ex post achievements. One can deserve an opportunity in the sense that one will make good use of it if it is offered.[16] In employment contexts, opportunities provided by affirmative action are largely vindicated in this way and thus do not violate meritocratic criteria (§7.4). In educational contexts, affirmative action does not close the racial gap in formal academic achievement. Hence, to vindicate affirmative action on meritocratic grounds in education requires appeal to criteria other than formal academic achievement. Compensatory affirmative action in education, if not supplemented by diversity or integrative rationales, does not satisfy meritocratic principles.

Whether violating meritocratic standards is an injustice is a separate matter. In educational contexts, the stress on merit is dubious since a main purpose of education is to *develop* people's merits. One can hardly justify depriving people of further education on meritocratic grounds, when the cause of their relative lack of educational qualifications can be traced to prior failures in the educational system. The stress on merit makes more sense in employment. One rationale for meritocratic hiring is efficiency. But efficiency is an institutional goal, not an outcome that actual or prospective participants in an organization have a right to demand as a matter of justice. A second rationale for meritocratic selection is to displace selection practices based on categorical inequality, such as opportunity hoarding and emulation. The classical liberal ideal of "careers open to talents" aimed at dismantling castelike systems of class subordination. Insofar as merit systems fail to achieve this, they cannot serve as standards of justice against which selection methods that better achieve this end should be evaluated.

Our interest in ending unjust categorical inequality suggests a different reason to respect meritocratic selection. Representations of blacks as unqualified and undeserving lie at the core of contemporary modes of racial stigmatization (§3.2). Affirmative action policies that violate apt meritocratic standards reinforce racial stigma. This is why it is important for affirmative action policies to respect, and publicize the ways they respect, meritocratic criteria—in part by expanding our understandings of what counts as merit, and how racialized status is related to merit.

Racial Divisiveness

Some critics of race-based affirmative action suggest that it conceives of society as essentially divided into mutually antagonistic racial blocs, each entitled to their proportionate share of goods. This objection interprets affirmative action as implementing a racial spoils system.[17] Other critics suppose that affirmative action is based on the idea of racial groups as creditor and debtor classes.[18] Both views of how racial groups are or ought to be related to each other are objectionable for being inherently divisive.

The most persuasive justifications of affirmative action avoid these criticisms. Affirmative action can be soundly grounded on individualistic claims (§7.2). Discrimination-blocking affirmative action views gaps between the racial composition of workers in each job and the racial composition of the pool of workers qualified for those jobs in the firm's locality as *evidence* of ongoing discrimination against and exclusion of individuals on account of their racialization, not as a per se unjust distribution of goods to racial groups (§7.4). Integrative affirmative action also depends on an individualistic conception of justice. Individuals have just claims against being segregated and stigmatized on the basis of race. Yet because they are stigmatized on the basis of their group identity, to destigmatize them may require addressing the stigmatization of their group through efforts to raise its status. The charge of conceiving of racial groups in divisive ways is especially inapt, since an aim of integrative affirmative action is to overcome racial division by forging a common in-group identity as citizens cooperating in constructing a democratic culture (§5.1, §5.4, §6.3, §6.4, §7.5).

Offense to Individuality

Some critics of race-based selection complain that it is based on racial stereotypes. This denies people's individuality by treating them as if all members of the same race were alike in some intrinsic characteristic. This is an expressive harm, an offense to people's dignity, even apart from whether the content of the stereotype is stigmatizing.[19] The criticism is valid as applied to statistical discrimination, when this is based on character race. It potentially applies as well to "cultural" understandings of diversity-based affirmative action, although not to the diversity model properly understood, which stresses the internal heterogeneity of racialized groups (§7.3). It is inapplicable to the other types of affirmative action. Compensatory and discrimination-blocking affirmative action treat membership in an unjustly racialized group as a proxy for liability to past or present discrimination. This is an *extrinsic* feature of individuals—a feature of their circumstances, not of their character or talents. Integrative affirmative action treats membership in an unjustly racialized group—an *extrinsic* feature of individuals—as causally relevant, not as a proxy for logically independent intrinsic characteristics. Since these representations are not about intrinsic characteristics, they are not racial stereotypes in any sense that offends individuality.

It might be thought that the contact, epistemic diversity, and accountability effects, on which part of the case for racial integration depends, invoke offensive racial stereotypes of *whites* as racially prejudiced, ignorant, and irresponsible. This errs in three ways. First, the characteristics in question are not features individuals have on account of their skin color, European ancestry, or any intrinsic characteristics thought to be correlated with the bodily marks and geographical origins associated with race. They are not stereotypes of minimal or character race, but rather generalizations about the *extrinsic* features of groups defined by their racialized status—in this case, their *external* circumstance as occupying a superior position in a system of categorical inequality. Second, even these generalizations are not about racialization. They rest on generic truths about the social psychological effects of being privileged by segregation, whether the basis of that segregation is race or any other social category (§1.3, §3.1). Third, the epistemic diversity and accountability effects are not about features of *individuals*, but rather of *cooperating groups defined by their institutional functions*. They claim not that whites are more ignorant and irresponsible than blacks, but rather that racially integrated groups are better informed and more responsible than racially homogeneous groups.

Our search for reasons to think that there is something *inherently* morally objectionable about racial preferences—that there is some ground for accepting color blindness as a moral *principle*, has come up empty-handed. The standard reasons offered by proponents of the color-blind principle, initially motivated by analyses of what is wrong with discrimination on the basis of minimal and character race, *fail to apply to race-conscious affirmative action and other integrative policies applied to racialized groups.*

The claim that color blindness is a moral principle faces two acute embarrassments. One is *Brown v. Board of Education,* which held that ending racial segregation was a constitutional imperative and a require-ment of justice, and its successor cases, notably *Swann v. Charlotte-Mecklenburg*

Board of Education, which held that race-conscious assignment of students to schools may be necessary to achieve this goal. It is hard to see how race-conscious selection can be simultaneously inherently morally wrong and required by justice. To account for this anomaly, advocates of the color-blind principle carve out an ad hoc exception: "there is only one circumstance in which the States may act by race to 'undo the effects of past discrimination': where that is necessary to eliminate their own maintenance of a system of unlawful racial classification."[20] This restriction on the systems of unjust racial classification that may be remedied by race-conscious means to *illegal* systems *maintained by the remedying agents* is morally arbitrary and legally absurd. There is no sound reason in justice or constitutional law why any agency in a position to dismantle unjust systems of racial stratification may not do so using race-conscious means, whether these systems are their own creation or that of other agents, and even if these systems are not illegal.[21] The state has interests in justice and democracy in counteracting legal "discrimination in contact" by actively promoting the racial integration of schools and workplaces.

The second embarrassment concerns the distinction between race-conscious means and race-conscious ends. Does the color-blind principle forbid only the use of race-conscious means, or does it also forbid the pursuit of race-conscious ends by race-neutral means? If only the means are forbidden but the ends allowed, then the elaborate system of facially race-neutral laws with the avowed purpose and effect of disenfranchising blacks throughout the Jim Crow South—including literacy tests, poll taxes, grandfather clauses, selective felon disenfranchisement, and arbitrary voter registration requirements—are permissible under the color-blind principle. To block this result, some advocates of color blindness argue that race-conscious *ends* should also be forbidden, even if they are pursued by race-neutral means.[22] This principle would forbid race-neutral selection policies, such as the University of Texas policy to admit the top 10 percent of each graduating high school class in the state, chosen with regard to their expected impact on the racial composition of the university. This policy was adopted for the purpose of mitigating the racial impact of *Hopwood v. Texas,* which forbad race-based affirmative action in the states covered by the 5th circuit.[23] A principle forbidding even race-neutral means to such race-conscious purposes would effectively require states to perpetuate and spread the devastating effects on disadvantaged racial groups of segregation and discrimination by actors other than themselves. It would give whites a right to lock in the relative advantages they enjoy due to continued segregation, stigmatization, and discrimination in society, and even to insist that these advantages be propagated and multiplied through the rest of society since any attempt to mitigate such effects would be impermissibly race-conscious.

Many advocates of color blindness reject such a patently unjust position. They acknowledge that the race-conscious ends of affirmative action are justified, and they object only to the use of race-conscious means.[24] But if the race-conscious ends are justified—if aiming at racial integration is fine—then how could it be wrong to achieve this aim by the most relevant and narrowly tailored means available, which is race-conscious selection? To object to race-conscious means while accepting the race-conscious end is to make a fetish of the superficial form of policy.[25]

8.4 The Costs of Race-Conscious Policy

Advocates of color-blind policy on consequentialist grounds attribute several bad consequences to racial preferences. They depress individual motivation and performance and lead to institutional inefficiency. They harm their intended beneficiaries, by placing them in institutions where they cannot compete. They increase racial resentment and divisiveness, racial prejudice and stigmatization.

We have already refuted the institutional efficiency argument. Integrative and diversity-based affirmative action contribute to institutional goals and so do not compromise efficiency. Discrimination-blocking affirmative action in the workplace has no adverse impact on worker productivity. Race-based affirmative action as practiced by academically selective schools depresses the average ex ante academic achievement of entering classes. However, the mission of these schools is not to maximize academic achievement, but to educate an elite best qualified to serve a democratic society. Fulfillment of that mission requires integration of people from all walks of life since an elite insulated from disadvantaged groups is an incompetent elite (§5.4).

More plausible is the claim that racial preferences depress the achievement motivation of their intended beneficiaries.[26] Why work so hard, if one will get into a selective school through affirmative action? Yet equally plausible is the claim that the presence of only token numbers of blacks in selective schools depresses motivation, by making life in such schools a lonely, alienating experience for blacks, lacking in social support and understanding, and by suggesting to blacks that they are academically so far behind that attempting to gain admission by working harder would be futile. It is impossible to choose between these hypotheses without empirical evidence, which appears to be lacking. Let us suppose that racial preferences do somewhat depress academic motivation. This would be a genuine cost, but trifling in comparison with the costs of perpetuating segregation.

Many critics of race-based affirmative action in education argue that it harms its intended beneficiaries by mismatching them to schools where they are unable to compete. Unprepared for the demanding curricula of selective colleges, they are more likely to drop out. Discouraged by how poorly they do relative to their better qualified white peers, they lower their aspirations and are less likely to pursue advanced degrees.[27] An important source of systematic evidence for the mismatch hypothesis is a paper by Linda Loury and David Garman, which found that the lower a black student's academic credentials were relative to those of the median student at his or her school, the less likely the student was to graduate. Because graduation affects economic prospects, blacks with low SAT scores who attended less selective schools had higher incomes than those who attended more selective schools.[28] Suggestive evidence for the mismatch hypothesis comes from the historically black colleges (HBCs). Most HBCs are unselective and educate a disproportionate percentage of economically disadvantaged students with low SAT scores. Although only 16 percent of black college students are enrolled at HBCs, they account for 27 percent of all black bachelors' degrees and 35 percent of black Ph.D.s.[29] Their graduation rates are 17 percent higher than the graduation rates of similarly qualified blacks at majority-white institutions.[30] The mismatch hypothesis claims that HBCs excel because of peer group effects: black students with mediocre academic credentials can shine at an HBC, but selective schools crush their confidence and ambition by ranking them at the bottom of the class.[31]

The most comprehensive study of the consequences of race-based affirmative action disconfirms the mismatch hypothesis, however. Controlling for standardized test scores, black students at more selective schools graduate and attain advanced degrees at higher rates, earn higher incomes, and report higher satisfaction with their college experience than do students at less selective schools.[32] Loury and Garman's findings have also been explained apart from the mismatch hypothesis: the *entire* favorable effect of lower college selectivity on black graduation rates is due to their inclusion of HBCs. Within majority-white schools, blacks at more selective schools have higher graduation rates and incomes than equally qualified blacks who attended less selective schools.[33] One might argue that black students would still be better off at majority-black HBCs than at any white college. However, the traditional advantages of HBCs for black students have been waning. Black students today who attend majority-white colleges have higher incomes than HBC graduates.[34]

Critics of race-based affirmative action charge that racial preferences are divisive and stigmatizing. Here, the charge applies not to how affirmative action conceives of its beneficiaries (§8.3), but to how it affects public beliefs and attitudes. Racial preferences are divisive, in that they cause whites to resent blacks. They are stigmatizing, in that people interpret affirmative action preferences in a patronizing way, as signs that blacks are not able to compete on their own. This theory predicts that black students in states where affirmative action has been banned should be less stigmatized and face less racial hostility than those who attend schools in states that allow affirmative action. Available data do not confirm this prediction.[35]

Suppose, however, that these are genuine costs of race-based affirmative action. They should not be accepted at face value. *Every* advance in the history of the struggle for black equality has been divisive, in the sense of arousing white resentment. Since this resentment is unjustified, its normative force should be drastically discounted.[36] Moreover, the alternatives—doing nothing, or working on segregation with much less effective race-neutral means (§8.5)—are also divisive, insofar as they allow segregation to persist.

The stigmatizing effects of race-based affirmative action also depend on unjustified racial stereotypes, based on the disposition to attribute blacks' relatively low human capital to their internal traits or cultural values rather than their circumstantial disadvantages (§3.2, §4.3). Given this disposition, the abolition of racial preferences would not reduce stigma, but merely shift its focus. Instead of targeting the beneficiaries of affirmative action for contempt, biased people will infer from the underrepresentation of disadvantaged racial groups in higher positions that members of these groups are generally incapable of functioning successfully in those positions. This is also stigmatizing. Given these biases, affirmative action may be divisive and stigmatizing. But given these biases, racial stigma and divisiveness will exist in any event. The only question is whether to pander to stigma by letting the legacies of white supremacy continue to exclude blacks from mainstream opportunities, or whether to take steps to undo those legacies.

8.5 Color-Blind Policy Is Empirically Misguided

Suppose the objectives of race-conscious policies—integration, destigmatization, and ending unjust racial discrimination—could be achieved by race-neutral means. If these means avoided the costs associated with race-based affirmative action, would it not be preferable to use them? Advocates of color-blind policy, if they support these objectives, favor race-neutral affirmative action and better enforcement of antidiscrimination law on this ground. But their confidence that these tools are effective and less costly means to achieve the objectives of race-conscious policies is misguided.

Consider first race-neutral affirmative action. Some advocates suppose that preferences based on class[37] or geographic location could function as reasonable proxies for race, while avoiding the costs of racial preferences. Class-based preferences would do little to advance racial integration, however. If class is defined in a race-neutral way, the number of lower-class whites who are otherwise academically qualified for selective schools so greatly exceeds the number of comparably qualified lower-class blacks that class-based affirmative action will not generate meaningful racial integration of selective schools.[38] There are also theoretical reasons to believe that it has worse effects on motivation, efficiency, and merit than race-based affirmative action.[39]

Geographical affirmative action, such as the University of Texas's top 10 percent admissions plan, yields higher racial diversity than class-based programs because it piggybacks on de facto racial segregation. However, given the vast differences in the quality of education provided by schools in different neighborhoods, the top 10 percent of the graduating class from the worst high schools in a state is substantially less academically qualified than even the top 40 percent of better schools. Geographical affirmative action would compromise academic standards for members of all races. My point is not that this compromises the principle of merit, which has doubtful application to educational contexts (§8.3). It is that schools must downgrade their curricula to fit students' background preparation. The worse prepared the students, the more course offerings must shift from advanced to remedial and introductory courses. This undermines the ability of selective schools to advance their missions of training an elite to the highest standards and preparing the next generation to carry out cutting-edge research.[40]

Consider next stricter race-neutral enforcement of antidiscrimination law. Justice Roberts, in striking down a school district's policy of using race-based assignments to advance racial integration, proclaimed that "[t]he way to stop discrimination on the basis of race is to stop discrimination on the basis of race."[41] If Justice Roberts thought he was expressing a tautology, he erred twice. First, to advance "stop[ping] discrimination on the basis of race" as a *policy instrument* is to direct people to consciously adopt it. His claim should therefore be translated as "the way to stop discrimination on the basis of race is to stop *conscious* discrimination on the basis of race." Second, "race" is an equivocal term. The question at stake is the legitimacy of discriminating on the basis of *unjust racialized status*. His claim should therefore be translated as follows: "the way to stop discrimination on the basis of character or purely minimal race is to stop discrimination on the basis of racialized status."

Both of these claims are empirically false. Consciously refusing to discriminate by race does nothing to stop unconscious prejudicial, anxious, or evaluative discrimination since these modes of discrimination are triggered by automatic mechanisms not under conscious control (§3.1, §3.5). This is why conscious discrimination in favor of unjustly racialized persons is sometimes needed to block unconscious discrimination against such persons (§7.4).

Stopping discrimination on the basis of racialized status for the purpose of promoting racial integration leaves racial segregation intact. Segregation causes discrimination on the basis of minimal and character race by numerous mechanisms (§3.1, §3.5). Integration, which may be brought about via discrimination on the basis of racialized status, reduces discrimination on the basis of minimal and character race by dismantling those mechanisms and triggering accountability effects (§5.3, §6.3, §7.5).

Underlying Justice Roberts's pronouncement is the confidence that simple enforcement of antidiscrimination laws under a color-blind interpretation is sufficient to end racial discrimination.[42] The history of enforcement efforts shows that this confidence is unjustified. Merely passing antidiscrimination laws without pressuring agents to take affirmative steps to include members of stigmatized groups achieves virtually nothing (§7.4). U.S. antidiscrimination law is riddled with weaknesses. Here is a catalog of the types of conduct causing systematic race-based disadvantage that antidiscrimination law fails to address.

Loopholes

Many forms of racial discrimination are not prohibited by law, including business-to-business discrimination on account of the race of the owner (except in the context of state contracting), discrimination by private schools and clubs not receiving state funds, employment discrimination by firms with fewer than fifteen employees,[43] housing discrimination concerning single-family homes put for sale or rental by the owner (as opposed to a real-estate agent),[44] and decisions of businesses (other than large banks, which are regulated by the Community Reinvestment Act) to direct their services to communities on the basis of their racial composition (§2.2). Proof requirements, combined with epistemic obstacles to discovering discrimination, create further loopholes. Title VII charges of discrimination in hiring (as opposed to discrimination against those already employed) are rare because individuals who are not employees are rarely in a position to discover whether employers used race as a factor in the hiring decision. Employers also often keep salary structures hidden from employees, preventing them from filing suit for pay discrimination.

Weak Enforcement

Enforcement of antidiscrimination laws is weak. The enforcement provisions of some laws, such as the Fair Housing Act, were deliberately limited so as to undermine the objectives of the law.[45] The Equal Employment Opportunity Commission lacked enforcement authority until 1972. Since then, it has been charged with enforcing an increasing number of laws (concerning discrimination on the basis of age and disability) without commensurate increases in budget or staff—even suffering cuts under the Bush administration.[46] Levels of enforcement, as measured by the ratio of resolutions to new complaints, have varied dramatically in response to political commitments, with Republican administrations dragging their feet and Democratic ones burdened with clearing the backlogs left by the former.[47]

Evaluative Discrimination

Evaluative discrimination is especially hard to prove when the qualities at stake are "soft" and subjectively assessed.[48] Courts generally defer to employers' subjective assessments of employee "soft skills."

Discrimination Laundering

I call "discrimination laundering" any conversion of the effects of an initial racially discriminatory act into a basis for legal discrimination on nonracial grounds (whether or not this conversion is intended). Racial discrimination in on-the-job training is illegal; however, discrimination on the basis of differences in human capital due to differences in on-the-job training is not. If employees do not promptly file suit over an employer's initial discrimination in providing on-the-job training—something that may be difficult to detect, given the extent to which such training is informal—employers are free to perpetuate and magnify the effects of their initial discrimination by appealing to differences in skill between favored and disfavored employees. This point is especially important since a principal source of divergent career trajectories between blacks and whites appears to be differential employer investment in training.[49] Once these effects become the basis for nonracial discrimination by other agents, they are beyond legal remedy. The effects of racial discrimination thereby spread and magnify across society, in ways color-blind antidiscrimination law is helpless to prevent.

Unconscious Discrimination

Equal protection doctrine provides no protection against unconscious discrimination. To violate equal protection, states must *purposely* discriminate by race.[50] This rule permits state actors to engage in unconscious and hence unintended racial discrimination. The evidence demanded by the Court to prove a discriminatory purpose is also often extraordinarily high. Even overwhelming statistical evidence of systematic juror bias in capital cases is not enough: plaintiffs must prove bias in their particular case—proof virtually never available if discriminating agents keep silent or are unaware of their motives.[51]

Aversive Racism

The structure of equal protection doctrine is virtually tailor-made to leave wide scope for state agents to engage in aversive racism—conduct disadvantaging a racial group when there is a race-neutral cover for such action (§3.1). Under contemporary doctrine, facially race-neutral policies are subject to a lax "rational basis" standard of review. In this test, states adopting a formally race-neutral policy do not have to prove that their purpose was innocent of invidious racial intent, even if the policy has a grossly disparate racial impact. In the absence of a "smoking gun," a credulous court will accept wholly speculative race-neutral justifications for formally race-neutral policies that grievously disadvantage blacks. This is important because every law aimed at dismantling the American system of racial caste has encountered massive resistance. Legally deprived of explicitly racial means to maintain segregation and subordination, whites have consistently invented subtler, formally race-neutral ways to keep blacks down. Sometimes this is deliberate, as in the case of the myriad formally race-neutral laws that achieved virtually complete black disenfranchisement in the South in the Jim Crow era. Unless the courts scrutinize such policies skeptically, such illegal actions will not be caught. If aversive racism is unconscious, current doctrine cannot cover it at all.

Racial Negligence

Equal protection doctrine permits states to act with gross negligence toward blacks. It permits states to give *zero* weight to blacks' interests, while giving extraordinary weight to the interests of whites, so long as they use race-neutral means, since the Fourteenth Amendment is violated only if the state adopts a policy "because of" and not "in spite of" its "adverse effects upon an identifiable group."[52] Race-neutral policies supported by voters out of ethnocentric motives (§3.6)—for instance, white support for cuts in school funding to avoid transferring resources from white taxpayers to black and Latino schoolchildren—are legal.

Second-Order Discrimination

Second-order discrimination occurs when a policy with a disparate racial impact is adopted because of its association with stigmatizing representations of the racial group disadvantaged by it (§§3.5–3.6). Perpetrators of certain crimes are punished more severely because their crimes are seen as "black." For example, congressional sentencing guidelines put those convicted of simple possession of user's amounts of crack cocaine in prison for the same amount of time as dealers of large quantities of powder cocaine.[53] Most of the street dealers in crack, and 85 percent of those convicted of simple possession, are black, whereas dealers and consumers of powder tend to be white. The hysteria leading to this sentencing disparity was stimulated by stigmatizing fantasies of black "crack babies" doomed to turn into "superpredators" upon reaching adolescence. Since the differential racial impact of the sentencing guidelines was not directly motivated by a desire to punish black drug dealers and users more severely than white ones, the equal protection clause cannot be used to overturn the disparity, even though it was inspired by racially stigmatizing images and grossly disadvantages black drug offenders.

Discrimination in Contact

While antidiscrimination law prohibits formal "discrimination in contract," it leaves untouched the vast informal realm of what Glenn Loury calls "discrimination in contact": discrimination in people's choices of friends, acquaintances, associates, and neighbors.[54] Our examination of social capital and its impact on the development of human and cultural capital demonstrates how important such informal contacts are to gaining economic opportunity (§2.3). While antidiscrimination laws should not cover such informal discrimination (§1.5), states should not be forbidden from taking effective steps to avoid reproducing and spreading the segregative effects of informal social avoidance of blacks in their own institutions. Removing the option of race-based school assignments drastically limits the ability of districts to racially integrate their schools, given the racial segregation of neighborhoods.

Color-blind interpretations of antidiscrimination law are grossly inadequate to the task of dismantling racial segregation and stigmatization, the two core causes of continuing systematic race-based injustice. They are based on empirically inadequate models of the myriad ways in which attitudes and ideas about race produce unjust racial disadvantage. With their static model of discrimination as always explicitly race-based, they fail to grasp the ways practices of social closure and opportunity hoarding continuously adapt to constraints. The result has been a set of doctrines that accommodates and reproduces the American racial caste system. This is evident in the evisceration of *Brown v. Board of Education*, which recognized that "separate educational facilities are inherently unequal."[55] After allowing enforcement of *Brown* to lapse for ten years, the federal courts briefly stood up to the task of integrating the schools. In *Green v. County School Board of New Kent County*,[56] the Court recognized that school boards guilty of de jure segregation could not satisfy equal protection requirements simply by ending race-based assignments of children to schools, while handing off the job of maintaining segregation to the private choices of students and their parents. They had an "affirmative duty to take whatever steps might be necessary to convert to a unitary [i.e., integrated] system."[57] The "constitutionally required end" is "the abolition of the system of segregation *and its effects*."[58] In *Swann v. Charlotte-Mecklenburg Board of Education*, the Court held that this end could justify the assignment of teachers and students to schools on the basis of their race.[59]

These convictions, and the courage to enforce them, faded in the face of overwhelming white resistance to school integration. *Milliken v. Bradley*[60] held that courts could not order interdistrict school integration, even if white flight from cities to suburbs made meaningful intradistrict school integration impossible. This enabled the laundering of illegal private housing discrimination into legal school segregation, as the state turned a blind eye to violations of the Fair Housing Act. In *San Antonio Independent School District v. Rodriguez*,[61] the Court upheld local financing of schools, notwithstanding the fact that local financing systems leave segregated, high-poverty school districts starved for resources. This further facilitated opportunity hoarding by wealthy, segregated white towns. In *Board of Education v. Dowell*,[62] the Court allowed desegregation orders to be dissolved once school boards have complied with them for a time, even if this results in immediate de facto resegregation of schools. In *Freeman v. Pitts*,[63] the Court established the presumption that school boards are not responsible for de facto school segregation due to neighborhood segregation, even if the school board or other state bodies had earlier fostered neighborhood segregation. In *Parents Involved v. Seattle School District*,[64] the Court restricted the freedom of school districts to counteract the segregative effects of white flight by using racial assignments to promote integration.

These decisions amount to a recipe for accommodating white opportunity hoarding: let white flight reproduce segregation across district lines; turn a blind eye to massive violations of the Fair Housing Act and state collusion in neighborhood segregation; permit segregated suburbs to hoard school revenues; let school districts transmit white preferences for racial segregation from neighborhoods to schools by allowing them to revert to neighborhood school assignments; and entitle whites to lock in the results of this segregation by blocking schools' race-conscious efforts to avoid spreading the effects of whites' private acts of social closure. Call this outcome "color-blind" and declare it a triumph of equal protection.

Could these weaknesses of antidiscrimination law be repaired within a framework that refuses to use race-based selection? One might argue that to identify and block unconscious discrimination, aversive racism, discrimination laundering, racial negligence, and second-order discrimination, one could vigorously challenge all policies with a differential racial impact, and establish a presumption that race-neutral policies must be justified by important interests and narrowly tailored to minimize differential impacts. This would certainly be an important step. Yet no one has figured out a way to avoid race-based selection when faced with recalcitrant discriminating agents. Moreover, to refuse racial goals and timetables is to permit de facto segregation to persist. Since de facto segregation causes discrimination and disadvantage, and there are limits to the caseloads any legal system can bear, to refuse racial selection, goals, and timetables effectively delays the remedy of severe and persistent race-based disadvantage. Similarly, to block active efforts to integrate institutions in the face of pervasive discrimination in contact effectively permits racial groups that shun blacks to spread the patterns of segregation they create in their private lives throughout civil society. Sometimes fire must be fought with fire.

8.6 The Ideal of Color Blindness in a Nonideal World

My critiques of color blindness as principle and policy leave the ideal of color blindness untouched. For all I have said, it is still legitimate to uphold an ideal of society in which no one ever draws racial distinctions or affiliates on the basis of race. Yet the ideal of color blindness has no *direct* application in our nonideal world. Given the consequences of de facto segregation and the social psychology of categorical inequality, it provides no support for color-blind policy or the color-blind principle under current and foreseeable circumstances. Given the ways segregation creates stigmatized racial identities, the only feasible way to realize the color-blind ideal is to assiduously practice racial integration. In addition, once stigmatized racial identities are created, those suffering from them may need to identify and affiliate on the basis of a self-understanding of collectively resisting their unjust racialization in order to cope with and overcome this injustice (chapter 9).

Suppose, however, we lived in an ideal world in which unjust racialization had never occurred or lay in the distant past. In such a world, racial classifications would not track anything of normative or enduring historical importance. Would the color-blind ideal be worthwhile for such a world? To the extent that it is derived from a comprehensive ideal to abandon all affiliation and in-group favoritism on the basis of morally arbitrary identities, it is futile. While it is a moral imperative to abandon character race, and feasible to abandon minimal race, as bases of social identity, human psychology does not appear to be capable of abandoning all arbitrary affiliation. Mere accidents of proximity, of arbitrary labeling and being thrown together, reliably trigger in-group identification and favoritism even when the ground of identity has no prior history, no meaningful content, and no credible future.[65]

Given that *some* arbitrary in-group affiliations are inevitable, is there any reason to reject minimal race as one such basis of identity? Iris Marion Young argues that ethnocentric affiliation on the basis of minimal or cultural ideas of race is morally innocent, once it is separated from any connections with racial hierarchy and oppression.[66] To evaluate this idea, it helps to have a positive account of when racial discrimination is morally objectionable. Young suggests that it is so when it embodies or causes race-based categorical inequality. This a correct but not exhaustive criterion. It fails to explain when discrimination against the racially privileged is morally objectionable. Racial discrimination is wrong when it expresses or causes unjust or undemocratic social relations (§1.5): when it embodies or causes relations of racial subordination or racial division (as in a racial spoils system), expresses antipathy toward or stigmatizing representations of racialized persons (as in prejudicial, evaluative, and second-order discrimination), or manifests ethnocentric partiality by an agent, such as the state, which is required to be impartial.

This would seem to leave room for "innocent" ethnocentric affiliation by private individuals, as Young desires. However, the account so far omits another unjust social relation: suppression of individuality. Individuals need to be free to forge their own identities, which requires that they be free to defy stereotypes and adopt out-group cultural practices. This entitles individuals to raise claims against forms of statistical discrimination that impede their freedom to pursue stereotype-defying roles. It also casts doubt on the legitimacy of conflating ancestry with culture. Norms of ethnocentric "cultural" affiliation threaten to unjustly deprive individuals of the freedom to participate in cultural practices because they have the "wrong" ancestry, and they may also stifle coethnics who wish to pursue different cultural practices. The ideal of a free and democratic culture of equals would therefore require that ideas of minimal race be substantially detached from ancestral group claims to control who gets to participate in cultural practices.

This leaves room for ethnocentric affiliation on minimal race, provided the notion of race at stake is minimal. Unfortunately, our psychologies seem built to impute ideas of group difference to minimal social categories, to vest them with social meanings.[67] There is still hope. Suppose society observed the following constraints. Ethnocentric affiliation may not be converted into categorical inequality. Individuals must be free to *dis*affiliate, to refuse to identify with any arbitrary group.[68] They must be free to identify with multiple, cross-cutting groups, defy group stereotypes, and participate in cultural practices of their own choice. No single parochial identity should be overarching, trumping all others. Rather, different social settings will make different, cross-cutting group identities salient. The rights citizens can claim against the state should not depend on their subgroup identities. The state must treat groups impartially. Such conditions could make ethnocentric affiliation compatible with justice, democracy, and individual freedom and equality. If these constraints are observed, then I am agnostic about the value of the color-blind ideal for an ideal world. Let the free culture of equals decide its fate.

Color blindness can be interpreted as a moral ideal or as a policy justified by a color-blind principle or by consequentialist considerations. In any interpretation, it must distinguish minimal and character racial concepts from the concept of a racialized group. The color-blind principle makes no sense as applied to race-based affirmative action and other integrative policies addressed to unjustly racialized persons because it fails to draw these conceptual distinctions. The objections it can offer against discrimination on the basis of minimal and character race do not apply to discrimination on the basis of unjust racialization. Consequentialist advocates of color-blind policy identify some possible costs to discrimination on the basis of unjust racialization, but none is so great as to undermine its use for integrative, discrimination-blocking, or compensatory purposes. Color-blind policies, including race-neutral affirmative action and more vigorous color-blind enforcement of existing discrimination laws, have costs of their own and fail to constrain or counteract much of the conduct that generates unjust systematic race-based disadvantage. Color blindness as an ideal retains some appeal. However, if categorical inequality were eliminated, individuals were free to repudiate racial identification, and ethnocentric affiliation on the basis of minimal race did not undermine the democratic imperatives of a common in-group identity for fellow citizens, the fate of such affiliation could be left to the dynamics of a culture of free and equal people.

· NINE ·

THE ORDEAL AND PROMISE OF INTEGRATION

9.1 The Ordeal of Integration Revisited

I have argued that integration is an indispensable goal in a society characterized by categorical inequality. It is necessary to block and dismantle the mechanisms that perpetuate unjust social inequality, and to realize the promise of a democratic state that is equally responsive and accountable to citizens of all identities. Yet integration does not proceed without cost. The experience of integration is often stressful and causes the loss or alteration of cherished racially homogeneous institutions. These costs have led both conservatives and various advocates on the left—multiculturalists and black nationalists—to reject integration as a goal of social policy.

The difficulties with the experience of integration must be acknowledged and confronted. "Color-blind" conservatives and advocates of racial identity politics are right to point out these problems. But they lack an adequate analysis of the material and social conditions of racial justice. So they cannot point the way forward. In making the case for racial integration, I also aim to reinforce the central methodological theme of this book: social and political philosophy needs to be grounded in an empirically adequate understanding of the problems we face and the effects of proposed solutions to these problems.

The integration of long segregated groups carries psychological costs. Conservatives point to high levels of racial conflict and self-segregation on more racially diverse campuses. Students at colleges with higher black enrollments report lower satisfaction with their educational experience. They also more often complain that they have experienced discrimination.[1] Conservatives therefore argue that "socially engineered" integration is self-defeating, in that it arouses racial discord and resentment.[2]

The experience of integration is particularly stressful for blacks. One influential study of black college students, summarizing its own findings in conjunction with prior studies, concludes that black students at majority-white colleges "emphasize feelings of alienation, sensed hostility, racial discrimination, and lack of integration."[3] This contrasts with their experiences at historically black colleges, where they feel accepted, encouraged, and supported, and report higher grades, occupational aspirations, and social involvement than their peers at majority-white colleges.[4] Black middle-class adults who work in majority-white firms also perceive discrimination.[5] Stress is particularly high among blacks who are "tokens" in their organization.[6]

Even more disturbing are reports of crime tied to integration. Many blacks living in white neighborhoods—not just new entrants but longstanding residents—experience violence and harassment at the hands of whites who aim to force them out.[7] On the other side, some have suggested that class-based integrative housing projects such as MTO have led to increased suburban crime, as former ghetto residents bring criminal habits with them.[8] If crime levels are tied to "tipping points" of concentrated poverty, and class integration programs increase the number of neighborhoods with moderate poverty concentration above the tipping point, then these integrative programs can end up increasing crime rates overall.[9]

To evaluate these claims, we must sort out the effects of integrative programs from other factors associated with integrated settings. The study by Rothman and colleagues finding higher dissatisfaction in more racially diverse schools has no implications for race-based affirmative action programs. This is because 80 percent of undergraduates attend institutions that accept all minimally qualified applicants, and hence do not practice affirmative action. Only the most selective institutions need affirmative action to achieve a racially integrated class—and these elite schools typically have *less* racial diversity than nonselective schools.[10] The race-neutral outcomes that Rothman and colleagues attribute to racial diversity, such as lower student satisfaction, perceptions of the quality of education, and perceptions of student work ethic, are more plausibly due to the lower academic preparation of the pool from which the school drew its students.

Similarly, the claim that integrative housing programs threaten (implicitly white) suburbs by bringing criminals into their midst is based on the unproven assumption that those committing crimes in areas of increasing crime rates are the beneficiaries of class-integrative programs. This ignores two important facts: that the vast majority of poor people entering suburban neighborhoods with increasing crime rates are not recipients of housing vouchers, and that the neighborhoods they are able to enter already tend to be in economic decline due to independent factors, such as housing foreclosures. Economically distressed neighborhoods typically experience higher crime rates even in the absence of new entrants.[11]

Such considerations cannot explain away the real race-specific costs of integration—experiences of increased racial conflict, discrimination, and alienation. Orlando Patterson refers to these costs as "the ordeal of integration."[12] They include not just experiences of interracial conflict, but discordant interpretations of the quality of race relations. Where whites tend to believe that antiblack discrimination has largely ended, blacks continue to perceive discrimination—a phenomenon whites chalk up to black "hypersensitivity." Patterson explains these costs as an inevitable consequence of integration. Segregation entails that blacks rarely interact with whites. They have few occasions to experience hostile or discriminatory treatment in face-to-face interaction. Integration exposes blacks to more whites—including more overtly racist whites. Even if the number of overtly racist whites has declined over time, integration increases the chance that blacks will encounter them. Thus, integration increases blacks' experience of white hostility, even while whites perceive that racism has declined within their group.

Patterson's analysis can be refined in light of recent research on the nature of racial attitudes. People often hold unconscious ideas that they do not endorse, but which are practically engaged (§3.1). Hence, whites who insult blacks out of racially stigmatizing ideas need not be overt racists; they may be genuinely unaware of what they are doing. Since introspection does not reveal their motive, such whites may unfairly accuse perceptive blacks of hypersensitivity. Overuse of the term "racist," which implies a stronger condemnation than warranted in the case of unconsciously stigmatizing acts, only reinforces white indignation and resistance to the possibility that their conduct, even if not evil, is racially unjust.

Add to this mix discordant ideas about what nonracist conduct looks like. Many whites worry that even *noticing* a person's race in interracial contexts may be perceived by blacks as racist; hence they pretend not to notice race even when faced with tasks where doing so can improve group performance. Blacks perceive such "color blindness" as disingenuous and absurd. Moreover, whites who strategically adopt a color-blind stance manifest discomfort with blacks in other ways—they avoid eye contact and appear less friendly.[13] This is a case of anxious racial discrimination, prompted by stereotype threat (white fear of confirming the stereotype of white racism) (§3.5). While such conduct is not racist, it is racially stigmatizing: it treats blacks as alien. Blacks naturally respond with feelings of alienation in settings with racially anxious whites.

Far from disconfirming the integrationist theory advanced in this book, these costs of integration are *predictions* of the theory. Segregation causes stigmatization. Integration does not instantly undo this effect. When people used to segregation meet in integrated settings, their interactions will predictably engage racially stigmatizing ideas, manifested in various forms of discrimination and unhappy interaction. The issue, then, is not whether racial conflict increases in more integrated settings. It is rather whether integration, over time, enables people to learn better ways of interacting across racial lines.

This is testable. If the conservative argument is right, then racial conflict would drive out positive experiences of interracial interaction, and people's tendencies to self-segregate would be stable or increase over time in response to the costs of integration. If the integrationist argument is right, then integration in settings of institutionalized support for cooperation initially increases both negative *and positive* interracial interaction. Over time, people will learn to better manage interracial relationships. Increased competence in interracial interaction will increase the returns to such interaction, and thereby induce people to choose more integrated lives. Studies consistently confirm the integrationist hypothesis. Students who attend more racially integrated schools lead more racially integrated lives after graduation: they have more racially diverse coworkers, neighbors, and friends than do students who attend less diverse schools (§6.2, §6.3).

9.2 The Limits of Multiculturalism

That integration in a world pervaded by segregation and stigmatization carries psychic costs, especially for the stigmatized, has important implications for integrationist ideals and policy. Given these costs, members of stigmatized groups need places of refuge, social settings in which they can count on unquestioned acceptance and affirmation, share their experiences with integration among themselves, and generate strategies for coping with the stresses of integration. The ideal of integration should therefore not be construed as to rule out or disparage the importance of preferential in-group affiliation among the disadvantaged at various times and in various settings. As Glenn Loury puts the point: "effective resistance to racial domination requires that the black victims of that domination organize and motivate themselves to collective action through the systematic practice of pro-black discrimination in contact."[14] What integration does rule out is pervasive self-segregation. It is one thing to associate ethnocentrically; quite another for black students "to confine their personal and extracurricular experiences almost exclusively" to same-race organizations and informal groups.[15] Such self-segregation deprives blacks of opportunities for enriching their social and cultural capital, deprives nonblack students of the experiences they need to overcome anti-black racial bias, and deprives us all of the joint perspective-taking we need to realize our culture as a democratic one.

Integration is not the same as assimilation (§6.1). The ideal of integration does not call for the elimination of group difference or group identity, nor for sweeping prohibitions on ethnocentric affiliation (§1.5), nor for the elimination of institutions in which stigmatized groups constitute a majority. In a just society, the fate of such identities and affiliations can be left to the free choice of equals (§8.6). Integration does call for full participation of members of salient social groups on terms of equality, cooperation, and mutual respect in all domains of civil society. This entails a rejection of strong forms of black nationalist separatism. It requires the construction of a superordinate group identity, a "we," from the perspective of which cooperative goals are framed, and appropriate policies selected and implemented. In a democratic society, this "we" is most importantly a shared identity as citizens.

Many on the multiculturalist left recoil from the idea of affirming national identities. They give racial identities priority over national identities. Can such ethnocentric identification priorities hope to realize a just society? Consider three prominent multiculturalist accounts of how this is supposed to work, which I shall call the identity development, benign ethnocentrism, and epistemological models.

Beverly Tatum, a leading theorist of the identity development model of ethnocentric affiliation, argues that self-segregation is needed for individuals to develop psychologically healthy and mature racial identities. Black self-segregation emerges among children as a way to cope with racism and negative images of blacks. Blacks turn to one another for a sympathetic ear in discussing encounters with whites, to forge more positive black identities than those prevalent in mainstream culture, and to share their experiences of interpersonal racism and learn how to deal with it.[16] The need not just to cope with racism but to belong to communities in which one is welcomed and affirmed persists through adulthood and justifies blacks' choices to live in self-segregated communities.

Iris Young advances a benign ethnocentric model of self-segregation. In this model, a social subgroup can legitimately prefer affiliating with "their own," without implying out-group prejudice. Residential clustering by race is morally permissible "when its purpose is mutual aid and culture-building among those who have affinity with one another, as long as the process of clustering does not exclude some people from access to benefits and opportunities. Such a clustering desire based on lifestyles or comfort is not wrong even when acted on by privileged or formerly privileged groups . . . if it can be distinguished from the involuntary exclusion of others and the preservation of privilege."[17] She argues that even white Afrikaners in postapartheid South Africa are entitled to their "own" neighborhoods to preserve their language, culture, and sense of history, provided they participate cooperatively in democratic politics.

Integration, Young argues, focuses on the wrong issues. The mere fact that neighborhoods are racially identifiable is no cause for concern. What matters is the equal allocation of benefits to different areas, not the equal allocation of racial groups to different areas. Her ideal of "differentiated solidarity," which accommodates benign ethnocentrism, claims to achieve this by moving benefits to the people. She complains that integration, in calling instead for people to move to the resources, forces disadvantaged groups, rather than advantaged ones, to change. Echoing conservative critiques, Young also argues that efforts to promote integration meet with resistance and failure. Finally, integration denies the validity of freedom of association. Differentiated solidarity upholds the rights of groups to choose with whom they will associate.[18]

Aimee MacDonald defends an epistemological model of self-segregation in the course of defending racial program houses on college campuses. Racial self-segregation provides a locus for generating knowledge from racially distinctive perspectives, which is needed to counter racism. Because race defines people's social locations, their opportunities, and the ways people perceive and treat them, people experience the social world differently by virtue of the ways they are racially classified. Arriving at an understanding of how this is so requires people to come to grips with their racial identities, which requires that people of the same race interpret their shared experiences together as a basis for antiracist action.

> The analysis of racial oppression and the formation of strategies for achieving political justice are contingent on communities of meaning that are racially identified. Thus anyone concerned with the long-range goal of securing broad-based freedom and autonomy should be committed to the continued existence of racially defined communities on the grounds that differentiated racial identities provide people with different experience of the world. If we are to have a hope of effectively interpreting the world, we need to draw on all epistemic resources. The preservation of racially defined communities of meaning secures the continued diversity of interpretations of the social world, thereby providing a richer array of knowledges from which to construct social, political, aesthetic, spiritual, and scientific accounts of our experience.[19]

Tatum, MacDonald, and Young offer powerful accounts of the benefits of self-segregation. I have just endorsed Tatum's account of these benefits and earlier argued that in racially segregated societies, racial diversity provides critical epistemic resources for democracy (§5.2). Young's idealized case of benign ethnocentrism abstracts from the fact that ethnocentrism today is inextricable from categorical inequality and stigmatization. Yet I allow that we can imagine just worlds in which ethnocentric affiliation is benign (§8.6). My complaint is not with these models' accounts of the benefits of self-segregation, but with the priority they give to ethnocentric self-segregation over integration on the basis of a common superordinate identity. None of these models is grounded in a realistic appraisal of the material and social conditions for advancing racial equality. For blacks to achieve racial equality, blacks need to change, whites need to change, and we need to change. These changes can happen only through racial integration. Let us recall why.

Young imagines a world in which racial equality can be achieved by moving resources to the people, rather than moving people to resources. Such a strategy could work if disadvantaged racial groups lacked only material resources. Yet black disadvantage is caused not simply by lack of material resources but by lack of social and cultural capital, which can be acquired only through interracial interaction (§2.3). Blacks need experience in integrated settings to acquire the skills needed to manage and lead racially integrated, majority-white institutions. This is a matter of acquiring cultural capital, not of assimilation. Integration does not assume that the habits learned and deployed at work and in other integrated settings must replace those prevailing in other settings. Racial equality therefore requires that blacks change, in that they acquire social and cultural capital that can be obtained only through social integration.

When blacks self-segregate, whites are of necessity racially isolated. Tatum imagines a world in which all-white groups construct positive, antiracist white identities for themselves, without burdening blacks with the thankless and stressful task of helping them deal with their prejudices.[20] Whites need to be aware of their own racial privilege for this to happen. Tatum and Young acknowledge that it is hard for whites to become aware of this if they are isolated from blacks. Even after acquiring such awareness, all-white groups are an inadequate setting for whites to learn how to advance racial equality. This is not just because when whites talk about race among themselves, what comes out may be, as in focus groups of working-class whites living in Detroit suburbs, "a profound distaste for blacks, a sentiment that pervades almost everything they think about government and politics. . . . Blacks constitute the explanation for their vulnerability and for almost everything that has gone wrong in their lives; not being black is what constitutes being middle class; not living with blacks is what makes a neighborhood a decent place to live."[21] This merely captures the problem of overt racists. The broader difficulty is that stigmatizing ideas operate unconsciously even among those who do not endorse them. To focus on changing whites' beliefs about racial privilege or their quest for a nonracist self-understanding is to suppose that acquiring a politically correct consciousness is what whites need to be able to treat blacks as equals. Yet what most urgently needs to change are people's unconscious habits of interracial interaction and perception. Such *practical* learning can take place only in integrated settings.

MacDonald imagines a world in which the critical epistemological communities are racially exclusive. Yet knowledge generated among blacks will have little impact if it does not inform the decisions of whites. It has little chance of doing that outside of integrated settings in which whites feel some accountability to fellow deliberators. Moreover, racial equality requires not just propositional knowledge, but practical knowledge of how to work together on terms of equality. Only racially integrated collective agents can generate this practical knowledge. Only by working and thinking *together* can *we* work out mutually respectful and cooperative habits of interaction.

MacDonald uses her epistemological argument to defend racial program housing in residential colleges. She rightly insists that blacks need to talk among themselves to develop strategies for coping with the stresses of integration. But she is wrong to suppose that the possibilities for generating this knowledge would be threatened by closing down racial program housing. Self-segregation is the default position of Americans of all races. Black students will find one another and develop coping strategies without segregated housing. MacDonald neglects the epistemological importance of the racially integrated "us." This is the most scarce, important, and difficult community of meaning we need to construct. This community cannot be achieved if black students institutionalize their self-segregation in as pervasive a form as racial program housing.[22] Classroom settings alone are not enough to make an integrated epistemic community.

MacDonald's epistemological argument is questionable on its own terms, in focusing on the *preservation* of racially exclusive communities. There is no legitimate point in preserving the races, understood as social positions in a racialized social hierarchy. There may be a point in preserving cultural meanings and practices that are independent of racism. This is why MacDonald, like Young, tends to slide from a structural to a cultural account of race. Certainly, cultural meanings and practices that originated in black communities have immeasurably enriched American culture. But only a spurious association of culture with ancestry can support the thought that racial self-segregation is needed to preserve or develop diverse cultural meanings and practices. Whites and Asians can, and do, play jazz. No group "owns" any particular cultural practice or is entitled to exclusive development rights to it. In a free and democratic society, culture is part of the commons and is no racial group's intellectual property. The demand to "preserve" particular cultural communities of meaning freezes culture in racialized cubicles, prevents its free engagement by others, and blocks its development by an integrated "us."

The idea that institutionalized self-segregation is needed to preserve epistemic diversity is equally spurious. It makes sense only against a background assumption that integration is the same as assimilation and cultural homogenization to a static mainstream culture. Yet integration is a constant generator of new cultural diversities and epistemic perspectives. Far from presuming that mainstream culture should remain static, integration aims to *change* it, especially to the extent that it embodies unconscious racial stereotypes and prejudices.

Integration insists on the centrality of forging a racially integrated "us" to advancing racial justice. Young, contrasting Kantian respect and communitarian solidarity, appears to deny this. Racial equality can be advanced on the basis of a "sense of commitment and justice owed to people, *but precisely not on the basis of a fellow feeling or mutual identification.*"[23] If she is merely saying that people can be induced to recognize obligations of justice to people for whom they have little affection, I agree. People do not need some *prior* sense of fellow feeling or mutual identification to have reasons to include one another as equals in cooperative projects. But the kind of inclusion entailed by seeing one another as fellow citizens joined in a common project of living together democratically *constitutes* a form of mutual identification. Unless this identification is invested with fellow feeling, the commitments we recognize as having to one another as citizens are liable to be thin. It is time for the Left to put behind its preference for racial identities at the expense of national identities, as if racial identities were inherently more authentic and worthy of emotional investment. This neglects the impact on whites of prioritizing ethnoracial self-segregation. It reinforces whites' alienation from disadvantaged groups, and their own tendencies to self-segregation. Given that it is impossible and undesirable to abolish informal routes to human and social capital development, and that whites control most of these routes, such a stance is self-defeating. Young's condition on the moral permissibility of white self-segregation—that it not exclude others from opportunities—is not satisfied in our society, where whites control most of the gates to opportunity. Excessive promotion of black self-segregation cannot help but entail white clubbishness, and thereby defeat the cause of racial justice.

I conclude that the integrated "us," not the self-segregated racial group, is the critical agent of racial justice that most urgently awaits deeper and richer construction. Neither justice nor democracy can be realized if the self-segregated racial group is celebrated as a more worthy site of identity and emotional investment than the integrated "us." Identity politics, in the form of ethnoracial nationalism, was a necessary moment in the struggle for racial equality.[24] In particular, overcoming subordinating role segregation required for a time the development of spatially segregated domains where blacks could attain leadership positions. But it is time to strike a new balance between moments of self-segregation and of integration, decidedly in favor of the racially inclusive "us."

9.3 The Hope for an Integrated Future

Comprehensive racial integration is a necessary condition for a racially just future. It is needed to overcome unjust racial inequality in opportunities, undo racial stigmatization, and realize a fully democratic society of equal citizens. For these reasons, I have advocated various integrative policies in this book: housing vouchers to promote black entry into non-black middle-class neighborhoods (§6.2), abolition of class-segregative zoning regulations (§4.2), extension and aggressive enforcement of Title VII–style differential impact standards of illegal discrimination to state action (§8.5), abolition of legal obstacles to voluntary integration programs based on the supposed value of color blindness (chapter 8), assiduous adoption of integrative programs by school districts, including within K–12 schools (§6.3), drawing boundaries to create integrated voting districts (§6.4), selection for racially integrated juries (§6.4), and extension of discrimination-blocking and integrative affirmative action programs in employment, education, and contracting (§§7.4–7.5).

But is racial integration just a pipe dream? While implementation of these mostly state-centered policies would have important effects, at foreseeable scales their impact would be modest compared to the vast scale of de facto segregation. Truly large-scale state-centered attempts to racially integrate K–12 schools, as took place in the busing era, consistently encounter massive white resistance and are not politically feasible. Hence the project of integration cannot be left to state initiative alone. Most of the work of integration inevitably rests with the spontaneous actions of citizens in civil society. Here there are a few promising, if small, signs— for example, of churches seeking integrated congregations and promoting programs of racial reconciliation.[25] Yet the overall picture is gloomy. Spontaneous residential racial integration of blacks proceeds at a glacial pace. Voter initiatives and state legislatures are rolling back affirmative action by public universities, while the Supreme Court is restricting voluntary integration by K–12 schools. Federal enforcement of key civil rights initiatives—*Brown v. Board of Education* and its successor cases, the 1964 Civil Rights Act, and the Fair Housing Act—is little more than perfunctory. Opinion research suggests that this state of affairs is just how whites want it—except that they think they are not getting it since they believe government is doing *too much* to help blacks.

This raises the question of what sort of realism is demanded in political philosophy. Throughout this book, I have stressed the centrality of nonideal theorizing in a sound political philosophy. Political philosophy should start with a diagnosis of what ails us, and construct remedies that are attentive to empirical constraints, including the limitations of human psychology. We are not nearly as rational, self-aware, and self-controlled as we imagine ourselves to be. Normative recommendations must take these limitations into account, lest they prescribe standards that are impossible for people to meet.

I have criticized both the multiculturalist Left and conservatives for their failure to live up to the demands of nonideal theorizing. Both sides fail to adequately diagnose the causes of racial inequality. They neglect the *multiple* ways de facto segregation propagates race-based injustice. Hence, they prescribe remedies—stricter race-neutral enforcement of antidiscrimination law, redistributing resources rather than people—that, in avoiding active steps toward integration, keep the fundamental causes of race-based injustice intact. Both sides also suggest psychologically unrealizable policies. Conservatives mistakenly suppose that people have the self-awareness and self-command to avoid acting on racially stigmatizing ideas that disadvantage blacks, simply by adopting a policy of color blindness. Multiculturalist advocates of race-based benign ethnocentrism mistakenly suppose that blacks can practice pervasive self-segregation under current conditions without reinforcing white social closure and self-flattering conceptions of white identity based on invidious comparisons with and alienation from blacks.

Is my integrationist theory unrealistic in these senses? No. It is based on an empirically grounded diagnosis of the causes of unjust race-based categorical inequality and pays close attention to the ability of integration to block or undo those causes and thereby reverse their effects (chapters 6, 7). It does not prescribe normative standards that are impossible or unreasonably difficult for people to meet, nor standards that fail to serve their objectives. Yet some theorists believe that a sound political philosophy must be realistic in another sense: that it must accommodate people's *unwillingness* to meet certain standards of justice. David Estlund argues that no one supposes that moral philosophy should be realistic in this sense: people's refusal to do what morality requires does not generate a valid claim on their part to be let off the moral hook. Why should matters be any different in normative political philosophy?[26]

This does not mean that political philosophy should ignore what people are willing to do. It is one thing to lay out an objective required by justice, another to implement policies capable of achieving that objective. Policy design must be sensitive to the responses of people to those policies. Court-ordered busing of schoolchildren, if it causes white flight, may fail to integrate schools. Integrative policies may need to adjust their scale and timing, and be joined with incentives and public education, to win public acceptance.

Given the glacial progress of white-black integration in the United States, this may seem to be a counsel of despair. Yet opposition to integration is based more on anticipatory fear than on evidence. The whites who are most opposed to integration are those with the least experience of it. As we have seen, people who have experienced integration earlier in their lives tend to lead more integrated lives as adults. In a book otherwise devoted to demonstrating the poor prospects for neighborhood integration in the United States, William Julius Wilson and Richard Taub observed that younger generations, who had more interracial contact and no experience with the struggle over busing in the 1960s and 1970s, were less racist than older generations and joined in multiracial alliances to improve the schools.[27]

As I was writing this book, the United States elected its first African American president. This does not portend an era of new policy initiatives aimed at overcoming race-based categorical inequality. President Obama was elected in part on an implicit promise not to make an issue of racial inequality, and nothing in his policy agenda suggests otherwise. Nevertheless, his election represents a moment of self-overcoming for democracy in America. In an act that was until very recently virtually inconceivable, a majority of Americans voting in 2008 chose to place their trust in a man who just fifty years ago would have been treated as unfit for collegial association with whites across the South, and in many domains outside the South. This gives us some reason to think that the horizon of realistic possibility for race relations in the United States extends beyond the low-altitude perspective of our current best estimates of feasibility. Notwithstanding the great obstacles to integration, we have grounds to hope for a better future.

NOTES

Chapter One
Segregation and Social Inequality

1. This striking pattern of white support for abstract principles of racial equality but opposition to or much lower support for their implementation has been regularly documented in survey research. See Howard Schuman, Charlotte Steeh, Lawrence Bobo, and Maria Krysan, *Racial Attitudes in America*, rev.ed. (Cambridge, Mass.: Harvard Univ. Press, 1997); Donald Kinder and Lynn Sanders, *Divided by Color* (Chicago: Univ. of Chicago Press, 1996); and David Sears, James Sidanius, and Lawrence Bobo, *Racialized Politics* (Chicago: Univ. of Chicago Press, 1999).

2. See, e.g., *Board of Education v. Dowell*, 498 U.S. 237 (1991) (allowing dissolution of desegregation orders once school boards have complied with them for a time, even if this results in immediate de facto resegregation); *Freeman v. Pitts*, 503 U.S. 467 (1992) (establishing presumption that a school board is not responsible for remedying de facto school segregation due to neighborhood segregation, even if it or other state bodies had earlier fostered neighborhood segregation); *Wessmann v. Gittens*, 160 F.3d 790, 810 (1st Cir. 1998) (rejecting "racial balancing" as goal of school admissions); *Parents Involved in Community Schools v. Seattle School District No. 1*, 525 U.S. 701 (2007) (rejecting unique focus on racial diversity in assigning transfer students to schools).

3. Gary Orfield and Chungmei Lee, *Brown at 50: King's Dream or Plessy's Nightmare?* (Cambridge, Mass.: Civil Rights Project, Harvard University, 2004), http://www.civilrightsproject.ucla.edu/research/reseg04/brown50.pdf.

4. Nancy Fraser, "From Redistribution to Recognition? Dilemmas of Justice in a 'Postsocialist' Age," in *Justice Interruptus* (New York: Routledge, 1997),11–39.

5. Stokely Carmichael and Charles Hamilton, *Black Power* (New York: Random House, 1967).

6. Nathan Glazer, *We Are All Multiculturalists Now* (Cambridge, Mass.: Harvard Univ. Press, 1997).

7. Sam Harper, John Lynch, Scott Burris, and George Davey Smith, "Trends in the Black-white Life Expectancy Gap in the United States, 1983–2003," *JAMA* 297 (2007): 1224–32.

8. Jamie Fellner, Marc Mauer, and Paul Hirschfield, *Losing the Vote: The Impact of Felon Disenfranchisement Laws in the United States* (Washington, D.C., and New York: The Sentencing Project and Human Rights Watch, 1998), 9, http://www.sentencingproject.org/doc/File/FVR/fd_losingthevote.pdf.

9. U.S. Census Bureau, *Annual Demographic Survey, March Supplement*, People Below 100% of Poverty, by Race, table 5 (Washington, D.C., 2006), http://pubdb3.census.gov/macro/032006/pov/new05_100.htm.

10. David Hollinger, *Postethnic America* (New York: Basic Books, 1995).

11. Important representatives of recent integrationist thought include Sheryll Cashin, *The Failures of Integration: How Race and Class Are Undermining the American Dream* (New York: Public Affairs, 2004); Cynthia Estlund, *Working Together: How Workplace Bonds Strengthen a Diverse Democracy* (Oxford: Oxford Univ. Press, 2005); Owen Fiss, *A Way Out: America's Ghettos and the Legacy of Racism* (Princeton, N.J.: Princeton Univ. Press, 2003); Douglas Massey and Nancy Denton, *American Apartheid* (Cambridge, Mass.: Harvard Univ. Press, 1993); Orlando Patterson, *The Ordeal of Integration: Progress and Resentment in America's "Racial" Crisis* (Washington, D.C.: Civitas/Counterpoint, 1997); and Robert Post "Introduction: After *Bakke*," in *Race and Representation: Affirmative Action*, ed. Robert Post and Michael Rogin (New York: Zone Books, 1998), 13–27.

12. John Dewey, *How We Think* (Boston: D. C. Heath, 1910), 196, 200.

13. Jean-Jacques Rousseau, *On the Social Contract*, trans. Donald Cress (Indianapolis: Hackett, 1987), 17.

14. John Rawls, *A Theory of Justice*, rev. ed. (Cambridge, Mass.: Harvard Univ. Press, 1999).

15. Charles Mills, *The Racial Contract* (Ithaca, N.Y.: Cornell Univ. Press, 1997) 17–19, 92–95; Lisa Schwartzman, *Challenging Liberalism: Feminism as Political Critique* (University Park: Pennsylvania State University Press, 2006).

16. Maria Krysan, "Community Undesirability in Black and White: Examining Racial Residential Preferences Through Community Perceptions," *Social Problems* 49.4 (2002): 522.

17. John Dewey, *Lectures on Ethics, 1900–1901*, ed. Donald F. Koch (Carbondale: Southern Illinois Univ. Press, 1991), 59–68, 229–30; John Dewey and James Tufts, *Ethics*, in *The Later Works of John Dewey, 1925–1953*, ed. Jo Ann Boydston (Carbondale: Southern Illinois Univ. Press, 1981), 189–91, 202–10.

18. John Dewey, *Human Nature and Conduct*, in *The Middle Works of John Dewey, 1899–1924*, ed. Jo Ann Boydston (Carbondale: Southern Illinois Univ. Press, 1976) 199, 208; Charles Taylor, "Explanation and Practical Reason," in *The Quality of Life*, ed. Martha Nussbaum and Amartya Sen (Oxford: Clarendon Press, 1993).

19. Charles Tilly, *Durable Inequality* (Berkeley and Los Angeles: Univ. of California Press, 1999).

20. Julia Isaacs, "International Comparisons of Economic Mobility," in *Getting Ahead or Losing Ground: Economic Mobility in America*, ed. Ron Haskins, Julia Isaacs, and Isabel Sawhill (Washington, D.C.: Brookings Institution, 2008), 38–39, http://www.brookings.edu/reports/2008/~/media/Files/rc/reports/2008/02_economic_mobility_sawhill/02_economic_mobility_sawhill.pdf.

21. Max Weber, *Economy and Society*, ed. Guenther Roth and Claus Wittich (Berkeley and Los Angeles: Univ. of California Press, 1968), 341–42.

22. Tilly, *Durable Inequality*, 10.

23. Charles Tilly, *Identities, Boundaries, and Social Ties* (Boulder, Colo.: Paradigm, 2005), chap. 10.

24. Kevin Bales, Laurel Fletcher, and Eric Stover, *Hidden Slaves: Forced Labor in the United States* (Washington, D.C.: Free the Slaves and University of California Human Rights Center, Berkeley, 2004), http://hrcberkeley.edu/pdfs/hiddenslaves_report.pdf.

25. Erik Olin Wright, "Metatheoretical Foundations of Charles Tilly's *Durable Inequality*," *Comparative Studies in Society and History* 42.2 (2000): 463.

26. Catharine MacKinnon, *Sexual Harassment of Working Women* (New Haven, Conn.: Yale Univ. Press, 1979).

27. Tilly, *Identities, Boundaries, and Social Ties*, 105–6.

28. I thank Eamonn Callan for this example.

29. "Usually one group of competitors takes some externally identifiable characteristic of another group of (actual or potential) competitors—race, language, religion, local or social origin, descent, residence, etc.—as a pretext for attempting their exclusion. It does not matter which characteristic is chosen in the individual case: whatever suggests itself most easily is seized upon." Weber, *Economy and Society*, 342.

30. Tilly, *Identities, Boundaries, and Social Ties*, 89.

31. Michael Walzer, *Spheres of Justice* (New York: Basic Books, 1983), identifies this as an important objectionable cause of inequality. In personal communication (January 28, 2007), Tilly agrees that leverage is important, too, without fitting it into his typology of causes of inequality.

32. Elizabeth Anderson, "What Is the Point of Equality?" *Ethics* 109 (1999): 321–25.

33. Iris Marion Young, *Justice and the Politics of Difference* (Princeton, N.J.: Princeton Univ. Press, 1990).

34. Adrienne Davis, "Slavery and the Roots of Sexual Harassment," in *Directions in Sexual Harassment Law*, ed. Catharine MacKinnon and Reva Siegel (New Haven, Conn.: Yale Univ. Press, 2004), 465.

35. Susan Fiske, "Stereotyping, Prejudice and Discrimination," in *Handbook of Social Psychology*, ed. Daniel Gilbert, Susan Fiske, and Gardner Lindzey (New York: McGraw-Hill, 1998), 380.

36. John Rawls, "Kantian Constructivism in Moral Theory," Dewey Lectures, *Journal of Philosophy* 77 (1980): 546.

37. Thomas Scanlon, *What We Owe to Each Other* (Cambridge, Mass.: Harvard Univ. Press, 1998).

38. I do not say that members of *all* groups are entitled not to be objects of violence, stigmatization, and so forth, because some groups, such as organized crime rings, terrorist groups, and aggressive states, are not prepared to behave justly toward others. These groups are properly subject to actions, including violent ones, that prevent them from realizing their unjust aims and punish them for acting on those aims.

39. See Anderson, "What Is the Point of Equality?"

40. In fact, various international relations—for example, those constituting the European Union—can give rise to claims that these relations be organized

democratically. However, an investigation of the conditions that give rise to democratic claims across international borders is beyond the scope of this book.

41. Marilynn Brewer, "The Psychology of Prejudice: Ingroup Love or Outgroup Hate?" *Journal of Social Issues* 55.3 (1999): 429–44.

42. John Dovidio, John Brigham, Blair Johnson, and Samuel Gaertner, "Stereotyping, Prejudice, and Discrimination: Another Look," in *Stereotypes and Stereotyping*, ed. Neil Macrae, Charles Stangor, and Miles Hewstone (New York: Guilford, 1996), 276–319.

43. I believe similar but not identical analyses can be offered of the injustices suffered by Latinos, Native Americans, and other ethnoracial groups in the United States. This does not mean that these other groups are entitled to claim remedies only insofar as their grievances resemble those of blacks, nor is it intended to deny the historical specificity of the practices that disadvantage them. On this point, see Ronald Sundstrom, *The Browning of America and the Evasion of Social Justice* (Albany, N.Y.: SUNY Press, 2008), chap. 3. The relational theory of group inequality offers only a schema that may be filled in with different mechanisms for different groups. For example, the historical origins of black-white inequality in the United States must be traced to conflicts over the control of black labor; of Native American–white inequality, to conflicts over the control of land and the power of Native Americans to govern themselves as sovereign nations. Yet we can still see spatial segregation, for example, playing a critical role in the impoverishment of Native Americans living on reservations—lands set aside for them often because they had negligible economic value. For lack of space, I set aside discussion of the disadvantages suffered by other ethnoracial groups, as well as consideration of the significance of interactions between blacks and these other groups. While these other interactions are interesting in their own right and have nontrivial impact, they do not require major revisions of the core narrative in my case study.

Chapter Two
Racial Segregation and Material Inequality in the United States

1. Elizabeth Arias, "United States Life Tables, 2004," National Center for Health Statistics, *National Vital Statistics Reports* 56.9 (Dec. 28, 2007): 4, http://www.cdc.gov/nchs/data/nvsr/nvsr56/nvsr56_09.pdf.

2. T. J. Mathews and Marian MacDorman, "Infant Mortality Statistics from the 2005 Period Linked Birth/Infant Death Data Set," National Center for Health Statistics, *National Vital Statistics Reports* 57.2 (July 30, 2008): 3–4, http://www.cdc.gov/nchs/data/nvsr/nvsr57/nvsr57_02.pdf; National Center for Health Statistics, *Health, United States, 2001* (Hyattsville, Md., 2001), table23,p. 156, http://www.cdc.gov/nchs/data/hus/hus01.pdf#023.

3. National Center for Health Statistics, *Health, United States, 2008*(Hyattsville, Md., 2009) 229–47, http://www.cdc.gov/nchs/data/hus/hus08.pdf; Robert Levine et al., "Black-white Inequalities in Mortality and Life Expectancy, 1933–1999: Implications for Healthy People 2010," *Public Health Reports* 116 (2001): 479.

4. Carmen DeNavas-Wait, Bernadette Proctor, and Jessica Smith, *Income, Poverty, and Health Insurance Coverage in the United States: 2007*, Current

Population Reports, P60-235 (Washington, D.C.: U.S. Census Bureau, 2008), 12, 48–49, http://www.census.gov/prod/2008pubs/p60–235.pdf.

5. Sarah Fass and Nancy Cauthen, *Who Are America's Poor Children?* (National Center for Children in Poverty, 2008), 2, http://www.nccp.org/publications/pdf/text_843.pdf.

6. Mary Corcoran, "Mobility, Persistence, and the Consequences of Poverty for Children: Child and Adult Outcomes," in *Understanding Poverty*, ed. Sheldon Danziger and Robert Haveman (New York: Russell Sage, 2001), 127–61.

7. DeNavas-Wait, Proctor, and Smith, *Income, Poverty, and Health Insurance*, 7, 32, 34.

8. Elena Gouskova and Frank Stafford, *Trends in Household Wealth Dynamics, 2003–5*, Panel Study of Income Dynamics Technical Series Paper no. 07-07 (Ann Arbor: Institute for Social Research, University of Michigan, 2007), 1, http://psidonline.isr.umich.edu/Publications/Papers/tsp/2007-07_Trends_in_Household_Wealth.pdf.

9. Julia Isaacs, "Economic Mobility of Black and White Families," in *Getting Ahead or Losing Ground: Economic Mobility in America*, ed. Ron Haskins, Julia Isaacs, and Isabel Sawhill (Washington, D.C.: Brookings Institution, 2008), 74–76, http://www.brookings.edu/reports/2008/~/media/Files/rc/reports/2008/02_economic_mobility_sawhill/02_economic_mobility_sawhill.pdf.

10. David Williams and Chiquita Collins, "Racial Residential Segregation: A Fundamental Cause of Racial Disparities in Health," *Public Health Reports* 116.5 (2001): 408.

11. Chinhui Juhn and Simon Potter, "Changes in Labor Force Participation in the United States," *Journal of Economic Perspectives* 20.3 (2006): 39.

12 Kurt Bauman and Nikki Graf, *Educational Attainment: 2000*, Census 2000 Brief (Washington, D.C.: U.S. Census Bureau, 2003), 5, http://www.census.gov/prod/2003pubs/c2kbr-24.pdf.

13. Jennifer Laird, Gregory Kienzl, Matthew DeBell, and Chris Chapman, *Dropout Rates in the United States: 2005*, NCES 2007-059 (Washington, D.C.: U.S. Department of Education, National Center for Education Statistics, 2007), 27, http://nces.ed.gov/pubs2007/2007059.pdf.

14. Jonathan Jacobson et al., *Educational Achievement and Black-White Inequality*, National Center for Education Statistics: Statistical Analysis Report 2001-061 (Washington, D.C.: U.S. Department of Education, 2001), 32, 37, http://nces.ed.gov/pubs2001/2001061.pdf.

15. Bureau of Justice Statistics, *Criminal Victimization in the United States, 2006 Statistical Tables*, NCJ 223436, National Crime Victimization Survey (Washington, D.C.: U.S. Department of Justice, 2008), table 5, http://www.ojp.usdoj.gov/bjs/pub/pdf/cvus06.pdf.

16. National Center for Injury Prevention and Control, *WISQARS Injury Mortality Reports, 1999–2006* (2006), http://webappa.cdc.gov/sasweb/ncipc/mortrate10_sy.html.

17. Heather West and William Sabol, *Prisoners in 2007*, NCJ 224280(Washington, D.C.: Bureau of Justice Statistics, 2009), 4, http://www.ojp.usdoj.gov/bjs/pub/pdf/p07.pdf.

18. Thomas Bonczar, *Prevalence of Imprisonment in the U.S. Population,*

1974–2001, Special Report NCJ 197976, Bureau of Justice Statistics (Washington, D.C.: U.S. Department of Justice, 2003), 8, http://www.ojp.usdoj.gov/bjs/pub/pdf/piusp01.pdf.

19. Bruce Western and Christopher Wildeman, "The Black Family and Mass Incarceration," *Annals of the American Academy of Political and Social Science* 621 (2009): 231.

20. Ibid., 223–27.

21. Jamie Fellner, Marc Mauer, and Paul Hirschfield, *Losing the Vote: The Impact of Felon Disenfranchisement Laws in the United States* (Washington, D.C., and New York: The Sentencing Project and Human Rights Watch, 1998), chap. 3, http://www.sentencingproject.org/tmp/File/FVR/fd_losingthevote.pdf.

22. Ryan King, *Expanding the Vote: State Felony Disenfranchisement Reform, 1997–2008* (Washington, D.C., and New York: The Sentencing Project and Human Rights Watch, 2008), 3, http://www.sentencingproject.org/Admin/Documents/publications/fd_statedisenfranchisement.pdf.

23. Fiske, "Stereotyping, Prejudice and Discrimination," 379.

24. John Logan, *Ethnic Diversity Grows, Neighborhood Integration Lags Behind* (Albany, N.Y.: Lewis Mumford Center, 2001), 1, 3, 11, 31, http://mumford1.dyndns.org/cen2000/WholePop/WPreport/page1.html.

25. Massey and Denton, *American Apartheid*, 74–78.

26. Gary Orfield and Chungmei Lee, *Historic Reversals, Accelerated Resegregation, and the Need for Integration Strategies* (Los Angeles: The Civil Rights Project/Proyecto Derechos Civiles/University of California, 2007), 24, table 9, http://www.civilrightsproject.ucla.edu/research/deseg/reversals_reseg_need.pdf.

27. Ibid., 29, table 11.

28. Ibid., 33.

29. Donald Tomaskovic-Devey, *Gender and Racial Inequality at Work: The Sources and Consequences of Job Segregation* (Ithaca, N.Y.: Cornell Univ. Press, 1993), 24.

30. Julie Kmec, "Minority Job Concentration and Wages," *Social Problems* 50.1 (2003): 38.

31. Barbara Reskin, Debra McBrier, and Julie Kmec, "The Determinants and Consequences of Workplace Sex and Race Composition," *Annual Review of Sociology* 25 (1999): 337.

32. Timothy Bates, *Banking on Black Enterprise* (Washington, D.C.: Joint Center for Political and Economic Studies, 1993), 140.

33. Kmec, "Minority Job Concentration and Wages," 49.

34. Ibid., 46.

35. Michael Emerson DeYoung, George Yancey, and Karen Chai Kim, *United by Faith: The Multiracial Congregation as an Answer to the Problem of Race* (New York: Oxford Univ. Press, 2003), 2.

36. Statistics constructed from Jason Fields, *America's Families and Living Arrangements: 2003*, Current Population Reports, P20-553 (Washington, D.C.: U.S. Census Bureau, 2004), 19, table 9, http://www.census.gov/prod/2004pubs/p20–553.pdf. Note that the U.S. Census counts Hispanics as an ethnicity that cross-cuts race, so the figure for Hispanics is not quite comparable to the figures for blacks and Asians.

37. Massey and Denton, *American Apartheid*, 85–88.

38. Mary Pattillo, "Extending the Boundaries and Definition of the Ghetto," *Ethnic and Racial Studies* 26.6 (2003): 1046–57.

39. John Kain, "Housing Segregation, Negro Employment, and Metropolitan Decentralization," *Quarterly Journal of Economics* 82.2 (1968): 175–97.

40. Keith Ihlanfeldt and David Sjoquist, "The Spatial Mismatch Hypothesis: A Review of Recent Studies and Their Implications for Welfare Reform," *Housing Policy Debate* 9.4 (1998): 880; Laurent Gobillon, Harris Selod, and Yves Zenou, "The Mechanisms of Spatial Mismatch," *Urban Studies* 44.12 (2007): 2401–27.

41. Judith Hellerstein, David Neumark, and Melissa McInerney, "Spatial Mismatch or Racial Mismatch?" *Journal of Urban Economics* 64.2 (2008): 464–79.

42. Susan Turner, "Barriers to a Better Break: Employer Discrimination and Spatial Mismatch in Metropolitan Detroit," *Journal of Urban Affairs* 19.2 (1997): 130.

43. Keith Ihlanfeldt and Madelyn Young, "Intrametropolitan Variation in Wage Rates: The Case of Atlanta Fast-Food Restaurant Workers," *Review of Economics and Statistics* 76.3 (1994): 425–33.

44. Keith Ihlanfeldt and David Sjoquist, "Job Accessibility and Racial Differences in Youth Employment Rates," *American Economic Review* 80.1 (1990): 267–76; Steven Raphael, "The Spatial Mismatch Hypothesis and Black Youth Joblessness: Evidence from the San Francisco Bay Area," *Journal of Urban Economics* 43 (1998): 79–111.

45. Gobillon, Selod, and Zenou, "Mechanisms of Spatial Mismatch"; Ihlanfeldt and Sjoquist, "Spatial Mismatch Hypothesis," 877–80.

46. Richard Martin, "The Adjustment of Black Residents to Metropolitan Employment Shifts: How Persistent Is Spatial Mismatch?" *Journal of Urban Economics* 50 (2001): 52–76.

47. Ihlanfeldt and Sjoquist, "Spatial Mismatch Hypothesis," 851, 872.

48. Stephan Thernstrom and Abigail Thernstrom, *America in Black and White: One Nation, Indivisible* (New York: Simon and Schuster, 1997), 249–50, 256.

49. Tilly, *Identities, Boundaries, and Social Ties*, chap. 10.

50. Jimy Sanders and Victor Nee, "Immigrant Self-Employment: The Family as Social Capital and the Value of Human Capital," *American Sociological Review* 61.2 (1996): 231–49.

51. Arthur Sakamoto and Hyeyoung Woo, "The Socioeconomic Attainments of Second-Generation Cambodian, Hmong, Laotian, and Vietnamese Americans," *Sociological Inquiry* 77.1 (2007): 44–75. Sakamoto and Woo (pp. 62, 64) find that while labor force characteristics—mainly education—explain virtually all of the variation in wages among second-generation Southeast Asian immigrant men compared to whites, blacks suffer a 12 percent earnings penalty relative to whites after controlling for these characteristics. This suggests that blacks face obstacles not faced by Southeast Asian immigrant groups.

52. Thernstrom and Thernstrom, *America in Black and White*, 251; Joleen Kirschenman and Kathryn Neckerman, "'We'd Love to Hire Them, but . . .': The Meaning of Race for Employers," in *The Urban Underclass*, ed. Christopher Jencks and Paul Peterson (Washington, D.C.: Brookings Institution, 1991), 203–32.

53. Amy Helling and David Sawicki, "Race and Residential Accessibility to Shopping and Services," *Housing Policy Debate* 14.1–2 (2003): 69–101.

54. Ibid.; John Metzger, "Clustered Spaces: Racial Profiling in Real Estate Investment," Lincoln Institute of Land Policy Conference Paper (Cambridge, Mass., 2001), http://www.lincolninst.edu/pubs/dl/606_metzger.pdf.

55. Metzger, "Clustered Spaces," 16–17.

56. Ibid., 10.

57. Ibid., 18–19.

58. Sharon Jackson, Roger Anderson, Norman Johnson, and Paul Sorlie, "The Relation of Residential Segregation to All-Cause Mortality: A Study in Black and White," *American Journal of Public Helath* 90.4 (2000): 616; Williams and Collins, "Racial Residential Segregation," 409.

59. Angus Deaton and Darren Lubotsky, "Mortality, Inequality and Race in American Cities and States," *Social Science and Medicine* 56 (2003): 1139–53.

60. Ingrid Ellen, "Is Segregation Bad for Your Health? The Case of Low Birth Weight," *Brookings–Wharton Papers on Urban Affairs: 2000* (2000); Sue Grady, "Racial Disparities in Low Birthweight and the Contribution of Residential Segregation: A Multilevel Analysis," *Social Science and Medicine* 63.12 (2006): 3013–29.

61. Williams and Collins, "Racial Residential Segregation," 411.

62. Latetia Moore and Ana Diez Roux, "Associations of Neighborhood Characteristics with the Location and Type of Food Stores," *American Journal of Public Health* 96.2 (2006): 325–31.

63. Kimberly Morland, Steve Wing, Ana Diez Roux, and Charles Poole, "Neighborhood Characteristics Associated with the Location of Food Stores and Food Service Places," *American Journal of Preventive Medicine* 22.1 (2002): 28.

64. Elizabeth Eisenhauer, "In Poor Health: Supermarket Redlining and Urban Nutrition," *GeoJournal* 53.2 (2001): 125–33.

65. Kevin Grumbach, "Physician Supply and Access to Care in Urban Communities," *Health Affairs* 16 (1997): 76, exhibit 1.

66. Miriam Komaromy et al., "The Role of Black and Hispanic Physicians in Providing Health Care for Underserved Populations," *New England Journal of Medicine* 334 (May 16, 1996): 1306–7.

67. Eli Ginzberg, "Improving Health Care for the Poor: Lessons from the 1980s," *Journal of the American Medical Association* 271.6 (1994): 464, 465.

68. Williams and Collins, "Racial Residential Segregation," 410.

69. Ibid.

70. Ibid., 411–12.

71. Max Weintraub, "Racism and Lead Poisoning," *American Journal of Public Health* 87.11 (1997): 1871–72.

72. Russ Lopez, "Segregation and Black/White Differences in Exposure to Air Toxics in 1990," *Environmental Health Perspectives* 110.Suppl 2 (2002): 289–95.

73. Rachel Morello-Frosch and Bill Jesdale, "Separate and Unequal: Residential Segregation and Estimated Cancer Risks Associated with Ambient Air Toxics in U.S. Metropolitan Areas," *Environmental Health Perspectives* 114.3 (2006): 386–93.

74. Dolores Acevedo-Garcia, "Residential Segregation and the Epidemiology of Infectious Diseases," *Social Science and Medicine* 51.8 (2000): 1143–61.

75. Williams and Collins, "Racial Residential Segregation," 404.

76. Kevin Krolicki, "Houses Cheaper Than Cars in Detroit," *Reuters* Mar. 19, 2007, http://www.reuters.com/article/topNews/idUSN1927997820070319.

77. Chenoa Flippen, "Unequal Returns to Housing Investments? A Study of Real Housing Appreciation among Black, White, and Hispanic Households," *Social Forces* 82.4 (2004): 1535.

78. Ibid., 1537.

79. Kathleen Engel and Patricia McCoy, "From Credit Denial to Predatory Lending: The Challenge of Sustaining Minority Homeownership," in *Segregation: The Rising Costs for America*, ed. James Carr and Nandinee Kutty (New York: Routledge, 2008), 81–124.

80. Melvin Oliver and Thomas Shapiro, *Black Wealth/White Wealth: A New Perspective on Racial Inequality* (New York: Routledge, 1997), 144–47, 149–54.

81. Gretchen Morgenson, "Baltimore Is Suing Bank over Foreclosure Crisis," *New York Times*, Jan. 8, 2008: A12.

82. Robert Fairlie, "The Absence of the African-American Owned Business: An Analysis of the Dynamics of Self-Employment," *Journal of Labor Economics* 17.1 (1999): 80, 96–97.

83. Thomas Boston, *Affirmative Action and Black Entrepreneurship* (New York: Routledge, 1999) 76–79.

84. Massey and Denton, *American Apartheid*, 161.

85. Ibid., 77.

86. Lee Sigelman and Susan Welch, "The Contact Hypothesis Revisited: Black-white Interaction and Positive Racial Attitudes," *Social Forces* 71.3 (1993): 1311.

87. James Coleman, "Social Capital in the Creation of Human Capital," *American Journal of Sociology*, suppl. vol. 94 (1988): S95–S120.

88. Robert Putnam, *Bowling Alone: The Collapse and Revival of American Community* (New York: Simon and Schuster, 2000), 21–23.

89. Mark Granovetter, "The Strength of Weak Ties," *American Journal of Sociology* 78.6 (1973): 1361.

90. Ibid.

91. Ibid., 1371.

92. Xavier de Souza Briggs, "Bridging Networks, Social Capital, and Racial Segregation in America," KSG Working Paper No. RWP02-011 (2003), http://ssrn.com/abstract=320243.

93. Peter Marsden, "The Hiring Process: Recruitment Methods," *American Behavioral Scientist* 37.7 (1994): 983.

94. Deirdre Royster, *Race and the Invisible Hand: How White Networks Exclude Black Men from Blue-Collar Jobs* (Berkeley and Los Angeles: Univ. of California Press, 2003); Roger Waldinger, *Still the Promised City: African-Americans and New Immigrants in Postindustrial New York* (Cambridge, Mass.: Harvard Univ. Press, 1996).

95. Briggs, "Social Capital and Segregation," 10.

96. Amy Wells and Robert Crain, "Perpetuation Theory and the Long-Term Effects of School Desegregation," *Review of Educational Research* 64.4 (1994): 546.

97. Sandra Susan Smith, *Lone Pursuit: Distrust and Defensive Individualism among the Black Poor* (New York: Russell Sage, 2007).

98. Coleman, "Social Capital in the Creation of Human Capital."

99. Glenn Loury, "A Dynamic Theory of Racial Income Differences," in *Women, Minorities, and Employment Discrimination*, ed. P. A. Wallace and A. LeMund (Lexington, Mass.: Lexington Books, 1977).

100. George J. Borjas, "Ethnic Capital and Intergenerational Mobility," *Quarterly Journal of Economics* 107 (1992): 123–50.

101. George J. Borjas, "Ethnicity, Neighborhoods, and Human-Capital Externalities," *American Economic Review* 85.3 (1995): 365–90. See also William Darity, Jason Dietrich, and David K. Guilkey, "Persistent Advantage or Disadvantage?: Evidence in Support of the Intergenerational Drag Hypothesis," *American Journal of Economics and Sociology* 60 (2001): 435–70 (replicating Borjas's findings).

102. Tanya Mohn, "Sometimes the Right Approach Is Putting the Best Face Forward," *New York Times*, May 7, 2006: sec. 10, p. 1.

103. Elijah Anderson, "The Code of the Streets," *Atlantic Monthly* (May 1994): 80–94.

104. Elijah Anderson, *Streetwise: Race, Class, and Change in an Urban Society* (Chicago: Univ. of Chicago Press, 1990), 190–206.

105. Kirschenman and Neckerman, "'We'd Love to Hire Them, but . . . .'"

106. Massey and Denton, *American Apartheid*, 162–65.

107. Patterson, *The Ordeal of Integration*, 68.

108. Michelle Johnson, *Working while Black: The Black Person's Guide to Success in the White Workplace* (Chicago: Lawrence Hill Books, 2004).

109. Ibid., 55–56.

110. Lauren Rivera, "Cultural Reproduction in the Labor Market: Homophily in Job Interviews" (Department of Sociology, Harvard University, 2009), 13–14, 36, http://www.kellogg.northwestern.edu/mors/faculty/seminars/LRivera.pdf.

111. George Wilson, Ian Sakura-Lemessy, and Jonathan West, "Reaching the Top: Racial Differences in Mobility Paths to Upper-Tier Occupations," *Work and Occupations* 26 (1999): 165–86.

112. Julian Betts, Kim Rueben, and Anne Danenberg, *Equal Resources, Equal Outcomes? The Distribution of School Resources and Student Achievement in California* (Public Policy Institute of California, 2000), 87, http://www.ppic.org/content/pubs/report/R_200JBR.pdf.

113. Jonathan Kozol, *The Shame of the Nation: The Restoration of Apartheid Schooling in America* (New York: Crown, 2005), 13–14, 41.

114. Deborah McKoy and Jeffrey Vincent, "Housing and Education: The Inextricable Link," in *Segregation: The Rising Costs for America*, ed. James Carr and Nandinee Kutty (New York: Routledge, 2008), 131.

115. Eric Hanushek, John Kain, and Steven Rivkin, "Why Public Schools Lose Teachers," *Journal of Human Resources* 39.2 (2004).

116. Eric Hanushek and Steven Rivkin, "School Quality and the Black-white Achievement Gap," NBER Working Paper no. W12651 (2006), http://ssrn.com/abstract=940600.

117. The New Jersey Supreme Court detailed many of the techniques of exclu-

sionary zoning in *Southern Burlington Cty. NAACP v. Township of Mt. Laurel*, 67 N.J. 151 (1975).

118. Nancy Burns, *The Formation of American Local Governments: Private Values in Public Institutions* (New York: Oxford Univ. Press, 1994); Gregory Weiher, *The Fractured Metropolis: Political Fragmentation and Metropolitan Segregation* (Albany, N.Y.: SUNY Press, 1991).

119. Gregg Ryzin, Douglas Muzzio, and Stephen Immerwahr, "Explaining the Race Gap in Satisfaction with Urban Services," *Urban Affairs Review* 39.5 (2004): 613–32.

120. Mark Schneider and Thomas Phelan, "Black Suburbanization in the 1980s," *Demography* 30 (1993): 270.

121. Ruth Hoogland DeHoog, David Lowery, and William Lyons, "Metropolitan Fragmentation and Suburban Ghettos: Some Empirical Observations on Institutional Racism," *Journal of Urban Affairs* 13 (1991): 488–90.

122. John Logan, *Separate and Unequal: The Neighborhood Gap for Blacks and Hispanics in Metropolitan America*, res. rept. (Albany, N.Y.: Lewis Mumford Center, 2002), http://mumford.albany.edu/census/SepUneq/SUReport/SURepPage1 .htm.

123. Thomas Phelan and Mark Schneider, "Race, Ethnicity, and Class in American Suburbs," *Urban Affairs Review* 31.5 (1996): 674.

124. John Logan and Richard Alba, "Locational Returns to Human Capital: Minority Access to Suburban Community Resources," *Demography* 30.2 (1993): 260.

125. Data confirming this claim may be found at the Lewis Mumford Center, *Separate and Unequal: Racial and Ethnic Neighborhoods in the 20th Century*, http://mumford1.dyndns.org/cen2000/SepUneq/PublicSeparateUnequal.htm, selected metropolitan region pages, "Effects of Income Class Differences on Neighborhood Characteristics." In a far from comprehensive survey, I personally confirmed this claim for the Newark, New York, Milwaukee, Oakland, Chicago, Atlanta, Los Angeles, St. Louis, Miami, Houston, and Boston metropolitan areas.

126. Mary Pattillo-McCoy, *Black Picket Fences: Privilege and Peril among the Black Middle Class* (Chicago: Univ. of Chicago Press, 1999), 28–30.

127. Massey and Denton, *American Apartheid*, 154–55.

128. Ibid., 158–59.

129. Mark Schneider and John Logan, "Suburban Racial Segregation and Black Access to Local Public Resources," *Social Science Quarterly* 63 (1982): 766–69; Schneider and Phelan, "Black Suburbanization in the 1980s," 274–77.

130. Phelan and Schneider, "Race, Ethnicity, and Class in American Suburbs," 673.

131. Jeffrey Cohan, "Local Taxes Display an Uneven Bite: County Residents Who Are Black or Poor, Pay More," *Pittsburgh Post-Gazette*, Mar. 8, 2004: A1.

132. Michael Greenberg, "Improving Neighborhood Quality: A Hierarchy of Needs," *Housing Policy Debate* 10.3 (1999): 607.

133. Douglas Massey, "Getting Away with Murder: Segregation and Violent Crime in Urban America," *University of Pennsylvania Law Review* 143.5 (1995): 1203–32; Massey and Denton, *American Apartheid*, 118–36.

134. Alexandra Natapoff, "Underenforcement," *Fordham Law Review* 75 (2006): 1729.

135. Ibid., 1725–27.

136. Ibid., 1733.

137. Sudhir Alladi Venkatesh, *Off the Books: The Underground Economy of the Urban Poor* (Cambridge, Mass.: Harvard Univ. Press, 2006); Natapoff, "Underenforcement."

138. Natapoff, "Underenforcement," 1752–53.

139. Melissa Marschall and Paru Shah, "The Attitudinal Effects of Minority Incorporation: Examining the Racial Dimension of Trust in Urban America," *Urban Affairs Review* 42 (2007): 629–58; Ryzin, Muzzio, and Immerwahr, "Explaining the Race Gap in Satisfaction with Urban Services."

140. Massey, "Getting Away with Murder."

141. Although the New York City Police Department did not admit that racial profiling played a role in the killing of Diallo, the city reached a $3 million settlement with Diallo's family in the face of racial profiling allegations. Alan Feuer, "$3 Million Deal in Police Killing of Diallo in '99," *New York Times*, Jan. 7, 2004: A1.

142. Randall Kennedy, *Race, Crime, and the Law* (New York: Vintage, 1997), 141–42, 152–53.

143. David Cutler and Edward Glaeser, "Are Ghettos Good or Bad?" *Quarterly Journal of Economics* 112.3 (1997): 847.

Chapter Three
Segregation, Racial Stigma, and Discrimination

1. Yueh-Ting Lee, Lee Jussim, and Clark McCauley, eds., *Stereotype Accuracy* (Washington, D.C.: APA, 1995).

2. Fiske, "Stereotyping, Prejudice and Discrimination," 362, 368, 371.

3. See Kenneth Arrow, "Some Mathematical Models of Race Discrimination in the Labor Market," in *Racial Discrimination in Economic Life*, ed. Anthony Pascal (Lexington, Mass.: Lexington Books, 1972), 187–203.

4. Glenn Loury, *The Anatomy of Racial Inequality* (Cambridge, Mass.: Harvard Univ. Press, 2002), 59. It might be thought that stereotypes of blacks as more likely to engage in crime than other groups are inherently stigmatizing. Matters are not so simple. The ratio of black to white imprisonment rates is 6.2:1. The ratio of male to female imprisonment rates is about 14:1. Heather West and William Sabol, *Prisoners in 2007*, NCJ 224280, Bureau of Justice Statistics Bulletin (Washington, D.C.: U.S. Department of Justice, 2009), 4, table 6, http://www .ojp.usdoj.gov/bjs/pub/pdf/p07.pdf. Few Americans would be surprised by this lopsided gender ratio. Yet men are not stigmatized by this familiar difference: they are not thereby regarded as presumptively untrustworthy, dangerous, or undeserving of positions of power and responsibility.

5. Fiske, "Stereotyping, Prejudice and Discrimination," 370.

6. Images from Yahoo! news archived by DvorakUncensored, "Blacks Are 'Looters' and Whites Are 'Finders'," *DvorakUncensored* (2005), http://www .dvorak.org/blog/images/katrina/.

7. Stigma need not represent the disfavored group as inferior. Henry Louis Gates observes that "[t]he racist believes that blacks are incapable of running anything by themselves. The anti-Semite believes . . . that thirteen rabbis rule the world." Henry Louis Gates, Jr., "Backlash," *New Yorker*, May 17, 1993: 42–43. Susan Fiske et al. "A Model of (Often Mixed) Stereotype Content: Competence and Warmth Respectively Follow from Perceived Status and Competition," *Journal of Personality and Social Psychology* 82.6 (2002): 878–902, explain that group stereotypes vary along two dimensions: competence and warmth. Groups such as Jews and Asians are stereotyped as competent but cold, a combination that inspires envy and suspicion; older people and those with disabilities as incompetent but warm, inspiring pity; poor and homeless people as incompetent and cold, inspiring contempt.

8. Douglas Massey, *Categorically Unequal: The American Stratification System* (New York: Russell Sage, 2007), 69.

9. Marilynn Brewer, "The Psychology of Prejudice: Ingroup Love or Outgroup Hate?" *Journal of Social Issues* 55.3 (1999): 429–44.

10. Fiske, "Stereotyping, Prejudice and Discrimination," 370; Samuel Gaertner and John Dovidio, "A Common Ingroup Identity: A Categorization-Based Approach for Reducing Intergroup Bias," in *Handbook of Prejudice, Stereotyping, and Discrimination*, ed. Todd Nelson (New York: Taylor and Francis, 2009), 491.

11. Curtis Hardin and Terri Conley, "A Relational Approach to Cognition: Shared Experience and Relationship Affirmation in Social Cognition," in *Cognitive Social Psychology: The Princeton Symposium on the Legacy and Future of Social Cognition*, ed. Gordon Moskowitz (Mahwah, N.J.: Erlbaum, 2001), 3–17.

12. David Hamilton and Steven Sherman, "Illusory Correlations: Implications for Stereotype Theory and Research," in *Stereotyping and Prejudice: Changing Conceptions*, ed. Daniel Bar-Tal, Carl Graumann, Arie Kruglanski, and Wolfgang Stroebe (New York: Springer-Verlag, 1989). The correlation in question need not be utterly false, but merely exaggerated, for the same mechanisms appear to underlie exaggeration of categorical differences ("category accentuation") and perception of nonexistent group differences. Jeffrey Sherman, et al., "Attentional Processes in Stereotype Formation: A Common Model for Category Accentuation and Illusory Correlation," *Journal of Personality and Social Psychology* 96.2 (2009): 305–23.

13. Barbara Reskin, *The Realities of Affirmative Action in Employment* (Washington, D.C.: American Sociological Association, 1998), 35–36.

14. Susan Fiske, "Controlling Other People: The Impact of Power on Stereotyping," *American Psychologist* 48 (1993): 621–28; Stephanie Goodwin, Alexandra Gubin, Susan Fiske, and Vincent Yzerbyt, "Power Can Bias Impression Processes: Stereotyping Subordinates by Default and by Design," *Group Processes & Intergroup Relations* 3.3 (2000): 227–56; Jennifer Richeson and Nalini Ambady, "Effects of Situational Power on Automatic Racial Prejudice," *Journal of Experimental Social Psychology* 39.2 (2003): 177–83.

15. John Jost, "Outgroup Favoritism and the Theory of System Justification: A Paradigm for Investigating the Effects of Socioeconomic Success on Stereotype Content," in *Cognitive Social Psychology: The Princeton Symposium on the*

Legacy and Future of Social Cognition, ed. Gordon Moskowitz (Mahwah, N.J.: Erlbaum, 2001), 89–102.

16. Anthony Greenwald and Mahzarin Banaji, "Implicit Social Cognition: Attitudes, Self-Esteem, and Stereotypes," *Psychological Review* 102.1 (1995): 4–27; Fiske, "Stereotyping, Prejudice and Discrimination," 364–72.

17. I thank Jorge Garcia for this point. Since my concern is racial stigmatization and racial injustice, rather than racism, I decline to offer a complete analysis of racism here.

18. Angela Smith, "Responsibility for Attitudes: Activity and Passivity in Mental Life," *Ethics* 115.2 (2005): 236–71; Angela Smith, "Conflicting Attitudes, Moral Agency, and Conceptions of the Self," *Philosophical Topics* 32.1–2 (2004): 331–52.

19. My discussion is indebted to Lawrence Blum, *"I'm Not a Racist . . . but": The Moral Quandary of Race* (Ithaca, N.Y.: Cornell Univ. Press, 2002), 1–32, who also distinguishes racism from racial injustice, for similar reasons.

20. See Samuel Gaertner and John Dovidio, "The Aversive Form of Racism," in *Prejudice, Discrimination, and Racism*, ed. John Dovidio and Samuel Gaertner (Orlando: Academic Press, 1986), 61–89; and Samuel Gaertner and John Dovidio, "Aversive Racism," in *Advances in Experimental Social Psychology*, vol. 36, ed. Mark Zanna (San Diego: Academic Press, 2004), 1–52. The label "aversive racism" is unfortunate for the reasons I have just discussed, but since it is a technical term I shall follow convention in using it to refer to the phenomenon in question.

21. Jennifer Crocker, Brenda Major, and Claude Steele, "Social Stigma," in *Handbook of Social Psychology*, vol. 2, ed. Daniel Gilbert, Susan Fiske, and Gardner Lindzey (New York: McGraw-Hill, 1998), 512.

22. John Dovidio and Samuel Gaertner, "Aversive Racism and Selection Decisions: 1989 and 1999," *Psychological Science* 11.4 (2000): 315–19.

23. Barbara Reskin, "The Proximate Causes of Employment Discrimination," *Contemporary Sociology* 29.2 (2000): 319–28.

24. Richard Apostle, Charles Glock, Thomas Piazza, and Marijean Suelzle, *The Anatomy of Racial Attitudes* (Berkeley: Univ. of California Press, 1983); Donald Kinder and Lynn Sanders, *Divided by Color* (Chicago: Univ. of Chicago Press, 1996) 115; Howard Schuman, Charlotte Steeh, Lawrence Bobo, and Maria Krysan, *Racial Attitudes in America*, rev. ed. (Cambridge, Mass.: Harvard Univ. Press, 1997), table 3.1, 104–8.

25. Thernstrom and Thernstrom, *America in Black and White*; Paul Sniderman and Thomas Piazza, *The Scar of Race* (Cambridge, Mass.: Belknap-Harvard University Press, 1993).

26. Such studies are too numerous to list. Representative examples include Harry Holzer, "Racial Differences in Labor Market Outcomes among Men," in *America Becoming: Racial Trends and Their Consequences*, vol. 2, ed. Neil Smelser, William Julius Wilson, and Faith Mitchell (Washington, D.C.: National Academies Press, 2001) (finding a persistent 20 percent gap in wages between black and white male workers after applying numerous controls); Stephen Ross and John Yinger, *The Color of Credit: Mortgage Discrimination, Research Methodology, and Fair-Lending Enforcement* (Cambridge, Mass.: MIT Press, 2002)

(finding a significant gap in loan approvals for equally credit-worthy black and white mortgage loan applicants).

27. Devah Pager and Hana Shepherd, "The Sociology of Discrimination: Racial Discrimination in Employment, Housing, Credit, and Consumer Markets," *Annual Review of Sociology* 34 (2008): 181–209; Michael Fix and Raymond Struyk, *Clear and Convincing Evidence: Measurement of Discrimination in America* (Washington, D.C.: Urban Institute Press, 1993); Helen Ladd, "Evidence on Discrimination in Mortgage Lending," *Journal of Economic Perspectives* 12.2 (1998): 41–62; John Yinger, "Evidence on Discrimination in Consumer Markets," *Journal of Economic Perspectives* 12.2 (1998): 23–40.

28. Ian Ayres, *Pervasive Prejudice? Unconventional Evidence of Race and Gender Discrimination* (Chicago: Univ. of Chicago Press, 2001); Yinger, "Evidence on Discrimination in Consumer Markets."

29. William Darity, Jr., and Patrick Mason, "Evidence on Discrimination in Employment: Codes of Color, Codes of Gender," *Journal of Economic Perspectives* 12.2 (1998): 63–90; Marianne Bertrand and Sendhil Mullainathan, "Are Emily and Greg More Employable than Lakisha and Jamal? A Field Experiment in Labor Market Discrimination," *American Economic Review* 94.4 (2004): 991–1013.

30. Devah Pager, "The Mark of a Criminal Record," *American Journal of Sociology* 108.5 (2003): 937–75.

31. Ellis Cose, *The Rage of a Privileged Class* (New York: HarperCollins, 1993); Joe Feagin and Melvin Sikes, *Living with Racism: The Black Middle-Class Experience* (Boston: Beacon, 1994).

32. Kirschenman and Neckerman, "'We'd Love to Hire Them, but...,'" 203–32; Philip Moss and Chris Tilly, *Stories Employers Tell: Race, Skill and Hiring in America* (New York: Russell Sage, 2001).

33. William Julius Wilson and Richard Taub, *There Goes the Neighborhood: Racial, Ethnic, and Class Tensions in Four Chicago Neighborhoods and Their Meaning for America* (New York: Knopf-Random, 2006).

34. Anthony Greenwald, Debbie McGhee, and Jordan Schwartz, "Measuring Individual Differences in Implicit Cognition: The Implicit Association Test," *Journal of Personality and Social Psychology* 74.6 (1998): 1464–80; Nilanjana Dasgupta, Debbie McGhee, Anthony Greenwald, and Mahzarin Banaji, "Automatic Preference for White Americans: Eliminating the Familiarity Explanation," *Journal of Experimental Social Psychology* 36 (2000): 316–28, http://faculty .washington.edu/agg/pdf/DasguptaEtAl.JESP2000.pdf.

35. Gaertner and Dovidio, "The Aversive Form of Racism"; Dovidio and Gaertner, "Aversive Racism and Selection Decisions."

36. Kinder and Sanders, *Divided by Color*; Schuman, Steeh, Bobo, and Krysan, *Racial Attitudes in America*; Sears, Sidanius, and Bobo, eds., *Racialized Politics*.

37. Kinder and Sanders, *Divided by Color*, 19.

38. Christopher Ruhm, "Labor Market Discrimination in the United States," in *Affirmative Action in Perspective*, ed. Fletcher Blanchard and Faye Crosby (New York: Springer, 1989), 149–58.

39. James Heckman, "Detecting Discrimination," *Journal of Economic Perspectives* 12.2 (1998): 101–16.

40. Thernstrom and Thernstrom, *America in Black and White*, 494–512.

41. Paul Sniderman and Michael Hagen, *Race and Inequality: A Study in American Values* (Chatham, N.J.: Chatham House, 1985).

42. Ross and Yinger, *The Color of Credit.*

43. Ibid.; Darity and Mason, "Evidence on Discrimination in Employment."

44. Dasgupta, McGhee, Greenwald, and Banaji, "Automatic Preference for White Americans."

45. Crocker, Major, and Steele, "Social Stigma," 522.

46. Donald Kinder and Tali Mendelberg, "Individualism Reconsidered: Principles and Prejudice in Contemporary American Opinion," in *Racialized Politics*, 44–74.

47. Kinder and Sanders, *Divided by Color.*

48. Irwin Katz and R. Glen Hass, "Racial Ambivalence and American Value Conflict: Correlational and Priming Studies of Dual Cognitive Structures," *Journal of Personality and Social Psychology* 55.6 (1988): 893–905.

49. P. J. Henry and David Sears, "The Symbolic Racism 2000 Scale," *Political Psychology* 23.2 (2002): 253–83; David Sears, "Symbolic Racism," in *Eliminating Racism: Profiles in Controversy*, ed. Phyllis Katz and Dalmas Taylor (New York: Plenum, 1988), 53–84.

50. John McConahay, "Modern Racism, Ambivalence, and the Modern Racism Scale," in *Prejudice, Discrimination, and Racism*, 91–125.

51. Crocker, Major, and Steele, "Social Stigma," 512–13, 538–41.

52. Joe Feagin, "The Continuing Significance of Race: Antiblack Discrimination in Public Places," *American Sociological Review* 56.1 (1991): 101–16; Anderson, *Streetwise.*

53. Loury, *Anatomy of Racial Inequality*, 23–33; Lee Jussim and Christopher Fleming, "Self-Fulfilling Prophecies and the Maintenance of Social Stereotypes: The Role of Dyadic Interactions and Social Forces," in *Stereotypes and Stereotyping*, ed. C. Neil Macrae, Charles Stangor, and Miles Hewstone (New York: Guilford, 1996), 161–92.

54. Ronald Ferguson, "Teachers' Perceptions and Expectations and the Black-white Test Score Gap," in *The Black-White Test Score Gap*, ed. Christopher Jencks and Meredith Phillips (Washington, D.C.: Brookings Institution Press, 1998), 273–317.

55. Crocker, Major, and Steele, "Social Stigma," 528–30.

56. Claude Steele, "Race and the Schooling of Black Americans," *Atlantic Monthly* (April 1992): 68–78.

57. Claude Steele and Joshua Aronson, "Stereotype Threat and the Intellectual Test Performance of African-Americans," *Journal of Personality and Social Psychology* 69.5 (1995): 797–811.

58. Crocker, Major, and Steele, "Social Stigma," 518–19, 533–38.

59. Douglas Massey, Camille Charles, Garvey Lundy, and Mary Fischer, *The Source of the River: The Social Origins of Freshmen at America's Selective Colleges and Universities* (Princeton, N.J.: Princeton Univ. Press, 2003), 184–96.

60. The vast majority of violent crime is intraracial. See Callie Rennison, *Violent Victimization and Race, 1993–98*, Bureau of Justice Statistics Special Re-

port NCJ 176354 (Washington, D.C.: U.S. Department of Justice, 2001), http://permanent.access.gpo.gov/lps19659/www.ojp.usdoj.gov/bjs/pub/pdf/vvr98.pdf.

61. However, according to the illusory correlation bias, segregated whites who learn about a crime involving a black offender are likely to form a negative stereotype about blacks on that basis.

62. Franklin Gilliam and Shanto Iyengar, "Prime Suspects: The Influence of Local Television News on the Viewing Public," *American Journal of Political Science* 44.3 (2000): 560–73.

63. Travis Dixon and Daniel Linz, "Overrepresentation and Underrepresentation of African Americans and Latinos as Lawbreakers on Television News," *Journal of Communication* 50.2 (2000): 131–54; Lori Dorfman and Vincent Schiraldi, *Off Balance: Youth, Race & Crime in the News* (Washington, D.C.: Building Blocks for Youth, 2001), http://www.buildingblocksforyouth.org/media/media.pdf.

64. Dorfman and Schiraldi, *Off Balance*, 12–17.

65. Gilliam and Iyengar, "Prime Suspects," 564.

66. Mary Beth Oliver, "Caucasian Viewers' Memory of Black and White Criminal Suspects in the News," *Journal of Communication* 49.3 (1999): 46–60. This study reproduces for the intrapersonal case the classic study of rumor transmission by Gordon Allport and Leo Postman, "The Basic Psychology of Rumor," *Transactions of the New York Academy of Sciences, 2nd Series* 8 (1945): 61–81. Participants were shown a picture of a white man holding a straight razor in a mixed-race subway scene and told to relate the story to another person, who told it to another, along a chain. Six tellings later, the story was of a black man holding the razor.

67. Mary Oliver and Dana Fonash, "Race and Crime in the News: Whites' Identification and Misidentification of Violent and Nonviolent Criminal Suspects," *Media Psychology* 4.2 (2002): 137–56.

68. Travis Dixon and Keith Maddox, "Skin Tone, Crime News, and Social Reality Judgments: Priming the Stereotype of the Dark and Dangerous Black Criminal," *Journal of Applied Social Psychology* 35.8 (2005): 1555–70, http://www.spcomm.uiuc.edu/tldixon/research_files/Dixon%20&%20Maddox%20(2005).pdf.

69. Anthony Greenwald, Mark Oakes, and Hunter Hoffman, "Targets of Discrimination: Effects of Race on Responses to Weapons Holders," *Journal of Experimental Social Psychology* 39 (2003): 399–405. This "shooter bias" is a product of stigma—mere awareness of the negative public image of blacks as violent—rather than personal belief, since it varies with awareness of the stereotype but not with its endorsement or with measures of personal prejudice. Joshua Correll, Bernadette Park, Charles Judd, and Bernd Wittenbrink, "The Police Officer's Dilemma: Using Ethnicity to Disambiguate Potentially Threatening Individuals," *Journal of Personality and Social Psychology* 83.6 (2002): 1325.

70. Birt Duncan, "Differential Social Perception and Attribution of Intergroup Violence: Testing the Lower Limits of Stereotyping of Blacks," *Journal of Personality and Social Psychology* 34.4 (1976): 590–98.

71. Samuel Sommers et al., "Race and Media Coverage of Hurricane Katrina:

Analysis, Implications, and Future Research Questions," *Analyses of Social Issues and Public Policy* 6.1 (2006): 6–7.

72. The distinction between ethnocentrism and out-group antipathy has been stressed by Brewer, "The Psychology of Prejudice." Conceptually, we can distinguish love vs. hate from ingroup vs. outgroup. Sometimes, people love groups to which they do not belong and hate groups to which they belong. Empirically, however, this phenomenon is not a significant source of categorical inequality. We should also distinguish outgroup antipathy, which may be directed at any group, from stigma, which applies specifically to publicly dishonored groups and ties in to categorical inequality.

73. Wilson and Taub, in *There Goes the Neighborhood*, offer a vivid account of the persistence of these attitudes in a Chicago neighborhood.

74. Gary Becker, *The Economics of Discrimination*, 2nd ed. (Chicago: Univ. of Chicago Press, 1971).

75. Thomas Pettigrew and Linda Tropp, "Allport's Intergroup Contact Hypothesis: Its History and Influence," in *On the Nature of Prejudice: Fifty Years after Allport*, ed. John Dovidio, Peter Glick, and Laurie Rudman (Malden, Mass.: Blackwell, 2005), 272.

76. John Dovidio, John Brigham, Blair Johnson, and Samuel Gaertner, "Stereotyping, Prejudice, and Discrimination: Another Look," in *Stereotypes and Stereotyping*, ed. Macrae, Stangor, and Hewstone, 276–319.

77. Kenneth Arrow, "The Theory of Discrimination," in *Discrimination in Labor Markets*, ed. Orly Ashenfelter and Albert Rees (Princeton, N.J.: Princeton Univ. Press, 1973), 3–33; Edmund Phelps, "The Statistical Theory of Racism and Sexism," *The American Economic Review* 62.4 (1972): 659–61.

78. One might object that stigmatization of vicious people is not unjust. Stigmatization of the morally vicious, however, has never grounded categorical inequality, which is perpetuated across generations on the basis of ascriptive social categories that are at least partially imposed and characteristically based on circumstances of birth.

79. Note that this is distinct from the common idea that what makes categorical discrimination unjust is that it is based on qualities that are involuntary or not under the control of the victim. Some genuine merits—for example, height for basketball players—are not under the control of the candidates for selection, but that does not make height an unjust basis of selection for basketball players. And some forms of categorical discrimination are based on identities from which individuals may opt out. Before World War I, thousands of Jews in Europe converted to Christianity to gain access to opportunities, such as civil service positions, reserved for Christians. That their status as Jews was under their control did not make categorical discrimination against Jews fair.

80. Dixon and Maddox, "Skin Tone, Crime News, and Social Reality Judgments."

81. Joni Hersch, "Skin-Tone Effects among African Americans: Perceptions and Reality," *American Economic Review* 96.2 (2006): 251–55; Joni Hersch, "Profiling the New Immigrant Worker: The Effects of Skin Color and Height," *Journal of Labor Economics* 26.2 (2008): 345–86.

82. Julie Kmec, "Minority Job Concentration and Wages," 38–59, finds that

workers of all races pay an 18 percent wage penalty if they work in predominantly black jobs, after controlling for human capital, unionization, location, length of time on the job, and other variables. Matt Huffman and Philip Cohen, "Racial Wage Inequality: Job Segregation and Devaluation across U.S. Labor Markets," *American Journal of Sociology* 109.4 (2004): 925, also find a substantial wage penalty after imposing similar controls.

83. Alberto Alesina, Reza Baquir, and William Easterly, "Public Goods and Ethnic Divisions," *Quarterly Journal of Economics* 114.4 (1999): 1243–84.

84. Henry and Sears, "The Symbolic Racism 2000 Scale."

85. Kinder and Sanders, *Divided by Color*, 116–21.

86. Eva Green, Christian Staerklé, and David Sears, "Symbolic Racism and Whites' Attitudes towards Punitive and Preventive Crime Policies," *Law and Human Behavior* 30.4 (2006): 435–54. These correlations remain even after controlling for race-neutral factors such as individualism, conservative ideology, and party identification.

87. Travis Dixon, "Psychological Reactions to Crime News Portrayals of Black Criminals: Understanding the Moderating Roles of Prior News Viewing and Stereotype Endorsement," *Communication Monographs* 73.2 (2006): 162–87; Gilliam and Iyengar, "Prime Suspects"; Mark Peffley and Jon Hurwitz, "The Racial Components of 'Race-Neutral' Crime Policy Attitudes," *Political Psychology* 23.1 (2002): 59–75.

88. Mark Peffley and Jon Hurwitz, "Persuasion and Resistance: Race and the Death Penalty in America," *American Journal of Political Science* 51.4 (2007): 996–1012.

89. Dixon and Maddox, "Skin Tone, Crime News, and Social Reality Judgments"; Franklin Gilliam, Shanto Iyengar, Adam Simon, and Oliver Wright, "Crime in Black and White: The Violent, Scary World of Local News," *Harvard International Journal of Press/Politics* 1.3 (1996): 6–23.

90. Jon Hurwitz and Mark Peffley, "Public Perceptions of Race and Crime: The Role of Racial Stereotypes," *American Journal of Political Science* 41.2 (1997): 375–401.

91. Loury, *Anatomy of Racial Inequality*, 71.

92. Martin Gilens, "Race and Poverty in America: Public Misperceptions and the American News Media," *Public Opinion Quarterly* 60.4 (1996): 515–41.

93. Ibid., 517; Martin Gilens, *Why Americans Hate Welfare: Race, Media and the Politics of Antipoverty Policy* (Chicago: Univ. of Chicago Press, 1999).

94. Weiher, *The Fractured Metropolis*, x.

Chapter Four
Racial Segregation Today

1. I set aside the hypothesis that black-white inequalities are due to black genetic deficiencies. No scientifically credible research program supports this hypothesis, and it is no longer taken seriously in public discourse either.

2. Stephen G. Meyer, *As Long as They Don't Move Next Door: Segregation and Racial Conflict in American Neighborhoods* (Lanham, Md.: Rowman and Littlefield, 2000); Kenneth Jackson, *Crabgrass Frontier: The Suburbanization of*

America (New York: Oxford Univ. Press, 1985); Thomas Sugrue, *The Origins of the Urban Crisis: Race and Inequality in Postwar Detroit* (Princeton, N.J.: Princeton Univ. Press, 1996); Massey and Denton, *American Apartheid*, 17–82.

3. See Casey Dawkins, "Recent Evidence on the Continuing Causes of Black-white Residential Segregation," *Journal of Urban Affairs* 26.3 (2004): 379–400; Margery Austin Turner, "Discrimination in Urban Housing Markets: Lessons from Fair Housing Audits," *Housing Policy Debate* 3.2 (1992): 185–215; John Yinger, *Closed Doors, Opportunities Lost* (New York: Russell Sage, 1995); Michael Fix and Raymond Struyk, *Clear and Convincing Evidence: Measurement of Discrimination in America* (Washington, D.C.: Urban Institute Press, 1993); Massey and Denton, *American Apartheid*, 96–114. Massey and Denton argue that levels of housing discrimination vary in response to white demands to keep the probability of random contact with blacks to 5 percent or less.

4. See Massey and Denton, *American Apartheid*, 186–216. As of May 18, 2007, the Department of Housing and Urban Development listed twenty-nine cases of race discrimination that it was prosecuting under the Fair Housing Act, most of which were filed in 2004. Only eight cases were initiated in 2006. http://www.hud.gov/offices/fheo/enforcement/hudcharges.cfm.

5. Massey and Denton, *American Apartheid*, 17–59; Jackson, *Crabgrass Frontier*.

6. Nancy Burns, *The Formation of American Local Governments: Private Values in Public Institutions* (New York: Oxford Univ. Press, 1994), 85–91.

7. The Supreme Court documented the existence of this practice and declared it unconstitutional in *Swann v. Charlotte-Mecklenburg Bd. of Ed.*, 402 U.S. 1 (1971). However, enforcement of the law on this point has been weak.

8. Weiher, *Fractured Metropolis*.

9. Thernstrom and Thernstrom, *America in Black and White*, 219–31.

10. Michael Emerson, Karen Chai, and George Yancey, "Does Race Matter in Residential Segregation? Exploring the Preferences of White Americans," *American Sociological Review* 66.6 (2001): 922–35.

11. Sheryll Cashin, "Middle Class Black Suburbs and the State of Integration: A Post-Integrationist Vision for Metropolitan America," *Cornell Law Review* 86.4 (2001): 729–76.

12. Maria Krysan and Reynolds Farley, "The Residential Preferences of Blacks: Do They Explain Persistent Segregation?" *Social Forces* 80.3 (2002): 937–80.

13. Howard Husock, "A Critique of Mixed Income Housing: The Problems with 'Gatreaux'," *Responsive Community* 5.2 (1995): 34–44.

14. See Ingrid Gould Ellen, *Sharing America's Neighborhoods: The Prospects for Stable Racial Integration* (Cambridge, Mass.: Harvard Univ. Press, 2000).

15. Thomas Schelling, "Models of Segregation," *American Economic Review* 59.2 (1969): 488–93; Thomas Schelling, *Micromotives and Macrobehavior* (New York: Norton, 1978).

16. Whether neighborhoods have tipping points depends on the structure of white tastes. Empirical evidence on white preferences appears to be inconsistent with the type of model needed to generate high segregation via a Schelling-style tipping point. See Elizabeth Bruch and Robert Mare, "Neighborhood Choice

and Neighborhood Change," *American Journal of Sociology* 112.3 (2006): 667–709.

17. Massey and Denton, *American Apartheid*, 97.

18. Emerson, Chai, and Yancey, "Does Race Matter in Residential Segregation?"

19. Ellen, *Sharing America's Neighborhoods*, 41.

20. Massey and Denton, *American Apartheid*, 57.

21. Gregory Mitchell and Philip Tetlock, "Antidiscrimination Law and the Perils of Mindreading," *Ohio State Law Journal* 67.5 (2006): 1088.

22. In a reply to critics, Mitchell and Tetlock shift their focus to doubts that a common measure of unconscious bias, the Implicit Association Test (IAT), is causally linked to discriminatory conduct. Gregory Mitchell and Philip Tetlock, "Facts Do Matter: A Reply to Bagenstos," *Hofstra Law Review* (2009), http://ssrn.com/abstract=1324367. However, the evidence that unconscious thoughts cause discrimination does not fundamentally rest on the IAT. Other sources of evidence, notably the experiments on aversive racism, in which people discriminate against blacks when a race-neutral justification is available but appear to be unaware of their discriminatory behavior, are more important. What the IAT does is offer evidence that people hold unconscious stereotypical representations of stigmatized groups. This makes more plausible the claim that people can really be unaware of thoughts that, if practically engaged, would cause them to discriminate. This in turn makes plausible the claim that people are not always aware of when they are discriminating, since they are not always aware of the thoughts that would make them discriminate.

23. Amy Wax, "Discrimination as Accident," *Indiana Law Journal* 74.4 (1999): 1129–1231.

24. Thomas Scanlon, *What We Owe to Each Other* (Cambridge, Mass.: Harvard Univ. Press, 1998); Angela Smith, "Responsibility for Attitudes."

25. Wax argues that the victims are "least cost avoiders" of the discriminatory harms of unconscious group-based stereotypes since they may be able to overwhelm negative stereotypes by making themselves obviously better workers than their nonstigmatized peers. Wax, "Discrimination as Accident," 1201–2. This ignores the fact that having to put in superior performance in order to get the same benefits as nonstigmatized peers is *constitutive* of discriminatory harm and hence cannot be a way to avoid that harm.

26. Reskin, "Proximate Causes of Employment Discrimination."

27. See Joshua Correll et al., "Across the Thin Blue Line: Police Officers and Racial Bias in the Decision to Shoot," *Journal of Personality and Social Psychology* 92.6 (2007): 1006–23, finding that untrained civilians displayed racial "shooter bias," but not well-trained police, and that training reduced the bias among civilians. It appears that police need training to avoid both direct *and* second-order discrimination in shooting. For Correll and colleagues cite evidence that police display shooter bias toward residents of neighborhoods perceived as disadvantaged, and that "the mere presence" of blacks in the neighborhood "is sufficient to evoke the perception of disadvantage" (1022).

28. Thernstrom and Thernstrom, *America in Black and White*.

29. In other work, I have criticized game-theoretic conceptions of cultural norms for their overly rationalistic, instrumental, egoistic conception of the motives underlying adherence to norms. Norms cannot survive under common knowledge of their grounds unless some people accept them as setting nonstrategically valid standards of conduct. Elizabeth Anderson, "Beyond *Homo Economicus:* New Developments in Economic Theories of Social Norms," *Philosophy and Public Affairs* 29.2 (2000): 170–200. A full understanding of norms must also incorporate the effects of cognitive, motivational, and behavioral biases and consider what they mean to the agents that follow them. These criticisms of game-theoretic models of norms should not be construed as rejecting the models altogether.

30. William Julius Wilson defends the necessity of integrating cultural with structural explanations of systematic group disadvantage in *More than Just Race: Being Black and Poor in the Inner City* (New York: Norton, 2009).

31. Arline Geronimus and Sanders Korenman, "The Socioeconomic Consequences of Teen Childbearing Reconsidered," *Quarterly Journal of Economics* 107.4 (1992): 1187–1214, find that poor teens pay no opportunity cost from early childbearing because their economic opportunities are already so constrained. David Ellwood, Ty Wilde, and Lilly Batchelder, "The Mommy Track Divides: The Impact of Childbearing on Wages of Women of Differing Skill Levels," working paper (New York: Russell Sage, 2004), http://www.russellsage.org/ publications/workingpapers/mommytrack, confirm that low-skill women pay little cost for early childbearing. Saul Hoffman, E. Michael Foster, and Frank Furstenberg Jr., "Reevaluating the Costs of Teenage Childbearing," *Demography* 30.1 (1993): 1–13, dispute this view. Whichever side is right, it is a safe bet that if it takes sophisticated statistical analysis to detect these costs, such that even experts disagree on whether they exist, they are unlikely to be evident enough to poor teens to affect their behavior.

32. Kathryn Edin and Maria Kefalas, *Promises I Can Keep: Why Poor Women Put Motherhood before Marriage* (Berkeley and Los Angeles: Univ. of California Press, 2005), 34, report that most of the single mothers they interviewed in Philadelphia and Camden "said they have no close friends, and many even distrust close kin"—a common experience in communities with concentrated poverty and high crime—and that the search for love is a powerful motive for young women to have children. Edin and Kefalas observe few differences among the perspectives of white, black, and Latino poor single mothers. This is powerful evidence that single teen childbearing is more a product of living in a community with concentrated poverty and marginalization than of race-specific cultural factors.

33. This is the "male marriagable pool" theory of why marriage rates have declined so precipitously in ghetto neighborhoods. See William Julius Wilson, *The Truly Disadvantaged* (Chicago: Univ. of Chicago Press, 1987). Kathryn Edin and Maria Kefalas argue that, while this theory does better than its rivals, it cannot explain all of the decline in marriage among the poor. They argue that changed conceptions of the value of marriage and the rise of feminism—values that are *shared* by the middle class and poor—also contributed to the decline in marriage rates. The poor are therefore not deviating from mainstream values about mar-

riage, but rather manifesting those values in disadvantageous circumstances. Edin and Kefalas, *Promises I Can Keep*, 198–202.

34. Elijah Anderson, *Code of the Street: Decency, Violence, and the Moral Life of the Inner City* (New York: Norton, 1999).

35. Massey, "Getting Away with Murder"; Dan Silverman, "Street Crime and Street Culture," *International Economic Review* 45.3 (2004): 761–86.

36. The phenomenon of joint and several liability reminds us that allocations of responsibility to additional agents need not reduce the responsibility assigned to given agents.

37. Thernstrom and Thernstrom, *America in Black and White*, 285.

38. Signithia Fordham and John Ogbu, "Black Students' School Success: Coping with the 'Burden of "Acting White"'," *Urban Review* 18.3 (1986): 176–206.

39. See the brief review of this literature in Massey, Charles, Lundy, and Fischer, *Source of the River*, 7–10.

40. Fordham and Ogbu, "Black Students' School Success," 202–3.

41. See, for example, Thernstrom and Thernstrom, *America in Black and White*, 383.

42. John McWhorter, *Losing the Race: Self-Sabotage in Black America* (New York: Free Press, 2000).

43. Disconfirming studies include James Ainsworth-Darnell and Douglas Downey, "Assessing the Oppositional Culture Explanation for Racial/Ethnic Differences in School Performance," *American Sociological Review* 63.4 (1998): 536–53; Philip Cook and Jens Ludwig, "The Burden of 'Acting White': Do Black Adolescents Disparage Academic Achievement?" in *The Black-White Test Score Gap*, ed. Christopher Jencks and Meredith Phillips (Washington, D.C.: Brookings Institution Press, 1998), 375–400; Massey, Charles, Lundy, and Fischer, *Source of the River*, 194–95; and Angel Harris, "I (Don't) Hate School: Revisiting Oppositional Culture Theory of Blacks' Resistance to Schooling," *Social Forces* 85.2 (2006): 797–834. Roland Fryer, Jr., and Paul Torelli, "An Empirical Analysis of 'Acting White'," working paper (Harvard University, 2006), http://www.economics .harvard.edu/faculty/fryer/papers/fryer_torelli.pdf, find that blacks in black schools and private schools pay no popularity penalty for high academic achievement, although there is a penalty for blacks in integrated public schools. This contradicts the oppositional culture hypothesis, which implies that the penalty should exist for blacks in all schools, especially black schools. That the penalty exists in integrated schools implicates high-achieving white students and not just black students since it shows that they also reject high-achieving black students.

44. David Hollinger argues against the idea that Asians and blacks are similarly situated, in "The One Drop Rule & the One Hate Rule," *Daedalus* 134.1 (2005): 18–28.

45. William Julius Wilson, *When Work Disappears: The World of the New Urban Poor* (New York: Knopf, 1996).

46. Sarah Lyall, "How the Young Poor Measure Poverty in Britain: Drink, Drugs and Their Time in Jail," *New York Times*, Mar. 10, 2007: A5. Similar findings obtain for disadvantaged neighborhoods in Cologne, Germany. See Jürgen Friedrichs and Jörg Blasius, "Social Norms in Distressed Neighbourhoods: Testing the Wilson Hypothesis," *Housing Studies* 18.6 (2003): 807–26.

Chapter Five
Democratic Ideals and Segregation

1. *Talbot v. Janson* 3 U.S. 133, 141 (1795) (recognizing, inter alia, the right of a U.S. citizen to renounce citizenship and become a citizen of another nation).

2. *Scott v. Sandford*, 60 U.S. 393, 407 (1867).

3. Here I gloss over a conceptual dispute. Republicans called the rights just listed "civil" or "public" rights to ward off the accusation that they were trying to force whites to befriend blacks or invite them into their homes. They agreed that the state was in no position to force such interracial intimacy. See, for example, *Civil Rights Cases* 109 U.S. 3, 59, 60 (1883) (Justice Harlan, dissenting). The rights listed above as social either are exercised in civil society, in facilities open to the public, or, in the case of marriage, presuppose the consent of the parties. However, white supremacists, in constructing the idea of social equality, conflated such public rights with supposed rights to force interracial intimacy, to incite fears of black men having sexual contact with white women. See Rebecca Scott, "Public Rights, Social Equality, and the Conceptual Roots of the *Plessy* Challenge," *Michigan Law Review* 106 (2008): 777–804.

4. Eric Foner, *Reconstruction, 1863–1877* (New York: HarperPerennial, 1989), 222–24, 227.

5. Ibid., 223.

6. Ibid., 199–209, 225, 277–79, 448.

7. See, for example, John Sherman, "Remarks in Favor of Civil Rights Amendment," *Congressional Globe*, 42nd Congress, 2nd Session, Senate (Washington, D.C., 1872), 843; George Downing, "Memorial of the National Convention of Colored Persons, Praying to Be Protected in Their Civil Rights," Mis. Doc. No. 21, *Congressional Record*, 43rd Congress, 1st Session, Senate (1873), 2.

8. Letter addressed to Sen. Charles Sumner, which he cited in his testimony in favor of the Civil Rights Amendment, January 17, 1872, *Congressional Globe*, 42nd Congress, 2nd Session, Senate (Washington, D.C., 1872), 432.

9. Charles Sumner, speech in favor of the Civil Rights Amendment, *Congressional Globe*, 42nd Congress, 2nd Session, Senate (Washington, D.C., 1872), 382.

10. Ibid., 381–82; *Civil Rights Cases* 109 U.S. 37–50 (1883) (Justice Harlan, dissenting).

11. Sumner, speech in favor of the Civil Rights Amendment, 383.

12. It follows that the conventional opposition of majority rule with minority rights is also confused. Many individual rights are constitutive of democracy. See John Hart Ely, *Democracy and Distrust: A Theory of Judicial Review* (Cambridge, Mass.: Harvard Univ. Press, 1980), 87–104.

13. Charles Sumner, "Equal Rights, Whether Political or Civil, by Act of Congress," letter to the Border State Convention at Baltimore, September 8, 1867, in *The Works of Charles Sumner*, vol. 12 (Boston: Lee and Shepard, 1877), 184–85.

14. *Sarah C. Roberts v. The City of Boston*, 59 Mass. (5 Cush.) (1850), 204.

15. Charles Sumner, "Equality Before the Law: Unconstitutionality of Separate Colored Schools in Massachusetts," argument before the Supreme Court of Mas-

sachusetts, in the case of *Sarah C. Roberts v. The City of Boston* (1849), in *The Works of Charles Sumner*, vol. 2 (Boston: Lee and Shepard, 1870), 370.

16. Ibid., 365.

17. Ibid., 371.

18. Ibid.

19. Ibid., 370–71.

20. Ibid., 372.

21. 109 U.S. 3 (1883) (Justice Bradley, opinion of the Court).

22. *Plessy v. Ferguson*, 163 U.S. 537 (1896).

23. Aldon Morris, *The Origins of the Civil Rights Movement: Black Communities Organizing for Change* (New York: Free Press, 1984), 257–74.

24. Raymond Wolfinger, ed., "Roundtable of Participants in the Passage of the Civil Rights Act of 1964," *This Constitution* 19 (1991): 30–32.

25. John Dewey, "Valuation and Experimental Knowledge," in *The Middle Works, 1899–1924*, vol. 13: *1921–1922* (Carbondale: Southern Illinois Univ. Press, 1976), 3–28.

26. Elizabeth Anderson, "The Epistemology of Democracy," *Episteme* 3.1–2 2006): 8–22.

27. William Chafe, *Civilities and Civil Rights: Greensboro, North Carolina, and the Black Struggle for Freedom* (New York: Oxford Univ. Press, 1980).

28. For a definitive account of the second-person perspective and its connections to claims of right and practices of accountability, see Stephen Darwall, *The Second-Person Standpoint: Morality, Respect, and Accountability* (Cambridge, Mass.: Harvard Univ. Press, 2006).

29. Plato, "Republic," in *The Collected Dialogues of Plato*, ed. Edith Hamilton and Huntington Cairnes, trans. Paul Shorey (Princeton, N.J.: Princeton Univ. Press, 1961), 339a.

30. Morris, *The Origins of the Civil Rights Movement*, 268.

31. Stanley Milgram, *Obedience to Authority: An Experimental View* (New York: Harper and Row, 1974).

32. Tilly, *Identities, Boundaries, and Social Ties*, 217.

33. *Talbot v. Janson* 3 U.S. 133, 141 (1795).

34. Elizabeth Anderson, "What Is the Point of Equality?" *Ethics* 109.2 (1999): 287–337; Samuel Scheffler, "Choice, Circumstance and the Value of Equality," *Politics, Philosophy & Economics* 4.1 (2005): 5–28.

35. James Oakes, *Slavery and Freedom: An Interpretation of the Old South* (New York: Knopf, 1990), 71–72.

36. Philip Pettit, *Republicanism: A Theory of Freedom and Government* (New York: Oxford Univ. Press, 1997), 4–5.

37. See Georg W. F. Hegel, *Hegel's Phenomenology of Spirit*, trans. Arnold Miller (Oxford: Oxford Univ. Press, 1977), paras. 178–96; and Alexander Kojève's famous interpretation of these passages in *Introduction to the Reading of Hegel: Lectures on the Phenomenology of Spirit*, ed. Allan Bloom, comp. Raymond Queneau, trans. James Nichols, Jr. (Ithaca, N.Y.: Cornell Univ. Press, 1980).

38. Don Herzog, *Poisoning the Minds of the Lower Orders* (Princeton, N.J.: Princeton Univ. Press, 1998), 350.

39. Oakes, *Slavery and Freedom*, 158–66.

40. Foner, *Reconstruction*, 132–40, 171–74.

41. Charles Sumner, "Powers of Congress to Prohibit Inequality, Caste, and Oligarchy of the Skin," speech in the Senate, February 5, 1869, in *The Works of Charles Sumner*, vol. 13 (Boston: Lee and Shepard, 1880), 37.

42. Pettit, *Republicanism*, 44–49.

43. John Locke, *Second Treatise of Government* (Indianapolis: Hackett, 1980), 4.22.

44. Ibid., 11.139.

45. Adrienne Davis, "Slavery and the Roots of Sexual Harassment," 457–78.

46. This is a necessary, not a sufficient, condition on justified powers of office. Many kinds of demeaning production relations cannot be justified, even if they are efficient in a technocratic sense. However, to investigate the further restraints that considerations of equality impose on productive relations is beyond the scope of this book.

47. John Stuart Mill, *Utilitarianism* (Indianapolis: Bobbs-Merrill, 1957), 40.

48. John Dewey, "Creative Democracy: The Task Before Us," in *The Later Works, 1925–1953*, vol. 14: *1939–1941, Essays*, ed. JoAnn Boydston (Carbondale: Southern Illinois Univ. Press, 1988), 227–28.

49. While *private* offices may properly aim to serve various private interests, they may do so only in ways consistent with the public interest. The more private offices are properly subject to regulation in the public interest, the more the argument in the text applies to them.

50. Lu Hong and Scott Page, "Groups of Diverse Problem Solvers Can Outperform Groups of High-Ability Problem Solvers," *Proceedings of the National Academy of Sciences* 101.46 (2004): 16385–89; Scott Page, *The Difference: How the Power of Diversity Creates Better Groups, Firms, Schools, and Societies* (Princeton, N.J.: Princeton Univ. Press, 2007).

Chapter Six
The Imperative of Integration

1. For an example of such confusion, see Iris Marion Young, *Inclusion and Democracy* (New York: Oxford UP, 2000), 197.

2. See Robert Post, "Prejudicial Appearances: The Logic of American Antidiscrimination Law," *California Law Review* 88.1 (2000): 5. ("The theme of self-expression, however, rests on the seemingly paradoxical notion that persons have the right both to use their appearance to communicate meanings . . . and simultaneously to require others to ignore these messages.")

3. Loury, *Anatomy of Racial Inequality*, 95–96.

4. Estlund, *Working Together*, 126–34.

5. *Hills v. Gautreaux*, 425 U.S. 284 (1976).

6. James Rosenbaum, "Black Pioneers—Do Their Moves to the Suburbs Increase Economic Opportunity for Mothers and Children?" *Housing Policy Debate* 2.4 (1991): 1188.

7. Ibid., 1198.

8. James Rosenbaum, Stefanie DeLuca, and Tammy Tuck, "New Capabilities in New Places: Low-Income Black Families in Suburbia," in *The Geography of Opportunity: Race and Housing Choice in Metropolitan America*, ed. Xavier de Souza Briggs (Washington, D.C.: Brookings Institution Press, 2005), 150–75.

9. James Rosenbaum, Susan Popkin, Julie Kaufman, and Jennifer Rusin, "Social Integration of Low-Income Black Adults in Middle-Class White Suburbs," *Social Problems* 38.4 (1991): 448–61.

10. Micere Keels et al., "Fifteen Years Later: Can Residential Mobility Programs Provide a Long-Term Escape from Neighborhood Segregation, Crime, and Poverty?" *Demography* 42.1 (2005): 51–73.

11. MTO aimed at socioeconomic (not racial) integration. Blacks in the treatment group moved to only modestly more racially integrated neighborhoods than blacks in the other two groups. John Goering, Judith Feins, and Todd Richardson, "What Have We Learned About Housing Mobility and Poverty Deconcentration?" in *Choosing a Better Life? Evaluating the Moving to Opportunity Social Experiment*, ed. John Goering and Judith Feins (Washington, D.C.: Urban Institute Press, 2003), 13, 20. Hence MTO does not directly test the effects of racial integration on blacks' opportunities. It offers an indirect test of my argument, since my theory entails that some of the disadvantages of racial segregation are due to the coincidence of race with class segregation. MTO results also bear on the general argument of §1.3, that segregation of any group from the more advantaged is a basic cause of inequality. Yet MTO outcomes relative to controls underestimate the effects of socioeconomic integration because the integration of treatment and control groups converged. While many in the control groups, taking advantage of an economic boom, moved to better neighborhoods, only about half of the experimental group managed to use the voucher due to other barriers, such as discrimination and lack of information about housing opportunities. Larry Orr et al., *Moving to Opportunity Interim Impacts Evaluation* (Washington, D.C.: U.S. Dept. of Housing and Urban Development, Office of Policy Development and Research, 2003), viii.

12. Orr et al., *Moving to Opportunity Interim Impacts Evaluation*, 66.

13. Jeffrey Kling, Jeffrey Liebman, and Lawrence Katz, "Experimental Analysis of Neighborhood Effects," *Econometrica* 75.1 (2007): 102.

14. Ibid., 103.

15. Jens Ludwig, Greg Duncan, and Helen Ladd, "The Effects of MTO on Children and Parents in Baltimore," in *Choosing a Better Life?*, 164; John Goering, Judith Feins, and Todd Richardson, "A Cross-Site Analysis of Initial Moving to Opportunity Demonstration Results," *Journal of Housing Research* 13.1 (2002): 1–30.

16. Orr et al., *Moving to Opportunity Interim Impacts Evaluation*, xii.

17. Ibid.

18. Ibid., xiii.

19. Xavier de Souza Briggs and Peter Dreier, "Memphis Murder Mystery? No, Just Mistaken Identity," *Shelterforce*, July 22, 2008: 5, http://www.shelterforce.org/article/special/1043/.

20. Kristin Turney et al., "Neighborhood Effects on Barriers to Employment:

Results from a Randomized Housing Mobility Experiment in Baltimore," *Brookings-Wharton Papers on Urban Affairs* (2006); Briggs and Dreier, "Memphis Murder Mystery?," 5.

21. Turney et al., "Neighborhood Effects on Barriers to Employment."

22. David Varady and Carole Walker, "Housing Vouchers and Residential Mobility," *Journal of Planning Literature* 18.1 (2003): 25.

23. Xavier de Souza Briggs, "Brown Kids in White Suburbs: Housing Mobility and the Many Faces of Social Capital," *Housing Policy Debate* 9.1 (1998): 208.

24. Karen Chapple, "Overcoming Mismatch: Beyond Dispersal, Mobility, and Development Strategies," *Journal of the American Planning Association* 72.3 (2006): 322–36.

25. James Coleman et al., *Equality of Educational Opportunity* (Washington, D.C.: GPO, 1966).

26. See, for example, Christopher Jencks and Marsha Brown, "The Effects of Desegregation on Student Achievement: Some New Evidence from the Equality of Educational Opportunity Survey," *Sociology of Education* 48.1 (1975): 126–40; Russell Rumberger and J. Douglas Willms, "The Impact of Racial and Ethnic Segregation on the Achievement Gap in California High Schools," *Educational Evaluation and Policy Analysis* 14.4 (1992): 377–96; and Eric Hanushek, John Kain, and Steven Rivkin, "New Evidence about Brown v. Board of Education: The Complex Effects of School Racial Composition on Achievement," NBER Working Paper no. 8741 (2002), http://www.nber.org/papers/w8741.pdf.

27. Jaekyung Lee, "Can Reducing School Segregation Close the Achievement Gap?," in *Lessons in Integration: Realizing the Promise of Racial Diversity in American Schools*, ed. Erica Frankenberg and Gary Orfield (Charlottesville: Univ. of Virginia Press, 2007), 74–97.

28. David Grissmer, Ann Flanagan, and Stephanie Williamson, "Why Did the Black-White Score Gap Narrow in the 1970s and 1980s?" in *The Black-White Test Score Gap*, ed. Christopher Jencks and Meredith Phillips (Washington, D.C.: Brookings Institution Press, 1998), 182–226.

29. Jacob Vigdor and Jens Ludwig, "Segregation and the Black-white Test Score Gap," NBER Working Paper no. 12988 (Cambridge, Mass., 2007), http://ssrn.com/abstract=975929; Lee, "Can Reducing School Segregation Close the Achievement Gap?"

30. Eric Hanushek, John Kain, and Steven Rivkin, "Why Public Schools Lose Teachers," *Journal of Human Resources* 39.2 (2004): 326–54.

31. Eric Hanushek and Steven Rivkin, "School Quality and the Black-white Achievement Gap," NBER Working Paper no. 12651 (2006), http://ssrn.com/abstract=940600; Russell Rumberger and Gregory Palardy, "Does Segregation Still Matter? The Impact of Student Composition on Academic Achievement in High School," *Teachers College Record* 107.9 (2005): 1999–2045. This effect may be reduced if integrated schools practice segregation at the classroom level and deploy less effective teaching strategies in classrooms with more blacks. Ronald Ferguson and Jal Mehta, "Why Racial Integration and Other Policies since Brown v. Board of Education Have Only Partially Succeeded at Narrowing the Achievement Gap," in *Achieving High Educational Standards for All*, National Research

Council Conference Summary, ed. Timothy Ready, Christopher Edley, Jr., and Catherine Snow (Washington, D.C.: National Academy Press, 2002), 183–217.

32. Eric Hanushek, John Kain, Jacob Markman, and Steven Rivkin, "Does Peer Ability Affect Student Achievement?" *Journal of Applied Econometrics* 18.5 (2003): 527–44; Jane Cooley, "Desegregation and the Achievement Gap: Do Diverse Peers Help?" (2009), http://www.ssc.wisc.edu/~jcooley/CooleyDeseg.pdf; Eric Hanushek, "Some U.S. Evidence on How the Distribution of Educational Outcomes Can Be Changed," in *Schools and the Equal Opportunity Problem*, ed. Ludger Woessman and Paul Peterson (Cambridge, Mass.: MIT Press, 2007), 159–90.

33. Steven Rivkin and Finis Welch, "Has School Desegregation Improved Academic and Economic Outcomes for Blacks?" in *Handbook of the Economics of Education*, ed. Eric Hanushek and Finis Welch (Amsterdam: Elsevier, 2006), 1019–47.

34. Janet Schofield, "Review of Research on School Desegregation's Impact on Elementary and Secondary School Students," in *Handbook of Research on Multicultural Education*, ed. James Banks and Cherry McGee Banks (New York: Macmillan, 1995), 597–616; Paul Wortman and Fred Bryant, "School Desegregation and Black Achievement: An Integrative Review," *Sociological Methods & Research* 13.3 (1985): 289–324.

35. David Armor, Abigail Thernstrom, and Stephan Thernstrom, "Brief as *Amici Curiae* in Support of Petitioners, Parents Involved in Community Schools v. Seattle School District No. 1" (2006), http://www.naacpldf.org/content/pdf/voluntary/Amic_Briefs_Support_Petitioners/DavidJArmor_etal%28Sea_Lou%29.pdf.

36. Although the Coleman Report denied that teacher quality has an impact on student achievement, more recent studies on larger samples indicate otherwise. See Hanushek, "Some U.S. Evidence on How the Distribution of Educational Outcomes Can Be Changed"; Ronald Ferguson, "Paying for Public Education: New Evidence on How and Why Money Matters," *Harvard Journal on Legislation* 28.2 (1991): 465–98.

37. Robert Crain and Rita Mahard, "The Effect of Research Methodology on Desegregation-Achievement Studies: A Meta-Analysis," *American Journal of Sociology* 88 (1983): 839–54, criticize the studies for failure to adopt adequate controls. Methodologically superior studies with a true experimental design and randomized assignment show stronger positive effects of desegregation. See Schofield, "Review of Research on School Desegregation's Impact on Elementary and Secondary School Students," for discussion of the methodological difficulties with both observational and busing studies.

38. Roslyn Mickelson, "Subverting Swann: First- and Second-Generation Segregation in the Charlotte-Mecklenburg Schools," *American Educational Research* 38.2 (2001): 215–52; Janet Eyler, Valerie Cook, and Leslie Ward, "Resegregation: Segregation within Desegregated Schools," in *The Consequences of School Desegregation*, ed. Christine Rossell and Willis Hawley (Philadelphia: Temple Univ. Press, 1983), 126–62.

39. Schofield, "Review of Research on School Desegregation's Impact on Elementary and Secondary School Students," 598.

40. Jencks and Brown, "The Effects of Desegregation on Student Achievement," 140; Rivkin and Welch, "Has School Desegregation Improved Academic and Economic Outcomes for Blacks?," 1042.

41. Richard Zweigenhaft and G. William Domhoff, *Blacks in the White Establishment?: A Study of Race and Class in America* (New Haven: Yale Univ. Press, 1991), 39.

42. Jonathan Guryan, "Desegregation and Black Dropout Rates," *American Economic Review* 94.4 (2004): 919–43.

43. Gary LaFree and Richard Arum, "The Impact of Racially Inclusive Schooling on Adult Incarceration Rates among U.S. Cohorts of African Americans and Whites since 1930," *Criminology* 44.1 (2006): 73–103.

44. Marvin Dawkins, "Black Students' Occupational Expectations: A National Study of the Impact of School Desegregation," *Urban Education* 18.1 (1983): 98–113; Robert Crain and Jack Strauss, *School Desegregation and Black Occupational Attainments: Results from a Long-Term Experiment*, Report for the National Institute of Education, UD 024 391 (Baltimore: Johns Hopkins University, Center for Social Organization of Schools, 1985), http://eric.ed.gov/ERICDocs/data/ericdocs2sql/content_storage_01/0000019b/80/33/16/32.pdf.

45. Jon Hoelter, "Segregation and Rationality in Black Status Aspiration Processes," *Sociology of Education* 55.1 (1982): 31–39; Amy Wells and Robert Crain, "Perpetuation Theory and the Long-Term Effects of School Desegregation," *Review of Educational Research* 64.4 (1994): 531–55.

46. Orley Ashenfelter, William Collins, and Albert Yoon, "Evaluating the Role of *Brown vs. Board of Education* in School Equalization, Desegregation, and the Income of African Americans," Princeton Law and Public Affairs Working Paper no. 05–001 (Princeton University, 2005), http://ssrn.com/abstract=747485.

47. Douglas Massey and Mary Fischer, "The Effect of Childhood Segregation on Minority Academic Performance at Selective Colleges," *Ethnic and Racial Studies* 29.1 (2006): 1–26.

48. Roland Fryer and Michael Greenstone, "The Causes and Consequences of Attending Historically Black Colleges and Universities," NBER Working Paper no. 13036 (Cambridge, Mass., 2007), http://www.economics.harvard.edu/faculty/fryer/files/fryer-greenstone%20HBCUs.pdf.

49. Jomills Henry Braddock II, "School Desegregation and Black Assimilation," *Journal of Social Issues* 41.3 (1985): 9–22; Jomills Henry Braddock II and James McPartland, "The Social and Academic Consequences of School Desegregation," *Equity and Choice* 4 (1988): 5–10, 63–73; Marvin Dawkins and Jomills Henry Braddock II, "The Continuing Significance of Desegregation: School Racial Composition and African American Inclusion in American Society," *The Journal of Negro Education* 63.3 (1994): 394–405; Wells and Crain, "Perpetuation Theory and the Long-Term Effects of School Desegregation."

50. Wells and Crain, "Perpetuation Theory and the Long-Term Effects of School Desegregation."

51. Gordon Allport, *The Nature of Prejudice* (Cambridge, Mass.: Addison-Wesley, 1954).

52. Estlund, *Working Together.*

53. Samuel Gaertner and John Dovidio, *Reducing Intergroup Bias: The Common Ingroup Identity Model* (Philadelphia: Psychology Press, 2000).

54. Marilynn Brewer and Norman Miller, "Beyond the Contact Hypothesis: Theoretical Perspectives on Desegregation," in *Groups in Contact: The Psychology of Desegregation*, ed. Norman Miller and Marilynn Brewer (Orlando: Academic Press, 1984), 281–302.

55. Jared Kenworthy, Rhiannon Turner, Miles Hewstone, and Alberto Voci, "Intergroup Contact: When Does It Work, and Why?" in *On the Nature of Prejudice: Fifty Years after Allport*, ed. John Dovidio, Peter Glick, and Laurie Rudman (Malden, Mass.: Blackwell, 2005), 287.

56. Ibid., 283, 285.

57. Miles Hewstone and Rupert Brown, "Contact Is Not Enough: An Intergroup Perspective on the 'Contact Hypothesis'," in *Contact and Conflict in Intergroup Encounters*, ed. Miles Hewstone and Rupert Brown (Oxford: Blackwell, 1986), 1–44.

58. Marilynn Brewer and Samuel Gaertner, "Toward Reduction of Prejudice: Intergroup Contact and Social Categorization," in *Blackwell Handbook of Social Psychology: Intergroup Processes*, ed. Rupert Brown and Samuel Gaertner (Oxford: Blackwell, 2003), 451–72; Kenworthy, Turner, Hewstone, and Voci, "Intergroup Contact"; Thomas Pettigrew, "Intergroup Contact: Theory, Research, and New Perspectives," *Annual Review of Psychology* 49 (1998): 65–85.

59. Pettigrew, "Intergroup Contact"; Thomas Pettigrew and Linda Tropp, "A Meta-Analytic Test of Intergroup Contact Theory," *Journal of Personality and Social Psychology* 90.5 (2006): 751–83.

60. Christopher Ellison and Daniel Powers, "The Contact Hypothesis and Racial Attitudes among Black Americans," *Social Science Quarterly* 75.2 (1994): 385–400; Linda Tropp and Thomas Pettigrew, "Differential Relationships between Intergroup Contact and Affective and Cognitive Dimensions of Prejudice," *Personality and Social Psychology Bulletin* 31.8 (2005): 1145–58; Shana Levin, Colette van Laar, and Jim Sidanius, "The Effects of Ingroup and Outgroup Friendships on Ethnic Attitudes in College: A Longitudinal Study," *Group Processes & Intergroup Relations* 6.1 (2003): 76–92.

61. Daniel Powers and Christopher Ellison, "Interracial Contact and Black Racial Attitudes: The Contact Hypothesis and Selectivity Bias," *Social Forces* 74.1 (1995): 205–26; Thomas Pettigrew, "Generalized Intergroup Contact Effects on Prejudice," *Personality and Social Psychology Bulletin* 23.2 (1997): 173–85.

62. Stephen Wright, Arthur Aron, Tracy McLaughlin-Volpe, and Stacy Ropp, "The Extended Contact Effect: Knowledge of Cross-Group Friendships and Prejudice," *Journal of Personality & Social Psychology* 73.1 (1997): 73–90.

63. Estlund, *Working Together*, 64–76.

64. Charles Moskos and John Butler, *All That We Can Be: Black Leadership and Racial Integration the Army Way* (New York: Basic, 1996), 2–5.

65. Ibid., 13–14, 38–47, 54–61.

66. Walter Stephan, "School Desegregation: An Evaluation of Predictions Made in *Brown v. Board of Education*," *Psychological Bulletin* 85.2 (1978): 217–38.

67. Schofield, "Review of Research on School Desegregation's Impact on Elementary and Secondary School Students," 609.

68. Ibid., 609; Janet Schofield and Rebecca Eurich-Fulcer, "When and How School Desegregation Improves Intergroup Relations," in *Applied Social Psychology*, ed. Marilynn Brewer and Miles Hewstone (Oxford: Blackwell, 2004), 186–205.

69. Eyler, Cook, and Ward, "Resegregation."

70. Rupert Brown, *Prejudice: Its Social Psychology* (Oxford: Blackwell, 1995), 251–52; Walter Stephan, "The Effects of School Desegregation: An Evaluation 30 Years after *Brown*," in *Advances in Applied Social Psychology*, vol. 3, ed. Michael Saks and Leonard Saxe (Hillsdale, N.J.: Erlbaum, 1986), 181–206; Robert Slavin, "Cooperative Learning and Desegregation," in *Effective School Desegregation: Equity, Quality, and Feasibility*, ed. Willis Hawley (Beverly Hills: Sage, 1981), 227–28.

71. Robert Slavin and Nancy Madden, "School Practices That Improve Race Relations," *American Educational Research Journal* 16.2 (1979): 169–80; Janet Schofield and H. Andrew Sagar, "Desegregation, School Practices, and Student Race Relations," in *The Consequences of School Desegregation*, ed. Christine Rossell and Willis Hawley (Philadelphia: Temple Univ. Press, 1983), 84.

72. Willis Hawley, "Designing Schools That Use Student Diversity to Enhance Learning of All Students," in *Lessons in Integration: Realizing the Promise of Racial Diversity in American Schools*, ed. Erica Frankenberg and Gary Orfield (Charlottesville: Univ. of Virginia Press, 2007), 31–56. Hawley reports mixed results on whether detracking reduces test scores for high achievers, but the evidence on this point appears weak (43). Carol Burris and Kevin Welner, "Classroom Integration and Accelerated Learning through Detracking," in *Lessons in Integration*, 207–27, discuss a successful detracking program that increased academic achievement for students of all abilities by offering a challenging curriculum to all, and that reduced the racial achievement gap as well.

73. James Moody, "Race, School Integration, and Friendship Segregation in America," *American Journal of Sociology* 107.3 (2001): 679–716.

74. Slavin and Madden, "School Practices That Improve Race Relations"; Slavin, "Cooperative Learning and Desegregation"; Robert Slavin and Robert Cooper, "Improving Intergroup Relations: Lessons Learned from Cooperative Learning Programs," *Journal of Social Issues* 55.4 (1999): 647–63; John McConahay, "Reducing Racial Prejudice in Desegregated Schools," in *Effective School Desegregation*, ed. Hawley, 35–53; Schofield and Sagar, "Desegregation, School Practices, and Student Race Relations"; David Johnson, Roger Johnson, and Geoffrey Maruyama, "Goal Interdependence and Interpersonal Attraction in Heterogeneous Classrooms: A Metanalysis," in *Groups in Contact*, ed. Miller and Brewer, 97–121.

75. Hawley, "Designing Schools That Use Student Diversity," 39–41.

76. Brewer and Miller, "Beyond the Contact Hypothesis," 286.

77. Elizabeth Cohen, "The Desegregated School: Problems in Status Power and Interethnic Climate," in *Groups in Contact*, ed. Miller and Brewer, 77–96.

78. Slavin, "Cooperative Learning and Desegregation."

79. Michael Emerson, Rachel Kimbro, and George Yancey, "Contact Theory Extended: The Effects of Prior Racial Contact on Current Social Ties," *Social Science Quarterly* 83.3 (2002): 745–61.

80. William Bowen and Derek Bok, *The Shape of the River: Long-Term Consequences of Considering Race in College and University Admissions* (Princeton, N.J.: Princeton Univ. Press, 1998), 238–40; Jomills Henry Braddock II, Marvin Dawkins, and William Trent, "Why Desegregate? The Effect of School Desegregation on Adult Occupational Desegregation of African Americans, Whites, and Hispanics," *International Journal of Contemporary Sociology* 31 (1994): 273–83; Patricia Gurin, "Expert Report of Patricia Gurin," in *The Compelling Need for Diversity in Higher Education. Gratz et al. v. Bollinger, et al., No. 97–75321 (E.D. Mich.), Grutter et al. v. Bollinger, et al., No. 97–75928 (E.D. Mich.)* (Ann Arbor: Univ. of Michigan, 1999), 133.

81. Jennifer Holme, Amy Wells, and Anita Revilla, "Learning through Experience: What Graduates Gained by Attending Desegregated High Schools," *Equity & Excellence in Education* 38.1 (2005): 14–24; Gurin, "Expert Report of Patricia Gurin."

82. Andrew Gelman, Jeffrey Fagan, and Alex Kiss, "An Analysis of the NYPD's Stop-and-Frisk Policy in the Context of Claims of Racial Bias," *Journal of the American Statistical Association* 102.479 (2007): 813–23; Jeffrey Fagan and Garth Davies, "Street Stops and Broken Windows: *Terry*, Race and Disorder in New York City," *Fordham Urban Law Journal* 28 (2000): 457–504; Billy Close and Patrick Mason, "Searching for Efficient Enforcement: Officer Characteristics and Racially Biased Policing," *Review of Law and Economics* 3.2 (2007): 263–321.

83. David Harris, "The Reality of Racial Disparity in Criminal Justice: The Significance of Data Collection," *Law and Contemporary Problems* 66.3 (2003): 96.

84. Robert Worden, "The Causes of Police Brutality: Theory and Evidence on Police Use of Force," in *Police Violence: Understanding and Controlling Police Abuse of Force*, ed. William Geller and Hans Toch (New Haven: Yale Univ. Press, 1996), 37.

85. Ian Ayers and Joel Waldfogel, "A Market Test for Race Discrimination in Bail Setting," in *Pervasive Prejudice? Unconventional Evidence of Race and Gender Discrimination*, ed. Ian Ayers (Chicago: University of Chicago Press, 2001), 233–311; Traci Schlesinger, "Racial and Ethnic Disparity in Pretrial Criminal Processing," *Justice Quarterly* 22.2 (2005): 170–92; Madeline Wordes, Timothy Bynum, and Charles Corley, "Locking Up Youth: The Impact of Race on Detention Decisions," *Journal of Research in Crime and Delinquency* 31.2 (1994): 149–65; Stephen Demuth and Darrell Steffensmeier, "The Impact of Gender and Race-Ethnicity in the Pretrial Release Process," *Social Problems* 51.2 (2004): 222–42.

86. Coramae Mann, *Unequal Justice: A Question of Color* (Bloomington: Indiana Univ. Press, 1993), 167, 183.

87. Rodger Jackson and Edward Pabon, "Race and Treating Other People's Children as Adults," *Journal of Criminal Justice* 28.6 (2000): 507–15.

88. Ojmarrh Mitchell, "A Meta-Analysis of Race and Sentencing Research: Explaining the Inconsistencies," *Journal of Quantitative Criminology* 21.4 (2005): 439–66; Ronald Everett and Roger Wojtkiewicz, "Difference, Disparity, and Race/Ethnic Bias in Federal Sentencing," *Journal of Quantitative Criminology* 18.2 (2002): 189–211; Stephen Demuth and Darrell Steffensmeier, "Ethnicity Effects on Sentence Outcomes in Large Urban Courts: Comparisons Among White, Black, and Hispanic Defendants," *Social Science Quarterly* 85.4 (2004): 994–1011.

89. Darrell Steffensmeier, Jeffery Ulmer, and John Kramer, "The Interaction of Race, Gender, and Age in Criminal Sentencing: The Punishment Cost of Being Young, Black, and Male," *Criminology* 36.4 (1998): 763–98; Rodney Engen, Sara Steen, and George Bridges, "Racial Disparities in the Punishment of Youth: A Theoretical and Empirical Assessment of the Literature," *Social Problems* 49.2 (2002): 194–220.

90. Kwabena Gyimah-Brempong and Gregory Price, "Crime and Punishment: And Skin Hue Too?" *American Economic Review* 96.2 (2006): 246–50; William Pizzi, Irene Blair, and Charles Judd, "Discrimination in Sentencing on the Basis of Afrocentric Features," *Michigan Journal of Race & Law* 10.2 (2005): 327–53.

91. Michael Tapia and Patricia Harris, "Race and Revocation: Is There a Penalty for Young, Minority Males?," *Journal of Ethnicity in Criminal Justice* 4.3 (2006): 1–25.

92. Mona Lynch, "Stereotypes, Prejudice, and Life-and-Death Decision Making: Lessons from Laypersons in an Experimental Setting," in *From Lynch Mobs to the Killing State: Race and the Death Penalty in America*, ed. Charles Ogletree Jr. and Austin Sarat (New York: New York Univ. Press, 2006), 182–207; Sara Steen, Rodney Engen, and Randy Gainey, "Images of Danger and Culpability: Racial Stereotyping, Case Processing, and Criminal Sentencing," *Criminology* 43.2 (2005): 435–68; Katherine Beckett, Kris Nyrop, Lori Pfingst, and Melissa Bowen, "Drug Use, Drug Possession Arrests, and the Question of Race: Lessons from Seattle," *Social Problems* 52.3 (2005): 419–41; Jackson and Pabon, "Race and Treating Other People's Children as Adults"; Michael Smith and Geoffrey Alpert, "Explaining Police Bias: A Theory of Social Conditioning and Illusory Correlation," *Criminal Justice and Behavior* 34.10 (2007): 1262–83.

93. I say "felonies" and not simply "rape" because there is little reason to believe that the factors that cause disproportionately high rates of false conviction for blacks in rape cases, where DNA evidence is available, are all absent in the case of blacks convicted of other felonies.

94. Samuel Gross et al., "Exonerations in the United States 1989–2003," *Journal of Criminal Law and Criminology* 95.2 (2005): 523–60.

95. Christian Meissner and John Brigham, "Thirty Years of Investigating the Own-Race Bias in Memory for Faces: A Meta-Analytic Review," *Psychology, Public Policy, and Law* 7.1 (2001): 3–35.

96. Alexandra Golby, John Gabrieli, Joan Chiao, and Jennifer Eberhardt, "Differential Responses in the Fusiform Region to Same-Race and Other-Race Faces," *Nature Neuroscience* 4.8 (2001): 845–50.

97. Sheri Johnson, "Black Innocence and the White Jury," *Michigan Law Review* 83.7 (1985): 1611–1708; Clem Turner, "What's the Story? An Analysis of

Juror Discrimination and a Plea for Affirmative Jury Selection," *American Criminal Law Review* 34.1 (1996): 289–323; Samuel Sommers and Phoebe Ellsworth, "How Much Do We Really Know about Race and Juries? A Review of Social Science Theory and Research," *Chicago-Kent Law Review* 78 (2003): 997–1031.

98. Turner, "What's the Story?"

99. Samuel Sommers and Phoebe Ellsworth, "White Juror Bias: An Investigation of Prejudice against Black Defendants in the American Courtroom," *Psychology, Public Policy, and Law* 7.1 (2001): 201–29; Samuel Sommers and Phoebe Ellsworth, "Race in the Courtroom: Perceptions of Guilt and Dispositional Attributions," *Personality and Social Psychology Bulletin* 26.11 (2000): 1367–79.

100. Samuel Sommers, "On Racial Diversity and Group Decision Making: Identifying Multiple Effects of Racial Composition on Jury Deliberations," *Journal of Personality and Social Psychology* 90.4 (2006): 604–5.

101. Hiroshi Fukurai and Richard Krooth, *Race in the Jury Box: Affirmative Action in Jury Selection* (Albany, N.Y.: SUNY Press, 2003).

102. Sommers, "On Racial Diversity and Group Decision Making," 605.

103. Ibid., 607.

104. Samuel Sommers, Lindsey Warp, and Corrine Mahoney, "Cognitive Effects of Racial Diversity: White Individuals' Information Processing in Heterogeneous Groups," *Journal of Experimental Social Psychology* 44.4 (2008): 1129–36.

105. Sommers, "On Racial Diversity and Group Decision Making," 603.

106. Ibid., 605–8.

107. Ibid., 608.

108. Ronald Weitzer, "White, Black, or Blue Cops? Race and Citizen Assessments of Police Officers," *Journal of Criminal Justice* 28.4 (2000): 313–24.

109. David Alan Sklansky, "Not Your Father's Police Department: Making Sense of the New Demographics of Law Enforcement," *Journal of Criminal Law and Criminology* 96.3 (2006): 1230–32.

110. Kenneth J. Meier, Joseph Stewart Jr., and Robert England, *Race, Class and Education: The Politics of Second-Generation Discrimination* (Madison: Univ. of Wisconsin Press, 1989), 94–103.

111. Shirley Hatchett and Howard Schuman, "White Respondents and Race of Interviewer Effects," *Public Opinion Quarterly* 39.4 (1975–1976): 523–28; Darren Davis, "Nonrandom Measurement Error and Race of Interviewer Effects among African Americans," *Public Opinion Quarterly* 61.1 (1997): 183–207.

112. Lynn Sanders, "Democratic Politics and Survey Research," *Philosophy of the Social Sciences* 29.2 (1999): 248–80.

113. Dewey, "Creative Democracy," 227–28.

114. Sanders, "Democratic Politics and Survey Research," 270.

115. Donald Kinder and Tali Mendelberg, "Cracks in American Apartheid: The Political Impact of Prejudice among Desegregated Whites," *Journal of Politics* 57.2 (1995): 402–24.

116. Diana Mutz, "Cross-Cutting Social Networks: Testing Democratic Theory in Practice," *American Political Science Review* 96.1 (2002): 111–26.

117. Lawrence Bobo and Franklin Gilliam Jr., "Race, Sociopolitical Participation, and Black Empowerment," *American Political Science Review* 84.2 (1990): 377–93.

118. David Canon, *Race, Redistricting, and Representation: The Unintended Consequences of Black Majority Districts* (Chicago: Univ. of Chicago Press, 1999).

119. Richard Pildes, "Is Voting-Rights Law Now at War with Itself? Social Science and Voting Rights in the 2000s," *North Carolina Law Review* 80.5 (2002): 1517–73.

Chapter Seven
Understanding Affirmative Action

1. 443 U.S. 193, 209–15 (1979).

2. 438 U.S. 265, 311–324 (1978). See also *Metro Broadcasting v. FCC*, 497 U.S. 547 (1990) (upholding, on diversity grounds, affirmative action in federal awards of broadcasting licenses).

3. 478 U.S. 421 (1986).

4. For histories of discrimination-blocking affirmative action, see Reskin, *The Realities of Affirmative Action in Employment*, 7–18; and John Skrentny, *The Ironies of Affirmative Action* (Chicago: Univ. of Chicago Press, 1996), 111–44.

5. 347 U.S. 483 (1954).

6. 402 U.S. 1 (1971).

7. 539 U.S. 306, 332 (2003). In "Racial Integration as a Compelling Interest," *Constitutional Commentary* 21 (2004): 15–40, I argue that *Grutter* follows the integrative logic of *Brown*.

8. "Amicus Briefs Filed with the U.S. Supreme Court in Grutter v. Bollinger," http://www.vpcomm.umich.edu/admissions/legal/gru_amicus-ussc/um.html.

9. See *Parents Involved in Community Schools v. Seattle School District #1*, 127 S. Ct. 2738 (2007) (barring a voluntary racial integration program by a school district not found to be guilty of unconstitutional segregation).

10. James Nickel, "Should Reparations Be to Individuals or to Groups?" *Analysis* 34.5 (1974): 154–60; Andrew Valls, "The Libertarian Case for Affirmative Action," *Social Theory and Practice* 25.2 (1999): 299–323.

11. George Sher, "Justifying Reverse Discrimination in Employment," *Philosophy and Public Affairs* 4.2 (1975): 159–70; Stephen Kershnar, "Uncertain Damages to Racial Minorities and Strong Affirmative Action," *Public Affairs Quarterly* 13.1 (1999): 83–98.

12. Paul Taylor, "Reverse Discrimination and Compensatory Justice," *Analysis* 33.6 (1973): 177–82; Owen Fiss, "Groups and the Equal Protection Clause," *Philosophy and Public Affairs* 5.2 (1976): 107–77.

13. It is frequently claimed that the equal protection clause of the Fourteenth Amendment prohibits state bodies from using racial preferences to remedy "societal discrimination," understood as any other discrimination than their own. I argue in "Integration, Affirmative Action, and Strict Scrutiny," *New York University Law Review* 77 (2002): 1254–66, that this is absurd as a moral norm and has no foundation in the Supreme Court opinions frequently cited on this point.

14. Gertrude Ezorsky, *Racism and Justice* (Ithaca, N.Y.: Cornell Univ. Press, 1991), 29–30.

15. Susan D. Clayton and Faye J. Crosby, *Justice, Gender, and Affirmative Action* (Ann Arbor: Univ. of Michigan Press, 1992).

16. William Banner, "Reverse Discrimination: Misconception and Confusion," *Journal of Social Philosophy* 10 (1979): 15–18.

17. See Adrian Vermeule, "Reparations as Rough Justice," University of Chicago Law and Economics, Olin Working Paper no. 260, 2005 (forthcoming in *Nomos 50: Transitional Justice*), for an application of this argument to the case of group reparations.

18. Nickel, "Should Reparations Be to Individuals or to Groups?"

19. As Justice Stevens argued in dissenting from the judgment of the Supreme Court in *Fullilove v. Klutznick*, 448 U.S. 448, 537–40 (1980). I oppose such a reparations program for two reasons. First, allocating lump-sum reparations to blacks is like serving water to the thirsty in a sieve. Unless the continuing causes of race-based disadvantage are dismantled, such reparations will offer only temporary relief. Second, reparations' focus on compensating for injustices in the past distracts attention from current injustices and is liable to encourage whites to feel that, once paid, they have done everything needed to end racial injustice, and to place all responsibility for continuing racial inequality on blacks alone.

20. *Bakke*, 438 U.S. 313.

21. *Theorists* of the diversity model argue that diversity promotes justice—for example, by breaking down racial stereotypes and promoting toleration and comfort in cooperating with diverse others. See, for example, Gurin, "Expert Report of Patricia Gurin," 99–234. *Practitioners* of the diversity model—most important, university administrators—tend to efface social justice rationales by assimilating racial diversity to cultural diversity. This is a response to legal constraint. Powell's *Bakke* opinion set up a sharp dichotomy between justice and diversity rationales, approving of only the latter. See Anderson, "Integration, Affirmative Action, and Strict Scrutiny," 25–27.

22. Sanford Levinson, "Diversity," *University of Pennsylvania Journal of Constitutional Law* 2 (2000): 593.

23. Institutional practitioners of diversity virtually never specify the types of expected differences in ideas and perspectives racial diversity is supposed to bring. Theorists also rarely spell this out. An exception is Iris Young, who, as I do, locates the source of epistemic diversity of racial groups in their different structural positions in the system of social stratification. See her *Inclusion and Democracy*, 92, 116–17. However, even Young sometimes slips into a cultural gloss on racial difference (see, e.g., 103–4, 216–17). Thus, even though few defenders of racial diversity embrace a cultural interpretation of it, the lack of specification combined with background multiculturalist rhetoric tends to promote a conflation of racial with cultural diversity.

24. Kwame Anthony Appiah, "Race, Culture and Identity: Misunderstood Connections," in *Color Conscious: The Political Morality of Race* (Princeton, N.J.: Princeton Univ. Press, 1996), 30–105; David Hollinger, "Group Preferences, Cultural Diversity, and Social Democracy: Notes toward a Theory of Affirmative Action," in *Race and Representation: Affirmative Action*, ed. Robert Post and Michael Rogin (New York: Zone Books, 1998), 97–109.

25. Cf. *Metro Broadcasting*, 497 U.S. 547, 621 (1990) (O'Connor, J., dissenting).

26. Richard Posner, "The DeFunis Case and the Constitutionality of Preferential Treatment of Racial Minorities," *Supreme Court Review* 1974 (1974): 1–32.

27. Charles O'Reilly, David Caldwell, and William Barnett, "Work Group Demography, Social Integration, and Turnover," *Administrative Science Quarterly* 34.1 (1989): 21–37.

28. Skrentny, *The Ironies of Affirmative Action*, 120–24.

29. This was the case in *Sheet Metal Workers v. EEOC*. A similar solution was affirmed by the Supreme Court in *United States v. Paradise*, 480 U.S. 149 (1987) (permitting quotas to remedy unrelenting discrimination in state trooper promotions).

30. Reskin, *The Realities of Affirmative Action in Employment*, 32. Reskin notes that word-of-mouth advertising is the most popular recruitment technique. Only 40 percent of job openings are formally advertised (33).

31. Barbara Bergmann, *In Defense of Affirmative Action* (New York: Basic Books, 1996), 78–79.

32. Michael Yelnosky, "The Prevention Justification for Affirmative Action," *Ohio State Law Journal* 64 (2003): 1385–1425.

33. Reskin, *The Realities of Affirmative Action in Employment*, 35.

34. Jerry Kang and Mahzarin Banaji, "Fair Measures: A Behavioral Realist Revision of 'Affirmative Action'," *California Law Review* 94 (2006): 1094–95.

35. Ibid., 1092–96.

36. Reskin, *The Realities of Affirmative Action in Employment*, 62–65.

37. Ibid., 64–65.

38. See, e.g., *Fullilove*, 448 U.S. 539, 542 (Stevens, J., dissenting); *Metro Broadcasting*, 497 U.S. 547, 614–17 (1990) (O'Connor, J., dissenting); *City of Richmond v. J.A. Croson Co.*, 488 U.S. 510.

39. Reskin, *The Realities of Affirmative Action in Employment*.

40. J. Ralph Lindgren, "The Irrelevance of Philosophical Treatments of Affirmative Action," *Social Theory and Practice* 7.1 (1981): 1–19.

41. Harry Holzer and David Neumark, "Are Affirmative Action Hires Less Qualified? Evidence from Employer-Employee Data on New Hires," *Journal of Labor Economics* 17.3 (1999): 534–69; Harry Holzer and David Neumark. "What Does Affirmative Action Do?," *Industrial and Labor Relations Review* 53.2 (2000): 240–71.

42. Donald Tomaskovic-Devey and Sheryl Skaggs, "An Establishment-Level Test of the Statistical Discrimination Hypothesis," *Work and Occupations* 26.4 (1999): 422–45.

43. Reskin, *The Realities of Affirmative Action in Employment*, 73.

44. Given the high involuntary unemployment rate among blacks and their well-documented willingness to accept what are regarded as undesirable jobs, such as fast-food work, employers should assume that racial disparities in the qualified applicant pool reflect insufficiently vigorous outreach rather than racial differences in taste for jobs.

45. For most entry-level jobs and trainee programs—the majority of places subject to employer-based affirmative action programs—differences in qualification are irrelevant to the hiring process because the standard personnel practice is to hire the first basically qualified applicant who appears in the job queue.

46. Kang and Banaji, "Fair Measures," 1098–1101; Laura Purdy, "In Defense of Hiring Apparently Less Qualified Women," *Journal of Social Philosophy* 15.2 (1984): 26–33.

47. This model also plausibly explains affirmative action in contracting. Government bodies may insist that their prime contractors set aside a certain percentage of subcontracts to businesses owned by members of traditionally excluded groups to avoid "passive participation" in the habitual discrimination of prime contractors. See *City of Richmond v. J. A. Croson Co.*, 488 U.S. 469, 491–92.

48. Kevin Stainback, Corre Robinson, and Donald Tomaskovic-Devey, "Race and Workplace Integration: A Politically Mediated Process?," *American Behavioral Scientist* 48.9 (2005): 1200–1228.

49. Aristotle, *Nicomachean Ethics*, trans. Terence Irwin (Indianapolis: Hackett, 1985), 1109b.

50. Joel Cantor, Joel, Erika Miles, Laurence Baker, and Dianne Barker, "Physician Service to the Underserved: Implications for Affirmative Action in Medical Education," *Inquiry* 33 (Summer 1996): 167–80; Miriam Komaromy et al., "The Role of Black and Hispanic Physicians in Providing Health Care for Underserved Populations," *New England Journal of Medicine* 334 (May 16, 1996): 1305–10; Vera Thurmond and Darrell Kirch, "Impact of Minority Physicians on Health Care," *Southern Medical Journal* 91 (Nov. 1998): 1009–13.

51. Timothy Bates, *Banking on Black Enterprise* (Washington, D.C.: Joint Center for Political and Economic Studies, 1993), 140.

52. Ibid., 16, 9–12, 90; Thomas Boston, *Affirmative Action and Black Entrepreneurship* (New York: Routledge, 1999), 1–4, 75.

53. See Mary Pattillo-McCoy, *Black Picket Fences: Privilege and Peril among the Black Middle Class* (Chicago: Univ. of Chicago Press, 1999), 28 (observing that the black middle class lives in neighborhoods with more poor people than the white middle class does); Bart Landry, *The New Black Middle Class* (Berkeley and Los Angeles: Univ. of California Press, 1987), 86 (discussing deep links of the black middle class to poor and working-class blacks); Bowen and Bok, *Shape of the River*, 158–64 (providing evidence that blacks at selective schools participate and lead community, neighborhood, social services, and youth organizations at a higher rate than their white classmates do).

54. See Michael Hout, "Status, Autonomy, and Training in Occupational Mobility," *American Journal of Sociology* 89 (1984): 1402–1404 (identifying fathers' status as self-employed professional as a key determinant of sons' upward occupational mobility).

55. See Ronald Dworkin, *A Matter of Principle* (Cambridge, Mass.: Harvard Univ. Press, 1985). Daniel Sabbagh elaborates on Dworkin's argument, with extensive empirical support, in *Equality and Transparency: A Strategic Perspective on Affirmative Action in American Law* (New York: Palgrave Macmillan, 2007).

56. See Bates, *Banking on Black Enterprise*, 13–14 (arguing that affirmative action in government contracting would have greater impact on black employment if it targeted college-educated, financially well-off black business owners because they are better able to generate economic development in ghettos).

57. Reskin, McBrier, and Kmec, "Determinants and Consequences of Workplace Sex and Race Composition," 348. A critical mass also appears to improve the performance of underrepresented groups by reducing stereotype threat (347).

58. Bowen and Bok, *Shape of the River*, 234–37.

59. It does use race as a proxy in the case of professional services to the disadvantaged. Given the urgency of such services, and the unreliability of alternatives, this proxy use of race may be justified. Alternative selection criteria are unreliable since ex ante declarations and even experience serving the underserved on the part of members of advantaged groups have little probative value for future service in the face of overwhelming ex post incentives and opportunities to serve advantaged groups once a professional degree is in hand. Race works as an effective proxy because those opportunities are mostly closed to blacks: most therefore find their best professional opportunities in serving the underserved.

60. Willis Hawley, "Designing Schools That Use Student Diversity to Enhance Learning of All Students," in *Lessons in Integration: Realizing the Promise of Racial Diversity in American Schools*, ed. Erica Frankenberg and Gary Orfield (Charlottesville: Univ. of Virginia Press, 2007), 31–56; Peter Wood and Nancy Sonleitner, "The Effect of Childhood Interracial Contact on Adult Antiblack Prejudice," *Journal of Intercultural Relations* 20.1 (1996): 1–17.

Chapter Eight
The Folly and Incoherence of Color Blindness

1. The following discussion is indebted to Sally Haslanger, "Gender and Race: (What) Are They? (What) Do We Want Them To Be?" *Nous* 34.1 (2000): 31–55; and Blum, *"I'm Not a Racist . . . but,"* 98–163.

2. Jacqueline Stevens, *Reproducing the State* (Princeton, N.J.: Princeton University Press, 1999), 191–92; Haslanger, "Gender and Race."

3. David Hollinger, *Postethnic America*, 8.

4. The asymmetries in the definitions of white and other races are due to the American rule of hypodescent, according to which no one with a non-European ancestor is white, and anyone with a black ancestor is black. The temporal conditions are needed to account for the facts that white South Africans are still white even though their parents were born in Africa, and that not everyone is black even though all humans can ultimately trace their ancestry back to Africa.

5. Blum, *"I'm Not a Racist . . . but,"* 147; Haslanger, "Gender and Race," 44.

6. *Fullilove v. Klutznick*, 448 U.S. 448, 525, quoting *Hirabayashi v. United States*, 320 U.S. 81, 100. Justice Thomas erred in a similar way in characterizing the University of Michigan Law School's interest in affirmative action as "aesthetic." *Grutter*, 123 S. Ct. 2325, 2352 n. 3 (Thomas, J., dissenting) ("the Law School wants to have a certain appearance, from the shape of the desks and tables in its classrooms to the color of the students sitting at them"). This supposes that the Law School took skin color to be the relevant characteristic, on the assumption that the only concept of race is minimal race.

7. Ibid.

8. *Civil Rights Cases*, 109 U.S. 3, 21 (1883) ("Congress has a right to enact all necessary and proper laws for the obliteration and prevention of slavery with all its badges and incidents").

9. Deborah Malamud also offers a concise account of the ways race-based factors specifically disadvantage the black middle class in "Affirmative Action,

Diversity, and the Black Middle Class," *University of Colorado Law Review* 68 (1997): 967–88.

10. I have defined biological races as a subset of character races, to capture the sense of race that figured in pseudoscientific racial doctrines of the last two centuries. This does not rule out the possibility that biological notions of race detached from ideas of virtue and talent—used, for example, to screen for vulnerability to certain diseases—may be scientifically useful. See Ian Hacking, "Why Race Still Matters," *Daedalus* 134.1 (2005): 102–16.

11. Statistical discrimination against groups disadvantaged by unjust racialization is morally objectionable because it reproduces categorical inequality in three ways. First, it stigmatizes these groups. Second, it violates equal opportunity and reproduces a caste system by denying those who possess the relevant underlying merits any chance to demonstrate that fact (§3.5). Third, it is often unfair to magnify and perpetuate group-based disadvantage by selecting for underlying characteristics that are themselves the product of group-based disadvantage. This complaint applies on behalf of those who are not equally qualified with their competitors, but who would develop such qualifications if they got the opportunity they are competing for.

12. "Narrow tailoring" refers to how well the means track the underlying purpose, so as to minimize the weighted sum of type I (overinclusion) and type II (underinclusion) error. When a group suffers from *pervasive* unjust disadvantage, failing to block or remedy discrimination against group members (type II error) is morally worse than offering advantages to group members who have not suffered or face little prospect of suffering discrimination or its effects. Such considerations support the "rough justice" rationale for compensatory affirmative action since individualized (nonproxy) remedies are vastly more underinclusive than affirmative action is overinclusive (§7.2). They also support the presumption behind affirmative action goals for discrimination-blocking affirmative action— that unexplained disparities between the racial composition of employees in a job and the racial composition of the qualified local work force reflect intentional, unconscious, or negligent discrimination (arbitrary and hence unjust obstacles to equal opportunity on the part of disadvantaged groups) (§7.4).

13. See, e.g., *Croson*, 488 U.S. 527–28 (Scalia, J., concurring) ("[T]hose who believe that racial preferences can help 'even the score' display, and reinforce, a manner of thinking by race that was the source of injustice"); Carl Cohen, "When Turnabout Is Not Fair Play," in *Contemporary Debates in Social Philosophy*, ed. Laurence Thomas (Oxford: Blackwell, 2008), 250–59.

14. See, for example, *Fullilove*, 448 U.S. 448, 529 (1980) (Stewart, J., dissenting) (complaining that Congress's racial set-aside constitutes "'discrimination for its own sake'," quoting *Bakke*, 438 U.S. 307); Carl Cohen, *Naked Racial Preference: The Case against Affirmative Action* (Lanham, Md.: Madison Books, 1995).

15. See *Adarand Constructors, Inc. v. Pena*, 515 U.S. 200, 240–41 (1995) (Thomas, J., concurring) (criticizing racial preferences for "stamp[ing] minorities with a badge of inferiority").

16. David Schmidtz, "How to Deserve," *Political Theory* 30.6 (2002): 778–84.

17. See, e.g., *Fullilove*, 448 U.S. 539, 542 (Stevens, J., dissenting).

18. See, e.g., *Adarand Constructors,* 515 U.S. 200, 239 (1995) (Scalia, J., concurring).

19. See *Miller v. Johnson,* 515 U.S. 900, 912 (1995): "Race-based assignments 'embody stereotypes that treat individuals as the product of their race.' " (Justice Kennedy, quoting Justice O'Connor in *Metro Broad., Inc. v. FCC,* 497 U.S. 547, 604 (1990), but omitting her qualification that this "may" be what race-based assignments do.)

20. *Croson,* 488 U.S. 524 (Scalia, J., concurring). Advocates of color blindness also allow that race-conscious policies may be permitted in life-threatening emergencies (521)—to separate prisoners in a race riot, for example.

21. As I argue in "Integration, Affirmative Action, and Strict Scrutiny," *New York University Law Review* 77 (2002): 1252–66.

22. Larry Alexander, "Rules, Rights, Options, and Time," *Legal Theory* 6.4 (2000): 391–404.

23. 78 F.3d 932, 951 (5th Cir. 1996). The Supreme Court overruled *Hopwood* in *Grutter v. Bollinger.*

24. See *Croson* 488 U.S. 469, 520, 526 (1989) (Scalia, J., concurring) (acknowledging that "compensating for social disadvantages" is "benign" purpose, but stressing that states can pursue this legitimate aim through race-neutral means); *Wessmann v. Gittens,* 160 F.3d 790, 810 (1st Cir. 1998) (Boudin, J., concurring) (conceding that Boston Latin School's race-conscious admissions is "a thoughtful effort to assist minorities historically disadvantaged"); *Hopwood,* 78 F.3d 934 (acknowledging that University of Texas acted "[w]ith the best of intentions" in employing race-conscious admissions). Even Justice Thomas acknowledges the legitimacy of special efforts to serve blacks as such. See *United States v. Fordice,* 505 U.S. 717, 748 (1992) (Thomas, J., concurring) (recognizing "'sound educational justification' for maintaining historically black colleges as such"). This implies the legitimacy of special efforts for blacks since it is inconceivable that he would approve the continuation of historically white colleges "as such."

25. I am not here presupposing the controversial consequentialist claim that it is permissible to violate an individual right in order to minimize the total number of rights-violations of the same type. Rather, I take the argument of §8.3 to have already established that there is no individual right not to be disfavored because one fails to possess a racial identity that is the ground of continuing categorical disadvantage.

26. Glenn Loury, "How to Mend Affirmative Action," *The Public Interest* 127 (Spring 1997): 33–43.

27. Thomas Sowell, *Black Education: Myths and Tragedies* (New York: McKay, 1972); Thernstrom and Thernstrom, *America in Black and White,* 386–422.

28. Linda Loury and David Garman, "College Selectivity and Earnings," *Journal of Labor Economics* 13.2 (1995): 289–308.

29. Ursula Wagener and Michael Nettles, "It Takes a Community to Educate Students," *Change* 30.2 (Mar./Apr 1998): 18–25.

30. Thomas Kane, "Racial and Ethnic Preferences in College Admissions," in *The Black-White Test Score Gap,* ed. Christopher Jencks and Meredith Phillips (Washington, D.C.: Brookings Institution Press, 1998), 445.

31. Stephan Thernstrom and Abigail Thernstrom, "Book Review: Reflections on *The Shape of the River*," *UCLA Law Review* 46.5 (June 1999): 1619.

32. Bowen and Bok, *Shape of the River*, 61, 65, 114–15, 143–45, 199. The mismatch hypothesis has been revived by Richard Sander with respect to law school admissions in "A Systemic Analysis of Affirmative Action in American Law Schools," *Stanford Law Review* 57 (2004): 367–483. However, many scholars challenge his statistical analysis. See, for example, Ian Ayres and Richard Brooks, "Does Affirmative Action Reduce the Number of Black Lawyers?" *Stanford Law Review* 57 (2004–2005): 1807–54.

33. Kane, "Racial and Ethnic Preferences in College Admissions," 445.

34. Fryer and Greenstone, "Causes and Consequences of Attending Historically Black Colleges and Universities."

35. Angela Onwuachi-Willig, Emily Houh, and Mary Campbell found no differences in external stigma or internalized feelings of stigmatization between black law students who attend schools with and without affirmative action. "Cracking the Egg: Which Came First—Stigma or Affirmative Action?" *California Law Review* 96 (2008): 1299–1352. Deirdre Bowen found that undergraduate science majors from underrepresented minorities experience higher hostility, external stigma, and internal stigma in states where affirmative action is banned than in states where it is allowed. "Brilliant Disguise: An Empirical Analysis of a Social Experiment Banning Affirmative Action," *Indiana Law Journal* (forthcoming), http://ssrn.com/abstract=1324076.

36. If stigmatization of affirmative action beneficiaries were based on principled, race-neutral support for meritocracy, rather than prior stigmatization of the disadvantaged, we would observe a similar stigmatization of men educated at Ivy League schools before the 1970s since all such men were beneficiaries of an extreme form of gender preference that categorically barred women from competing with them. We would also observe a willingness to drop all doubts about the qualifications of affirmative action beneficiaries once they demonstrated their deservingness post hoc, through successful performance in the role they gained.

37. Richard Kahlenberg, *The Remedy: Class, Race, and Affirmative Action* (New York: Basic Books, 1996).

38. Deborah Malamud, "Assessing Class-Based Affirmative Action," *Journal of Legal Education* 47 (1997): 465–66.

39. Roland Fryer, Glenn Loury, and Tolga Yuret, "Color-Blind Affirmative Action," NBER Working Paper no. 10103, Cambridge, Mass., 2003, http://people.bu.edu/gloury/papers/colorblind%20affirmative%20action.pdf.

40. Samuel Issacharoff, "Can Affirmative Action Be Defended?" *Ohio State Law Journal* 59 (1998): 669–95.

41. *Parents Involved in Community Schools v. Seattle School District No. 1*, 551 U.S. 701, 748 (2007).

42. John Arthur makes the same error in *Race, Equality, and the Burdens of History* (New York: Cambridge Univ. Press, 2007), 262–63. Contrary to his claim that affirmative action is "the wrong tool for the job," racial goals and timetables are precisely what "effective enforcement of antidiscrimination laws" looks like (§7.4).

43. 42 U.S.C. §2000e(b).

44. 42 U.S.C. §3603(b)(1).

45. Massey, *Categorically Unequal*, 67–68. The Fair Housing Act was amended to enhance the enforcement capabilities of the Department of Housing and Urban Development, including nontrivial fines and the power to issue cease-and-desist orders. 42 U.S.C. §3612(g). However, these powers depend on the willingness to use them, which has often been low (§4.1).

46. Christopher Lee, "EEOC Is Hobbled, Groups Contend: Case Backlog Grows as Its Staff Is Slashed, Critics Say," *Washington Post*, June 14, 2006: A21.

47. B. Dan Wood, "Does Politics Make a Difference at the EEOC?" *American Journal of Political Science* 34.2 (1990): 517–19. Michael Connelly, general counsel to President Reagan, suspended litigation of several types of discrimination cases, including complaints of sexual harassment, pay discrimination, age discrimination, and class actions. Clarence Thomas, EEOC head under Reagan, expressed similar hostility to class action suits—the only effective litigation remedy for systematic discrimination—and allowed thousands of age discrimination cases to lapse (509, 523–25). Under President George W. Bush, the EEOC again allowed a backlog of unresolved race-discrimination complaints to accumulate. U.S. Equal Employment Opportunity Commission, "Race-Based Charges FY 1997-2007," http://www.eeoc.gov/stats/race.html.

48. Cecilia Conrad, "Do Black Workers Lack Soft Skills?" in *Building Skills for Black Workers: Preparing for the Future Labor Market*, vol. 2: *The Black Worker in the 21st Century*, ed. Conrad (Lanham, Md.: Univ. Press of America, 2004), 105–25.

49. Donald Tomaskovic-Devey, Melvin Thomas, and Kecia Johnson, "Race and the Accumulation of Human Capital across the Career: A Theoretical Model and Fixed-Effects Application," *American Journal of Sociology* 111.1 (2005): 58–89; William Rodgers III, "Racial and Ethnic Differences in the Impact of Job Training on Wages," in *Building Skills for Black Workers*, ed. Conrad, 77–103.

50. *Washington v. Davis*, 426 U.S. 229 (1976).

51. *McKlesky v. Kemp*, 481 U.S. 279 (1987).

52. *Personnel Administrator of Mass. v. Feeney*, 442 U.S. 256, 279 (1979) (upholding the constitutionality of an absolute lifetime preference for veterans in the Massachusetts civil service, notwithstanding its extreme adverse impact on women, the lack of any rationale for replicating the military's preference for men in civilian domains, and the grossly excessive weight and duration of the preference relative to the state's expressed interest in helping veterans reintegrate into civilian life).

53. In *Kimbrough v. U.S.*, 552 U.S. 85 (2007), the Supreme Court ruled that judges may deviate from guidelines calling for a 100 to 1 sentencing disparity between crack and powder cocaine, observing that the disparity is not rationally related to legitimate sentencing objectives (street-level crack dealers were punished more severely than the powder dealers who sold them the cocaine they turned into crack). The U.S. Sentencing Commission amended the guidelines to modestly reduce the disparity, but full correction of the problem awaits congressional action. Adam Liptak, "Whittling Away, but Leaving a Gap," *New York Times*, Dec. 17, 2007.

54. Loury, *Anatomy of Racial Inequality*, 95–103.

55. 347 U.S. 495 (1954).

56. 391 U.S. 430 (1968).

57. Ibid., 437–38 (rejecting "freedom of choice" plan for assigning students to schools).

58. Ibid., 440, quoting Bowman v. County School Board, 382 F.2d 326, 333 (C.A.4th Cir.1967) (concurring opinion) (emphasis added).

59. 402 U.S. 1, 19, 28 (1971) (rejecting claim that the Constitution requires teachers to be assigned to schools on a "color-blind" basis, when de jure teacher assignments had enabled schools to be racially identified; rejecting "racially neutral" student assignments when they "fail to counteract the continuing effects of past school segregation"; and requiring race-conscious "affirmative action" to achieve desegregation).

60. 418 U.S. 717, 743–44 (1974).

61. 411 U.S. 1 (1973).

62. 498 U.S. 237 (1991).

63. 503 U.S. 467 (1992).

64. 551 U.S. 701 (2007).

65. Muzafer Sherif et al., *Experimental Study of Positive and Negative Intergroup Attitudes between Experimentally Produced Groups: Robbers Cave Experiment* (Norman: Univ. of Oklahoma Press, 1954); Robyn Dawes, Alphonse van de Kragt, and John Orbell, "Cooperation for the Benefit of Us—Not Me, or My Conscience," in *Beyond Self-Interest*, ed. Jane Mansbridge (Chicago: Univ. of Chicago Press, 1990).

66. Young, *Inclusion and Democracy*.

67. Sherif et al., *Experimental Study of Positive and Negative Intergroup Attitudes*.

68. Hollinger, *Postethnic America*.

Chapter Nine
The Ordeal and Promise of Integration

1. Stanley Rothman, Seymour Martin Lipset, and Neil Nevitte, "Does Enrollment Diversity Improve University Education?" *International Journal of Public Opinion Research* 15.1 (2003): 8–26.

2. John Arthur, *Race, Equality, and the Burdens of History* (New York: Cambridge Univ. Press, 2007), 266–68; Peter Schuck, *Diversity in America: Keeping Government at a Safe Distance* (Cambridge, Mass.: Belknap Press, 2003), 178–79.

3. Walter Allen, "The Color of Success: African-American College Student Outcomes at Predominantly White and Historically Black Public Colleges and Universities," *Harvard Educational Review* 62.1 (1992): 39.

4. Ibid., 37.

5. Ellis Cose, *The Rage of a Privileged Class* (New York: HarperCollins, 1993); Joe Feagin and Melvin Sikes, *Living with Racism: The Black Middle-Class Experience* (Boston: Beacon, 1994).

6. Pamela Jackson, Peggy Thoits, and Howard Taylor, "Composition of the Workplace and Psychological Well-Being: The Effects of Tokenism on America's Black Elite," *Social Forces* 74.2 (1995): 543–57.

7. Jeannine Bell, "Policing Neighborhood Boundaries: Violence, Racial Exclusion, and the Persistence of Segregation," Indiana Legal Studies Research Paper no. 74 (2007), http://ssrn.com/abstract=963476.

8. See Hanna Rosin, "American Murder Mystery," *The Atlantic* (July/Aug 2008): 40–54 (suggesting that recipients of section 8 housing vouchers designed to enable class [not racial] integration are causing a crime wave in Memphis, based on the overlap between areas of rising crime and addresses of section 8 recipients); Solomon Moore, "As Program Moves Poor to Suburbs, Tensions Follow," *New York Times*, Aug. 8, 2008: A1.

9. George Galster, "Consequences from the Redistribution of Urban Poverty during the 1990s: A Cautionary Tale," *Economic Development Quarterly* 19.2 (2005): 119–25.

10. Bowen and Bok, *Shape of the River*, 15.

11. Briggs and Dreier, "Memphis Murder Mystery?"

12. Patterson, *The Ordeal of Integration*.

13. Michael Norton et al., "Color Blindness and Interracial Interaction: Playing the Political Correctness Game," *Psychological Science* 17.11 (2006): 949–53.

14. Loury, *Anatomy of Racial Inequality*, 97.

15. Patterson, *The Ordeal of Integration*, 68.

16. Beverly Tatum, *"Why Are All the Black Kids Sitting Together in the Cafeteria?" and Other Conversations about Race* (New York: Basic Books, 1997), 54–74.

17. Young, *Inclusion and Democracy*, 217.

18. Ibid., 216, 221, 227.

19. Aimee MacDonald, "Racial Authenticity and White Separatism: The Future of Racial Program Housing on College Campuses," in *Reclaiming Identity: Realist Theory and the Predicament of Postmodernism*, ed. Paula Moya and Michael Hames-Garcia (Berkeley and Los Angeles: Univ. of California Press, 2000), 213.

20. Tatum, *"Why Are All the Black Kids Sitting Together in the Cafeteria?"*, 90–113.

21. Thomas Edsall and Mary Edsall, *Chain Reaction: The Impact of Race, Rights and Taxes on American Politics* (New York: Norton, 1991), 182.

22. I leave open the possibility that student housing based on themes of racial identity, but managed for racial integration (where blacks, say, might be a bare majority or plurality within the house, and a majority of blacks in student housing live elsewhere), would meet integrative goals. There is much to be said for the educative and democratic value of having many nonblacks participate in settings where blacks predominate.

23. Young, *Inclusion and Democracy*, 222–23.

24. Patterson, *The Ordeal of Integration*, 65–66.

25. Kathleen Garces-Foley, "New Opportunities and New Values: The Emergence of the Multicultural Church," *Annals of the American Academy of Political and Social Science* 612 (2007): 209–24.

26. David Estlund, *Democratic Authority: A Philosophical Framework* (Princeton, N.J.: Princeton Univ. Press, 2008), 12–13.

27. Wilson and Taub, *There Goes the Neighborhood*, 27–31.

INDEX

246 · INDEX